The Essentials of Conditioning and Learning

MICHAEL DOMJAN
University of Texas at Austin

BROOKS/COLE PUBLISHING COMPANY

I(T)P™ An International Thomson Publishing Company

Pacific Grove • Albany • Bonn • Boston • Cincinnati • Detroit • London • Madrid • Melbourne
Mexico City • New York • Paris • San Francisco • Singapore • Tokyo • Toronto • Washington

Sponsoring Editor: *Vicki Knight*
Marketing Representative: *Heather Dutton*
Editorial Associate: *Lauri Ataide*
Production Editor: *Tessa A. McGlasson*
Manuscript Editor: *Mary P. O'Briant*
Permissions Editor: *Cathleen S. Collins*

Cover and Interior Design: *Vernon T. Boes*
Cover Photo: *Jim Cummins/FPG*
Interior Illustration: *Kathy Joneson*
Photo Editor: *Kathleen Olson*
Typesetting: *Graphic World, Inc.*
Printing and Binding: *Malloy Lithographing, Inc.*

For more information, contact:

BROOKS/COLE PUBLISHING COMPANY
511 Forest Lodge Road
Pacific Grove, CA 93950
USA

International Thomson Editores
Campos Eliseos 385, Piso 7
Col. Polanco
11560 México D. F. México

International Thomson Publishing—Europe
Berkshire House 168-173
High Holborn
London WC1V 7AA
England

International Thomson Publishing GmbH
Königswinterer Strasse 418
53227 Bonn
Germany

Thomas Nelson Australia
102 Dodds Street
South Melbourne, 3205
Victoria, Australia

International Thomson Publishing—Asia
221 Henderson Road
#05-10 Henderson Building
Singapore 0315

Nelson Canada
1120 Birchmount Road
Scarborough, Ontario
Canada M1K 5G4

International Thomson Publishing—Japan
Hirakawacho Kyowa Building, 3F
2-2-1 Hirakawacho
Chiyoda-ku, Tokyo 102
Japan

Printed in the United States of America.

10 9 8 7 6 5 4 3 2

Domjan, Michael, [date]
    The essentials of conditioning and learning / Michael Domjan.
        p.   cm.
    Includes bibliographical references and indexes.
    ISBN 0-534-23730-4
    1. Conditioned response.   2. Reinforcement (Psychology)
3. Learning, Psychology of.   I. Title.
BF319.D653   1995
053.1'526—dc20   95-43643
                                                     CIP

To Neil D. Kent, D. W. Tyler, and S. Siegel,
Who Got Me Started in Conditioning and Learning

BRIEF CONTENTS

ONE   *Basic Concepts and Definitions*   1

TWO   *The Structure of Unconditioned Behavior*   11

THREE   *Habituation and Sensitization*   23

FOUR   *Pavlovian Excitatory Conditioning*   37

FIVE   *Stimulus Relations in Pavlovian Conditioning*   53

SIX   *Instrumental and Operant Conditioning*   70

SEVEN   *Schedules of Reinforcement and Response Choice*   87

EIGHT   *Theories of Reinforcement*   102

NINE   *Extinction*   116

TEN   *Stimulus Control of Behavior*   131

ELEVEN   *Avoidance Learning*   149

TWELVE   *Punishment*   166

THIRTEEN   *Memory Mechanisms*   178

CONTENTS

CHAPTER ONE
Basic Concepts and Definitions   1

Fundamental Features of Learning 2
  Learning and Other Forms of Behavior Change 2
  Learning, Performance, and Levels of Analysis 4
  A Definition of Learning 6
Investigative Strategies for the Study of Learning
    and Behavior 6
  The Fundamental Learning Experiment 7
  The Control Problem in Studies of Learning 9
Technical Terms 10

CHAPTER TWO
The Structure of Unconditioned Behavior   11

Shaping and Homogeneous versus Heterogeneous Substrates
    of Behavior 12
The Concept of the Reflex 13
Complex Forms of Elicited Behavior 15
  Modal Action Patterns 15
  Sign Stimuli 17
The Organization of Behavior 18
  Motivational Factors Influencing Elicited Behavior 19

Appetitive and Consummatory Behavior   19
Behavior Systems   20
Suggested Readings   21
Technical Terms   22

CHAPTER THREE

Habituation and Sensitization   23

General Principles of Regulation   25
Effects of the Repeated Presentation of an
    Eliciting Stimulus   26
Characteristics of Habituation Effects   27
Characteristics of Sensitization Effects   31
Mechanisms of Habituation and Sensitization   32
The S-R System and the State System   32
Implications of the Dual-Process Theory   34
Suggested Readings   36
Technical Terms   36

CHAPTER FOUR

Pavlovian Excitatory Conditioning   37

Pavlov's Proverbial Bell   38
Common Misconceptions about Pavlovian Conditioning   38
Contemporary Pavlovian Conditioning Preparations   40
Appetitive Conditioning   40
Aversive Conditioning   41
The Nature of the Conditioned Response   42
Skeletal versus Glandular Conditioned Responses   42
Similarity of Conditioned and Unconditioned Responses   43
The Behavior System Approach   43
The Contents of Pavlovian Associations   44
Effects of US Devaluation   45
Effects of US Inflation   47
Are All Conditioned Stimuli Equally Conditionable?   47
The Control Problem in Pavlovian Conditioning   49
Suggested Readings   52
Technical Terms   52

CHAPTER FIVE

Stimulus Relations in Pavlovian Conditioning   53

Temporal Relation between CS and US   54
  Simultaneous Conditioning   54
  Delayed Conditioning   55
  Trace Conditioning   55
  Effects of the CS-US Interval   55
Signal Relation between CS and US   57
  The Blocking Effect   57
  CS/US Contingency   59
Higher-Order Relations in Pavlovian Conditioning:
  Conditioned Inhibition   60
  Inhibitory Conditioning Procedures   60
  Behavioral Manifestations of Conditioned Inhibition   62
  Stimulus Relations in Conditioned Inhibition   64
Higher-Order Relations in Pavlovian Conditioning:
  Conditioned Facilitation   66
  Stimulus Relations in Conditioned Facilitation   66
  Distinguishing between B-US and B(A-US) Relations   67
Suggested Readings   68
Technical Terms   69

CHAPTER SIX

Instrumental and Operant Conditioning   70

The Traditions of Thorndike and Skinner   72
  Methodological Considerations   73
The Establishment of an Instrument or
  Operant Response   76
  Learning Where and What to Run For   77
  Combining Familiar Responses in New Ways   77
  Shaping New Responses   77
The Importance of Immediate Reinforcement   80
Event Relations in Instrumental Conditioning   81
  The S-R Association: Thorndike's Law of Effect   82
  S-S* and S(R-S*) Relations   83

Two-Factor and Three-Factor Theories of
Instrumental Learning   84
Neurophysiological Implications   *84*
Implications for Constraints on Instrumental Conditioning   *85*
Suggested Readings   86
Technical Terms   86

CHAPTER SEVEN
*Schedules of Reinforcement
and Response Choice*   *87*
The Cumulative Record   88
Simple Schedules of Reinforcement   89
Ratio Schedules   *90*
Interval Schedules   *91*
Chained Schedules of Reinforcement   93
Heterogeneous Chains   *94*
Homogeneous Chains   *94*
Training Response Chains   *95*
Concurrent Schedules   96
Mechanisms of Schedule Performance   98
Feedback Functions for Ratio Schedules   *98*
Feedback Functions for Interval Schedules   *99*
Feedback Functions and Schedule Performance   *100*
Suggested Readings   100
Technical Terms   101

CHAPTER EIGHT
Theories of Reinforcement   *102*
Thorndike and the Law of Effect   103
Hull and Drive Reduction Theory   104
Primary Reinforcers   *105*
Secondary Reinforcers and Acquired Drives   *106*
Sensory Reinforcement   *106*
Reinforcers as Responses   107
The Premack Principle   *107*
The Premack Revolution   *108*

Applications of the Premack Principle   108
Theoretical Problems   109
The Response Deprivation Hypothesis   109
    Response Deprivation and the Law of Effect   110
    Response Deprivation and Response Probability   110
    Response Deprivation and the Locus of Reinforcement Effects   111
The Behavioral Regulation Approach   111
    The Behavioral Bliss Point   112
    Imposing an Instrumental Contingency   112
    Responding to Schedule Constraints   114
    Contributions of Behavioral Regulation   114
Suggested Readings   115
Technical Terms   115

CHAPTER NINE

Extinction   116

Extinction of Pavlovian Conditioned Behavior   118
    Extinction and Habituation   118
    Extinction as Unlearning   119
    Extinction as a Form of Inhibition   120
    Clinical Implications   121
    Extinctive Inhibition versus Conditioned Inhibition   121
Extinction of Instrumentally Conditioned Behavior   122
    The Partial Reinforcement Extinction Effect   123
    Explanations of the PREF   124
Suggested Readings   129
Technical Terms   129

CHAPTER TEN

Stimulus Control of Behavior   131

Measurement of Stimulus Control   132
    Identifying Relevant Stimuli   133
    Identifying Relevant Stimulus Features   134
    Measurement of the Degree of Stimulus Control   135
Determinants of Stimulus Control:
    Stimulus and Organismic Factors   138
    Sensory Capacity   138
    Sensory Orientation   139

Stimulus Intensity or Salience   139
Motivational Factors   140

Determinants of Stimulus Control: Learning Factors   141
Pavlovian and Instrumental Conditioning   141
Stimulus Discrimination Training   142
Multiple Schedules of Reinforcement   144
Differential Reinforcement and Stimulus Control   144
Interdimensional versus Intradimensional Discriminations   146

Suggested Readings   148
Technical Terms   148

CHAPTER ELEVEN

Avoidance Learning   149

Dominant Questions in the Analysis of
   Avoidance Learning   150
Origins of the Study of Avoidance Learning   151
Contemporary Avoidance Conditioning Procedures   152
Discriminated Avoidance   152
Nondiscriminated or Free-Operant Avoidance   154
Theoretical Approaches to Avoidance Learning   156
Test of the Role of the Instrumental Contingency   156
Two-Factor Theory of Avoidance   157
Conditioned Temporal Cues   159
Safety Signals in Avoidance Learning   160
Avoidance Learning and Unconditioned Defensive Behavior   162
Suggested Readings   165
Technical Terms   165

CHAPTER TWELVE

Punishment   166

Effective and Ineffective Punishment   167
When Punishment Fails   168
When Punishment Succeeds   169
Research Evidence on Punishment   170
Response-Reinforcer Contingency   170
Response-Reinforcer Contiguity   170
Intensity of the Aversive Stimulus   171
Signaled Punishment   171

*Punishment and the Mechanisms Maintaining the
    Punished Response   173*
Punishment and Reinforcement of Alternative Behavior   174
Paradoxical Effects of Punishment   174
Can and Should We Create a Society Free
    of Punishment?   175
Suggested Readings   177
Technical Terms   177

CHAPTER THIRTEEN
Memory Mechanisms   178

Stages of Information Processing   179
The Matching-to-Sample Procedure   180
Simultaneous and Delayed Matching-to-Sample   181
Procedural Controls for Memory   182
Types of Memory   182
Reference Memory and Working Memory   182
Active and Passive Memory   184
Retrospective and Prospective Memory   185
Sources of Memory Failure   188
Interference   188
Retrieval Failure   190
Suggested Readings   192
Technical Terms   192

GLOSSARY   193

REFERENCES   206

NAME INDEX   221

SUBJECT INDEX   224

MICHAEL DOMJAN is Professor of Psychology at the University of Texas at Austin, where he has been teaching undergraduate and graduate courses in learning since 1973. He has served as Editor of the *Journal of Experimental Psychology: Animal Behavior Processes* and Associate Editor of *Learning and Motivation*. He is noted for his research on food-aversion learning and learning mechanisms in sexual behavior. He is a recipient of the G. Stanley Hall Award of the American Psychological Association, and his research on sexual conditioning was selected for a MERIT Award by the National Institutes of Mental Health. His textbook *The Principles of Learning and Behavior* is now in its third edition.

PREFACE

The principles of conditioning and learning are used in many areas of psychology and allied disciplines. The purpose of this book is to provide a concise, current, and sophisticated summary of the essentials of conditioning and learning for students and professionals in those areas.

Concepts from conditioning and learning have been used in the design of behavior therapy procedures, and in various educational settings, including special education, rehabilitation training, and elementary education. The principles of conditioning and learning are also important in behavioral neuroscience, physiological psychology, developmental psychology, psychopharmacology, and comparative psychology. Researchers in these areas are interested in how nonverbal organisms learn, process, and remember information. Asking animal and nonverbal human subjects how they learn and think invariably requires using conditioning procedures in some way. Therefore, interpretation of the results of such experiments necessitates understanding the underlying processes and mechanisms that are responsible for conditioning and learning effects.

The basic procedures of habituation, classical conditioning, and instrumental conditioning have not changed in the past fifty years and are familiar to many students and professionals. However, interpretations of basic conditioning phenomena have changed, with the result that common presumptions about learning are no longer valid. Consider, for example, the following claims:

- Learning can be directly observed in the behavior of organisms, just like aggression, maternal behavior, and other important activities.
- Pavlovian conditioning involves the learning of new conditioned responses to previously ineffective stimuli.
- Extinction is the opposite of conditioning and involves the unlearning of an association.
- Avoidance responses occur because they prevent the delivery of an aversive event.

- Using a larger reinforcer makes instrumental behavior more resistant to extinction.

All of these claims seem reasonable, but none of them is valid in light of contemporary perspectives. The purpose of this book is to summarize contemporary perspectives to enable students and professionals to use concepts from conditioning and learning more effectively in their work.

The book can serve as the primary source for an introductory course on conditioning and learning. It can also serve as a supplemental text for courses related areas. Finally, the book can be used to provide the foundations for an advancd course in which students are required to read a collection of specialized articles.

In preparing this book, I was guided by my students, who over the past quarter century have encouraged me to keep searching for ways to explain concepts simply and directly. I acknowledge the insightful reviewers who helped keep me on track: Robert Allan, Lafayette College; George Cicala, University of Delaware; Dale Dick, University of Wisconsin–Eau Claire; Nelson Freedman, Queen's University; David Gast, University of Georgia; Judith Goggin, University of Texas at El Paso; Teresa Jacob, Grossmont College and University of California, San Diego; Bruce Menchetti, Florida State University; and Tim Shearon, Albertson College of Idaho. I would also like to thank Vicki Knight of Brooks/Cole for encouraging me to write the book, and Tessa McGlasson, who guided the book through the production process.

Michael Domjan

Chapter One

Basic Concepts and Definitions

D I D   Y O U   K N O W   T H A T :

- Learning can result either in an increase or a decrease in responding.
- Learning is a special type of cause of behavior.
- Learning may be investigated at the cellular, neurophysi-ological, or behavioral level.
- Learning is not always evident in the actions of an organism.
- Learning can only be investigated with experimental methods.
- Learning is an inference based on a difference in behavior between subjects given a particular type of experience and subjects lacking that experience.
- The design of a control procedure is as important in studies of learning as the design of various training or experimental procedures.

Learning is a widespread phenomenon in the animal kingdom. It has been found in species as diverse as fruit flies, sea slugs, honeybees, rodents, birds, monkeys, and people. It is a basic feature of **behavior.**

Fundamental Features of Learning

Many aspects of human behavior are learned. We learn to recognize friends as different from strangers. We learn to hold a telephone and to pick it up when it rings. We learn to swim, to ride a bicycle, and to avoid stepping in potholes. In all of these cases, *learning is identified by a change in behavior.* An experienced swimmer or bike rider acts very differently than someone who has not learned to swim or ride a bike yet.

Learning to swim or ride a bicycle involves acquiring new hand, leg, and body movements or responses that facilitate balance and forward locomotion. However, learning does not always involve the acquisition of new responses. We also learn to *not do* certain things. Children have to learn to keep quiet during a sermon, to hold still when being examined by a doctor, and to not be alarmed when they are picked up by a grandparent rather than by a parent. Learning to inhibit or suppress behavior is often as important as learning new responses. Riding a bicycle, for example, requires learning to pedal as well as learning not to lean too much to one side or the other. Thus, *the change in behavior that is used to identify learning can be either an increase or a decrease in responding.*

LEARNING AND OTHER FORMS OF BEHAVIOR CHANGE

Although all learning is identified by some kind of a change in behavior, not all cases in which behavior is altered are instances of learning (see Figure 1.1). Therefore, it is important to distinguish learning from other sources of behavior change. One such alternative is **maturation.**

Children are better able to lift heavy objects and to reach a cookie jar on a high shelf when they are 10 years old than when they are 5 years old. However, these changes are not due to learning. Rather, they result from physical growth and maturation. Children become taller and stronger between their fifth and tenth birthdays, and they become able to lift heavier objects and reach higher shelves as a result of that physical growth and maturation.

Behavioral changes due to learning and changes due to maturation can be interrelated and difficult to distinguish. As a child becomes stronger and taller with age, those physical changes facilitate the learning of new skills. However, one important difference between learning and maturation is that maturation does not require practice with things specifically related to the change in behavior that occurs. A little girl, for example, will become better able to reach high shelves as she gets older whether or

Sources of Behavior Change

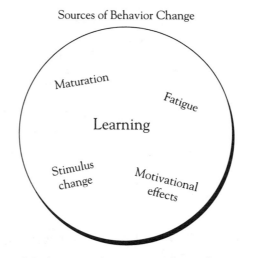

FIGURE 1.1   Mechanisms that can result in changes in behavior.

not she ever practices reaching for cookies. In contrast, practice is required for learned responses.

Practice is obviously necessary to learn a skill such as swimming or riding a bicycle. A person cannot become a good swimmer without extensively practicing the required strokes and cannot learn to ride a bicycle without extensively practicing pedaling, steering, and balancing. In contrast, other things can be learned very quickly. Touching an electric outlet once is enough to teach a child to avoid touching outlets ever again. However, regardless of the amount of practice involved, all *learning requires some practice or experience specifically related to the change in behavior.*

Another difference between maturation and learning is that the same maturational process can produce behavioral changes in a wide variety of situations. As a girl grows taller, she will be able to reach taller shelves, climb taller trees, and catch butterflies that are flying higher off the ground. Physical growth and maturation can result in changes in behavior in many different contexts. In contrast, *behavior changes due to learning tend to be specific to the practiced response.* For example, practice in turning on an electric stove will not improve a person's skill in building a cooking fire outdoors. What is learned about one situation may generalize to other situations to some extent, however. Practice in turning on a particular electric stove will improve a person's ability to turn on other, similar electric stoves. Practice with electric stoves will not be as useful, however, to someone trying to cook with a microwave oven.

Another important feature of learning is that *the results of learning are relatively long-lasting.* This serves to distinguish learning from temporary changes in behavior. Physiological changes such as **fatigue** and drowsiness can cause widespread and large changes in behavior (all of a person's actions may become slower and less vigorous). However, such changes are temporary and can be easily reversed by sufficient rest. Other dramatic changes in behavior can be caused by changes in **motivation** (people do different things when they are hungry than just after they have eaten) and changes in **stimulus** conditions (a fire alarm can quickly turn a quietly seated audience into an anxiously scrambling mob). Such changes are temporary, however, and are restricted to a particular motivational state or stimulus condition. Learning involves longer-term changes. For example, a woman cannot be considered to have learned another woman's name if she cannot remember it the next day. The assumption is that once something is learned, it will be remembered for some time.

LEARNING, PERFORMANCE, AND LEVELS OF ANALYSIS

Although the occurrence of learning can only be identified by observing a change in behavior, the change in behavior may be evident only under special circumstances. A young man taking physics, for example, may not be able to provide an adequate definition of a quark, suggesting that he has not learned the concept. However, the same student may be able to pick out the correct definition from a list of alternative possibilities. Children can learn many things about driving a car by watching adults drive. They may learn what to do with the gas and brake pedals, for example, but they may show no evidence of this knowledge until they are old enough to take driving lessons. These examples illustrate that *sometimes learning is behaviorally silent*—it does not produce a visible change in behavior. In such cases, special procedures must be used to determine what has been learned.

Learning may not be evident in the actions of an organism for a variety of reasons. One possibility is that what is learned is a relationship between stimuli or events in the environment rather than a particular response. For example, we may learn to associate the color red with ripe apples. The learning of an association between two stimuli is called **stimulus learning.** A learned association between red and ripeness will not be reflected in what we do unless we are given a special task, such as judging the ripeness of apples. Stimulus learning is usually not evident in the actions of an organism unless special test procedures are used.

The things an individual does—a person's observable actions—are collectively referred to as **performance.** Performance depends on many things, including motivation and the stimulus conditions or behavioral opportunities provided by the environment. Learning is just one of the many factors that determine performance. A person may be an excellent flute player, but without the opportunity or inclination to play the flute, no one will be able to tell how well that person has learned to play an instrument.

I will describe a number of behaviorally silent forms of conditioning and

Level of Investigation   Type of Learning Mechanism

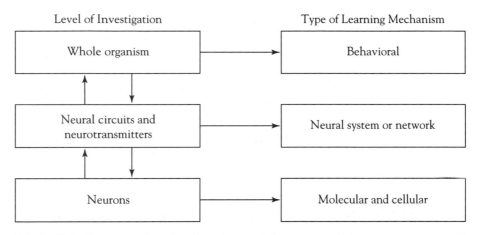

FIGURE   1.2   **Levels of analysis of learning: whole organism, neural circuits, and transmitter systems, and nerve cells or neurons.**

learning in the following chapters. Examples of behaviorally silent learning suggest that learning cannot be equated with changes in behavior. Rather, learning involves a change in the kinds of actions an organism might perform. Learning involves a change in the potential for doing something. *Learning involves a potential change in performance.*

Where does the change in the potential for action reside? Behavior is regulated by the nervous system. Therefore, learning involves long-lasting changes in the neural mechanisms of behavior. In fact, early neuroscientists such as Ivan Pavlov used behavioral studies of learning in their efforts to study how the nervous system works. They regarded learning procedures as techniques for the investigation of neural function.

Because learning involves changes in the nervous system, it may be investigated at different levels of analysis (see Figure 1.2). We may study learning at the level of molecular changes within nerve cells or neurons. We may also study changes in neurotransmitter systems or neural circuits associated with learning. Finally, we may study learning at the level of changes in the behavior of intact organisms.

Studies of learning began at the organismic level, where learning is manifest in changes in observable behavior; learning has been investigated most extensively at that level. However, with recent advances in the neurosciences, concepts and terms that have been developed for the behavioral analysis of learning have been also applied to investigations at the level of neural circuits and neurotransmitter systems and at cellular and molecular levels. One of the challenges facing the study of learning in the coming years will be to integrate the findings from these diverse levels of analysis.

A DEFINITION OF LEARNING

I identified a number of characteristics of learning in the preceding discussion. Learning involves a change in the potential or neural mechanisms of behavior. The change is relatively long-lasting and is the result of experience with environmental events specifically related to the behavior in question. These characteristics are combined in the following definition:

> Learning is a relatively enduring change in the neural mechanisms of behavior resulting from experience with environmental events specifically related to that behavior.

Investigative Strategies for the Study of Learning and Behavior

Behavior occurs in many ways and in many situations. However, just two basic approaches to the study of behavior are available—naturalistic observations and experimental observations. **Naturalistic observations** involve observing and measuring behavior as it occurs under natural conditions, in the absence of interventions or manipulations introduced by the investigator. In contrast, **experimental observations** involve measuring behavior under conditions specifically designed by the investigator to test particular factors or variables that might influence the learning or performance of the behavior.

Consider, for example, activities involved in foraging for food by tree squirrels. Foraging can be investigated using naturalistic observations. An observer could watch squirrels in a park and count how often they picked a particular type of seed, how often they ate the seed right away, and how often they buried the seed for later retrieval. Making such observations throughout the day would provide detailed information about the foraging behavior of the squirrels in that park. However, such observations would not reveal why the squirrels did what they did. Observing squirrels foraging undisturbed cannot tell us why they select one type of seed instead of another, why they devote more effort to foraging in one part of the day than another, or why they eat some seeds right away and bury others to eat later. Naturalistic observations cannot provide answers to questions that probe the causes of behavior. They may help us formulate questions or hypotheses about why animals do certain things, but naturalistic observations cannot provide the answers.

The causes of behavior can only be discovered using experimental observations. Experimental observations require the investigator to manipulate the environment in special ways that allow reaching causal conclusions. Using naturalistic observations, a researcher may find that squirrels bury more seeds in the fall than in the winter. What might cause this outcome? Naturalistic observations cannot answer this question because environmental conditions in the fall differ from conditions in the winter in many respects. Food is more plentiful in the fall than in the winter. The climate is warmer in the fall than in the winter. Daylight gets shorter from day to day in the fall and longer in the winter; and trees have more leaves in the fall than in the winter, making it easier for squirrels to hide seeds without being seen.

To determine what factors encourage squirrels to bury seeds, the environment has to be manipulated to isolate each possible causal variable. Consider, for example, whether the availability of excess food causes seed burying. We could test this possibility by comparing squirrels under two different conditions. In one condition, the squirrels would be provided with excess food by spreading lots of store-bought peanuts in the observation area. In the second condition, only a subsistence food supply would be available. The squirrels would not be provided with store-bought peanuts, and some of the food growing in their habitat would be harvested by the experimenter to reduce the food supply. In all other relevant respects, the two test conditions would be the same. Temperature, changes in daylight from day to day, and extent of foliage in the trees would be identical. Given these identical conditions, if the squirrels buried more seeds when food was plentiful than when food was scarce, we could conclude that excess food encourages or causes squirrels to bury seeds.

Although experimental observations permit drawing conclusions about the causes of behavior, it is important to realize that the causes of behavior cannot be observed directly. Rather, causes are inferred from the data. When we conclude that excess food causes seed burying, we are not describing something we have actually observed. What we have seen in our hypothetical experiment is that squirrels bury more seeds when food is plentiful than when food is scarce. The conclusion that excess food causes seed burying is an inference arrived at from comparing the two experimental conditions. *Causal conclusions are inferences based on experimental observations.* Causes cannot be observed directly.

Uncontrolled naturalistic observations can provide a wealth of descriptive information about behavior. We have learned a great deal about foraging for food, courtship and sexual behavior, maternal behavior, parental behavior, and defensive and territorial behavior from naturalistic observations. Considering that learning is ultimately also evident in the behavior of humans and other animals, one might suppose that observational techniques also can be useful in the study of learning. In fact, some have advocated that detailed investigations of learning should begin with naturalistic observations of learning phenomena (Miller, 1985). However, naturalistic observations are inherently unsuitable for studies of learning.

THE FUNDAMENTAL LEARNING EXPERIMENT

According to the definition I have developed, learning is a relatively enduring change in the mechanisms of behavior resulting from experience with environmental events specifically related to that behavior. A critical aspect of this definition is that learning is a result of past experiences. As such, learning is a particular type of cause of behavior, a cause that involves past experience with relevant environmental events. To conclude that learning has occurred, the researcher must be sure that the observed change in behavior is caused by past experience.

As I noted, causes cannot be observed directly. Instead, they have to be inferred from experimental observations. This idea has profound implications for the study of learning. Because learning is a particular type of cause of behavior, it cannot be observed directly. Rather, learning can only be investigated with experimental manipulations that serve to isolate a specific past experience as the cause of a change in behavior.

To conclude that a change in behavior is due to a specific past experience, subjects with and without that experience must be compared under otherwise identical circumstances. Consider, for example, the fact that most 8-year-old children can ride a bicycle proficiently whereas 4-year-olds cannot. A reasonable interpretation is that 8-year-olds are expert riders because they have had a lot more chance to practice riding a bicycle. That is, the change in behavior from 4 to 8 years of age may be caused by experience with bicycles. To support this conclusion, it is not enough to point to the fact that 8-year-olds are better riders than 4-year-olds. Such an age difference could be due to physical growth and maturation. Some kind of an experiment has to be conducted to prove that proficient riding is a result of past experience or practice with bicycles.

One way to prove that bicycle riding is a learned skill would be to conduct an experiment with 4-year-old children who have never ridden a bicycle. Children could be assigned randomly to one of two treatment groups—an experimental group and a control group. Then, the experimental group would receive three 1-hour lessons in riding a bicycle. The control group would also receive three 1-hour lessons through which they would also become familiar with bicycles. However, the control group would not be taught to ride. Rather, they would be told about various parts of a bicycle and how the parts fit together. At the end of the lessons, both groups of children would be tested for their skill in riding. If proficient riding is learned through relevant practice, then the children in the experimental group should be much more proficient than the children in the control group.

The above example illustrates *the fundamental learning experiment*. To conclude that a behavior change is a result of learning, the behavior of subjects must be compared under two conditions. In one condition, subjects are provided with the relevant environmental experience or training. This is called the **experimental condition**. In the other condition, subjects do not receive the relevant training but are treated identically in all other respects. This is called the **control condition**. The occurrence of learning is inferred from a comparison between the two conditions. A researcher cannot conclude that learning has occurred by observing subjects in just one condition or the other. Conclusions about learning require a comparison between the experimental and the control conditions.

THE CONTROL PROBLEM IN STUDIES OF LEARNING

There are some special consequences of the fact that learning can only be inferred from a comparison of subjects with a particular training history and subjects that are otherwise comparable but lack that history. One important consequence is that learning cannot be investigated with naturalistic observations. Under natural circumstances, subjects with a particular training history often differ in a number of respects from subjects lacking that history. Therefore, the requirements of the fundamental learning experiment are difficult to satisfy under entirely natural circumstances.

A second important consequence of the fact that learning depends on the comparison of an experimental and a control condition is that the control procedure has to be designed with as much care as the experimental procedure. In fact, some landmark contributions to the study of learning have come not from analyses of experimental procedures but from analyses of control procedures (for example, Church, 1964; Rescorla, 1967). Different training procedures require different control procedures. I will discuss the various types of control procedures as I describe various types of learning in the following chapters. Let it suffice to say here that the design of control procedures is dictated by the particular aspect of past experience the researcher wishes to isolate and show to be responsible for the change in behavior of interest.

In my example of children learning to ride a bicycle, the question was whether practice in riding is critical for becoming a skillful rider. Children who practice riding also learn a lot about how a bicycle works (how the pedals make the wheels turn, for example). Notice that the procedure for the control group is designed so that the children in that group got to learn about the parts of a bicycle and how those parts go together. However, the children in the control group were not provided with practice in sitting on a bicycle and pedaling it. Thus, the design of the control procedure allowed the isolation of practice in riding a bicycle as the critical factor involved in learning to ride.

A third important consequence of the fact that learning can only be inferred from a comparison of experimental and control conditions is that learning is usually investigated with at least two independent groups of subjects—an experimental group and a control group. Learning can also be inferred from extensive investigations of the behavior of an individual subject. However, even single-subject experiments involve comparisons between experimental and control conditions (see Figure 1.3).

Single-subject experiments involve some unique methodological considerations (Sidman, 1960). Basically, they require that the individual's behavior be understood well enough to permit accurate assumptions about

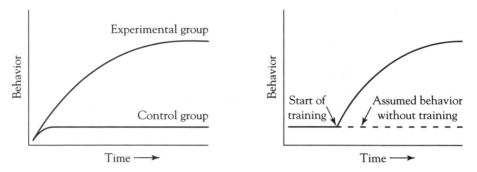

FIGURE   1.3 Two versions of the fundamental learning experiment.
In the left panel, two groups of subjects are compared. The training procedure
is provided for subjects in the experimental group but not for subjects in the
control group. In the right panel, a single subject is observed before and during
training. The subject's behavior during training is compared to how the subject is assumed to behave without training.

how the subject would have behaved without having received a training
procedure.

Consider, for example, a 4-year-old boy who is unable to catch a ball
tossed to him. If his parents spend several hours a day teaching the child how
to catch a ball, he might become proficient within a few days. From this, we
may conclude that the child has learned to catch a ball. Notice, however,
that this conclusion is based on our assumption that the child would not have
acquired the skill so rapidly if he had not received instruction. Only if we
have sufficient knowledge to make this assumption can we infer that the
child has learned to catch the ball.

Technical Terms

Behavior   Motivation
Control conditon   Naturalistic observation
Experimental condition   Performance
Experimental observation   Single-subject experiment
Fatigue   Stimulus
Learning   Stimulus learning
Maturation

CHAPTER TWO

The Structure of Unconditioned Behavior

DID YOU KNOW THAT:

- Learning is constrained by the subject's unconditioned behavior.
- Unconditioned behavior is organized in complex and systematic ways.
- Organized elicited behavior can result in well-coordinated social interactions.
- Species-typical behavior is not invariant.
- Some forms of elicited behavior are modulated by the subject's motivational state.
- Behavior in a complex environment can be governed by small, isolated stimulus features.

Learning enables organisms to benefit from experience. Through learning, behavior can be altered in ways that make the subject more effective in interacting with its environment. Animals can forage more effectively by learning where and when food is likely to be available (for example, Kamil & Clements, 1990). They can defend themselves more successfully by learning when and where they are likely to encounter a predator (for example, Hollis, 1990); and, they can be more effective in reproduction by learning when and where they are likely to encounter an available sexual partner (Domjan, 1994; Hollis, 1990).

Shaping and Homogeneous versus Heterogeneous Substrates of Behavior

In all instances of learning, the behavior of an organism is modified or shaped by its prior experience. B. F. Skinner introduced the term *shaping* in reference to a particular type of conditioning procedure that I will describe in greater detail in Chapter 6. For present purposes, it is sufficient to point out that through shaping, an organism's behavior can be gradually changed to enable the subject to perform entirely new responses. A child's crude swings of a bat, for example, can be gradually shaped to enable the child to become an expert hitter.

Skinner chose the term *shaping* by analogy with how a sculptor gradually changes and molds a lump of clay into a recognizable object (Skinner, 1953). A sculptor interested in making a statue of a swan, for example, starts with an unformed lump of clay, then cuts away excess clay here and there, and molds what remains in special ways. As this process continues, a recognizable swan gradually emerges. In an analogous fashion, learning can change or shape an organism's behavior, with the result that the subject comes to respond in ways that are entirely new.

The analogy of molding a block of clay into a swan captures some aspects of changing behavior through learning. However, the analogy has a serious shortcoming. Clay is a homogeneous substance that can be molded in any direction with equal ease. In contrast, behavior is not like that. Behavior cannot be changed in any direction with equal ease. Changes in behavior occur in the context of genetically programmed predispositions that make certain changes easier to produce than others. For example, it is much easier to train animals to approach and manipulate food-related stimuli (Hearst & Jenkins, 1974) than it is to train them to release or withdraw from stimuli related to food (Breland & Breland, 1961; Timberlake, Wahl, & King, 1982).

Learning procedures do not shape new behavior in the way that a sculptor shapes clay into a new object. A more apt analogue for the behavioral substrate for learning is wood rather than clay (Rachlin, 1976). Unlike clay, wood has a heterogeneous or uneven consistency. It is grainy and has knots. Cutting with the grain is easier and results in a smoother line than cutting against the grain, and cutting around knots is easier than cutting through them. Because of this heterogeneity, a person carving a statue out of wood must pay close attention to how the statue is oriented in relation to the grain and the knots in the wood. In an analogous fashion, learning psychologists have to pay close attention to how what they are trying to teach an organism fits with the animal's preexisting behavioral tendencies.

All instances of learning reflect an interaction between the training procedures that are used and the subject's preexisting behavior. Changes brought about by learning are not imposed on a homogeneously modifiable substrate. Rather, changes in behavior produced by learning are superimposed on a heterogeneous preexisting behavioral structure. Understanding how learning occurs requires an appreciation of the heterogeneous behavioral substrate that organisms bring into a learning situation.

Although all conditioning procedures are superimposed on preexisting behavioral tendencies, this dependence of learning on unlearned aspects of behavior has been emphasized in some areas of conditioning more than in others. The interaction of conditioned and unconditioned aspects of behavior has been the focus of attention in studies of Pavlovian conditioning and avoidance conditioning (see Chapters 4 and 11). However, I will give numerous examples of how learning effects depend on unlearned behavioral tendencies in analyses of other aspects of instrumental conditioning as well.

The Concept of the Reflex

The smallest unit of unconditioned behavior is the **reflex** (see Figure 2.1). The concept of a reflex was formulated by the French philosopher René Descartes (1596–1650). Descartes made numerous contributions to Western philosophy, including ideas about behavior that are familiar to most of us today but were innovative in his time. As did other philosophers of his time, Descartes believed that important aspects of human behavior were voluntary. However, he was also impressed with the seemingly automatic and involuntary nature of some actions, and he proposed the concept of the reflex to characterize involuntary behavior.

Descartes based his concept of the reflex on animated statues that he had seen in public parks in France. Sophisticated animated characters, such as those created by Disney Studios, were not around when Descartes lived, but some of the parks Descartes frequented contained statues whose limbs would move when someone walked by. The statues moved because their limbs were attached with joints. Through a series of levers and linkages, the limbs and joints were connected to stepping stones along the walkway near the statue. Whenever someone stepped on one of these stones, the pressure was transferred to the statue, causing the statue's arm or leg to move.

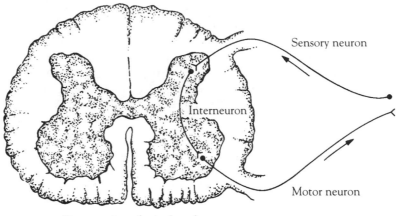

Cross-section of spinal cord

FIGURE 2.1 Neural organization of simple reflexes.
The environmental stimulus for the reflex response activates a sensory neuron, which transmits the sensory message to the spinal cord. Here the neural impulses are relayed to an interneuron, which in turn passes the impulses to the motor neuron. The motor neuron activates muscles involved in the reflex response. (Domjan & Burkhard, 1993.)

The moving statues appeared lifelike, and it occurred to Descartes that some aspects of human and animal behavior were similar to the behavior of the statues. Descartes pointed out that animals and people also perform certain actions in response to a particular environmental stimulus. For example, we quickly withdraw our finger when we touch a hot stove, we instinctively flinch when we hear a sudden noise, and we extend our arm when we lose our footing. Such responses to particular stimuli are examples of **elicited behavior.**

In the moving statues Descartes saw, the movements were in a sense reflections of the eliciting stimulus or force that was applied to the associated stepping stone. Descartes coined the term *reflex* to capture this idea of behavior being a reflection of an eliciting stimulus. The entire unit from stimulus input to response output was termed the **reflex arc.**

Reflexes are involved in many aspects of behavior important for sustaining critical life functions. Respiratory reflexes provide us with sufficient air intake. The suckling reflex provides a newborn's first contact with milk; chewing, swallowing, and digestive reflexes are important in obtaining nutrients throughout life; postural reflexes enable us to maintain stable body positions, and withdrawal reflexes protect us from focal sources of injury.

For several hundred years after Descartes, investigations of reflexes were primarily concerned with physiological questions. Scientists studied the neural circuitry of the reflex arc, the mechanisms of neural conduction, and the role of reflexes in various physiological systems. These investigations continued in an accelerated fashion in the twentieth century. In addition, the idea of elicited behavior came to be extended to more complex forms of overt behavior. Much of this work was done in the newly emerging field of **ethology,** which is a specialty within biology concerned with the evolution and development of behavior (Baerends, 1988).

Complex Forms of Elicited Behavior

Ethologists discovered that complex social behavior in various species is often made up of response components that are elicited by social stimuli. Male stickleback fish, for example, establish a small territory and build a nest tunnel during the mating season. After the territory has been set up, the approach of a male intruder elicits an aggressive defensive response from the resident. In contrast, if a female enters the territory, the resident male engages in courtship zig-zag swimming motions (see Figure 2.2). The courtship zig-zag motions stimulate the female to follow the resident male to the nest tunnel. Once the female is in the tunnel, with her head at one end and her tail at the other, the male prods the base of the female's tail. This causes the female to release her eggs. The female then leaves the nest and the male enters and fertilizes the eggs. After that, he chases the female away and fans the eggs to provide oxygen until the eggs hatch (Tinbergen, 1952).

In this complex behavioral duet, the male and female each have their special roles. Stimuli provided by the female trigger certain actions on the part of the resident male (zig-zag swimming); the male's behavior in turn provides stimuli that trigger other responses on the part of the female (following the resident male to the nest); the female's behavior then leads to further responses from the male, and so on. The outcome is a sequence of nicely coordinated social responses. The behavior sequence progresses only if the male's behavior provides the necessary stimulation to elicit the next response from the female, and vice versa. If the response of one participant is inadequate to stimulate the next response in the other fish, the sequence of actions will be interrupted and the social interaction may end.

MODAL ACTION PATTERNS

Careful observations by ethologists have revealed numerous examples of complex social and nonsocial behavior that are made up of sequences of elicited responses of the sort illustrated by the sexual behavior of stickle-backs. Elicited responses have been shown to be involved in, among other things, nest building, incubation, parental feeding of the young, groom-

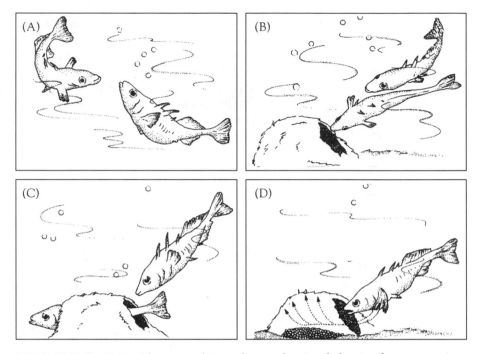

FIGURE 2.2 The courtship and reproduction behavioral sequence in the stickleback.
(A) The male swims toward the female with zig-zag motions. (B) The male guides the female to the nest. (C) The female enters the nest and releases her eggs. (D) After fertilizing the eggs, the male fans them to provide sufficient oxygen for development. (Based on Tinbergen, 1952.)

ing, foraging, and defensive behavior (Alcock, 1993). Each unit of elicited behavior is made up of a characteristic response and its corresponding eliciting stimulus.

The units of elicited behavior I have been describing are technically called **modal action patterns** or MAPs. The term *action pattern* is used instead of *response* because the activities involved are not restricted to a single muscle movement such as the blink of the eye or the flexion of a leg muscle. Elicited responses involved in grooming, foraging, and sexual and parental behavior require a coordinated set of a number of different muscles. The term *modal* is used to signify that most members of a species perform the action pattern in question and they do so in a similar fashion. The action pattern is a modal characteristic of the species. For example, infant mammals typically feed by suckling; infant gulls typically feed by gaping and receiving food from a parent; and infant chickens typically feed by pecking small spots on the ground. Because modal action patterns are characteristic of a species, they are examples of **species-typical behavior.**

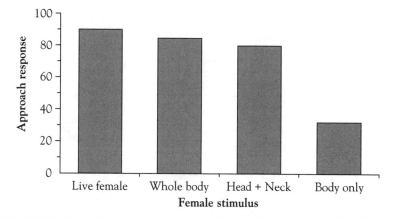

F I G U R E 2.3 Approach response of sexually experienced male quail to a live female and to taxidermic models consisting of the whole body of a female, a female's head and neck only, or a female's body without the head and neck. (Based on Domjan & Nash, 1988.)

SIGN STIMULI

Modal action patterns occur in the context of rich and complex arrays of stimulation. Consider, for example, a male quail or turkey that becomes sexually attracted to a female who comes into view. The female is a source of many visual cues. Visual cues are provided by her various body parts (head, neck, torso, legs) and her movements. She may also provide auditory and olfactory stimulation, and if she comes close enough to the male, she provides tactile stimulation. Interestingly, most of these cues are not critical for eliciting male sexual behavior.

To determine which of the various stimuli provided by a female are sufficient to elicit male sexual behavior, experimenters have tested males with live females and with taxidermic models of females. In one study (Domjan & Nash, 1988), some of the models consisted of the head and the entire body of a female. Other models consisted of just the head and neck of the female or just the body without the head. Figure 2.3 shows the tendency of male quail to approach and remain near these various types of female stimuli.

The male quail responded as vigorously to a complete taxidermic model of a female as they responded to a live female. This result shows that movement cues and auditory and olfactory stimuli provided by a live female are not necessary to elicit the approach response. The birds also responded vigorously to just the visual cues of a female's head and neck. In fact, they approached the head + neck model almost as often as they responded to a complete female model. This is a remarkable outcome. Evidently, male quail

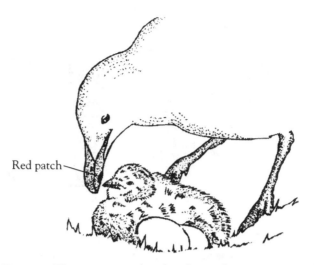

Red patch

FIGURE 2.4   The sign stimulus for the pecking response of gull chicks: a red spot near the tip of the parent's bill. (Domjan & Burkhard, 1993.)

can identify females only by the visual cues of the female's head and neck. The rest of her body, auditory cues, olfactory cues, and cues related to the female's movement are all unnecessary.

The restricted set of stimuli that are required to elicit a modal action pattern is called a **sign stimulus.** With male quail and turkeys, the female's head and neck is the "sign" that she is a female (Schein & Hale, 1965).

A sign stimulus is often a remarkably small part of the total number of cues that ordinarily precede a modal action pattern. The pecking response of gull chicks, for example, is elicited by a prominent red spot on the parent's bill (see Figure 2.4). The pointed shape of the parent's bill, together with this prominent spot, stimulates the chicks to peck the parent's bill, which then causes the parent to regurgitate the food that she brought back to the nest. Other aspects of the parent (the shape of her head, her eyes, how she lands on the edge of the nest, and the noises she makes) are not important (Tinbergen & Perdeck, 1950).

The Organization of Behavior

If each reflex or modal action pattern occurred automatically whenever its eliciting stimulus was encountered, behavior would be a bit disorganized. Elicited responses do not occur independently of each other; rather, they are organized in special ways. As I will show in the following chapters, some of this organization is a result of experience. Currently, I will discuss aspects of behavioral organization that are not obviously a product of learning.

MOTIVATIONAL FACTORS INFLUENCING ELICITED BEHAVIOR

One prominent factor that serves to coordinate modal action patterns is the internal state of the organism. The occurrence of many action patterns depends on the subject's motivational state. For example, in numerous species, courtship and sexual responses occur only during the breeding season. In fact, the situation can be even more restrictive. For male sticklebacks to court a female, they not only have to be in the breeding season but they first have to set up a territory and build a nest. These preconditions serve to prime or create the motivation for courtship behavior.

Motivational substrates have been identified for a variety of modal action patterns, including aggression, feeding, and various aspects of parental behavior. The motivational state sets the stage for a modal action pattern, whose actual occurrence is then triggered by a sign stimulus. In a sense, the sign stimulus releases the modal action pattern when the subject is in a particular motivational state. Because of this, a sign stimulus is also sometimes referred to as a **releasing stimulus.**

Ethologists considered the motivational state of the organism to be one of the key factors involved in the organization of behavior (for example, Lorenz, 1981). Using motivational concepts, they formulated an influential model for how modal action patterns are organized that is referred to as the **hydraulic model** of behavior. The hydraulic model assumes that certain factors lead to the buildup of a particular type of motivation or drive. The hunger drive, for example, is created by the expenditure of energy and the utilization of nutrients. This drive in turn induces selective attention to food-related stimuli and lowers the threshold for activating food-related modal action patterns. Once food is found and eaten, the motivational state of hunger is discharged. Thus, the motivational state facilitates modal action patterns related to eating, and the opportunity to perform those responses in turn reduces the motivational state.

APPETITIVE AND CONSUMMATORY BEHAVIOR

Motivational states determine which modal action patterns occur in combination with the eliciting stimuli an organism encounters. Ethologists characterized the response sequence involved in the discharge of a drive state as consisting of two major components. The first of these is **appetitive behavior.** In the case of the feeding system, appetitive behavior consists of responses involved in searching for a patch of food. Appetitive behavior is fairly variable and occurs in response to general spatial cues. In searching for a patch of food, a squirrel will focus on spatial cues that help it to identify trees and bushes that potentially contain nuts and fruit. Appetitive behavior tends to occur over a wide area and involves a range of activities. During the course of its foraging, the squirrel may run across open grass, climb over rocks, climb trees, and jump from one tree limb to another.

Once the squirrel encounters an edible nut, its behavior becomes much

FIGURE 2.5   Components of the feeding behavior system.
The feeding behavior sequence begins with a general search for potential food sites. Once a potential food site has been identified, the animal engages in a focal search of that site. Upon finding the food, the animal engages in food handling and ingestion responses.

more stereotyped and restricted. Now the squirrel remains in one place, sits back on its hind legs and tail, takes the nut in its front paws, cracks it open, and chews and swallows the food. These more stereotyped species-typical responses are called **consummatory responses.** The elicited behavior sequence ends with these modal action patterns because these responses discharge the motivation or drive state. The term *consummatory* is used to refer to the completion or consummation of the response sequence. In the feeding system, consummatory behavior involves the consumption of food, but that is just a coincidence. We can talk about the completion or consummation of other response sequences as well. For example, in the sexual behavior system, consummatory behavior consists of the copulatory responses that serve to complete a sexual interaction.

Another way to think about appetitive and consummatory behavior is that appetitive behavior consists of activities that enable an organism to come into contact with stimuli that will elicit the modal action patterns that serve to end the response sequence. A male's appetitive sexual behavior involves searching for a female. Once the female is encountered, the stimuli provided by the female elicit a more restricted range of courtship and copulatory responses. Copulatory responses then discharge the motivation to engage in sexual behavior.

BEHAVIOR SYSTEMS

More recent research on the structure of unconditioned behavior has suggested that elicited behavior sequences involve more than just the two response components, appetitive and consummatory behavior. Timberlake (1994), for example, has characterized the feeding system as consisting of at least three components (see Figure 2.5). According to this more detailed view, the feeding behavior sequence starts with a **general search mode.** In the general search mode, the subject reacts to general features of the environment with responses that enable it to come in contact with a variety of potential sources of food. A honeybee, for example, may fly all around looking for bushes or other plants with flowers.

Once an animal has identified a potential source of food, it switches to a more restricted response mode, the **focal search mode.** In the focal search mode, the bee will concentrate on one bush, going from flower to flower. Upon encountering a specific flower, the behavior of the bee will change to the **food handling and consumption mode.** This response mode is similar to what ethologists referred to as consummatory behavior and consists of responses required to extract nectar from the flower and ingest the nectar.

Behavior systems have been described for a variety of different functions that organisms have to accomplish in their lives. There are behavior systems for the caring of young, for grooming, for defense, and for reproduction. Several features of behavior systems are noteworthy:

1. Behavior systems often consist of a sequence of three or more different modes of behavior rather than just appetitive and consummatory behavior. An animal moves from one mode of responding to another (general search to focal search) depending on the environmental events it encounters.

2. The sequence of response modes is linear in that the subject typically moves from one response to the next without skipping a step in the sequence. A squirrel cannot handle food, for example, without first having encountered the food in a focal search mode.

3. Although the response sequence is linear, it is not one-directional. An animal may go forward or back in the sequence depending on its circumstances. If, through its focal search behavior, a squirrel does not find nuts that are worth the trouble to break open and eat, it will move back to a more general search mode.

4. Finally, each response mode involves not only characteristic responses but also increased sensitivity or attention to particular kinds of stimuli. In the general search mode, a foraging bee is likely to be looking for flowering bushes as opposed to ones that don't have flowers. In a focal search mode, it is apt to focus on where the flowers are in the bush it has chosen to search. Finally, in the food-handling mode, it will focus on the part of the flower that contains the nectar. Thus, various modes of behavior differ not only in terms of the type of responses that are involved but also in terms of the types of stimuli that guide the behavior.

Suggested Readings

BAERENDS, G. P. (1988). Ethology. In R. C. Atkinson, R. J. Herrnstein, G. Lindzey, & R. D. Luce (Eds.), *Stevens' handbook of experimental psychology* (Vol. 1, pp. 765–830). New York: Wiley.

RACHLIN, H. (1976). *Behavior and learning* (pp. 102–154). San Francisco: W. H. Freeman.

TIMBERLAKE, W. (1994). Behavior systems, associationism, and Pavlovian conditioning. *Psychonomic Bulletin & Review, 1,* 405–420.

TINBERGEN, N. (1951). *The study of instinct.* Oxford: Clarendon Press.

Technical Terms

Appetitive behavior

Consummatory responses

Elicited behavior

Ethology

Focal search mode

Food handling and
    consumption mode

General search mode

Hydraulic model

Modal action pattern

Reflex

Reflex arc

Releasing stimulus

Sign stimulus

Species-typical behavior

CHAPTER THREE

Habituation and Sensitization

DID YOU KNOW THAT:

- Reflexive behavior is not automatic.
- Reflexive behavior can increase or decrease as a result of experience.
- Behavioral systems are maintained in a stable state by opponent processes.
- Habituation effects are evident in decreased responding.
- Sensitization effects are evident in increased responding.
- Both habituation and sensitization effects can be short-lasting.
- Habituation is an inherent property of elicited behavior.
- Sensitization reflects a modulatory influence on the mechanisms of elicited behavior.

In this chapter, I will discuss two of the simplest and most pervasive ways in which behavior can change as a result of experience: *habituation* and *sensitization*. Habituation and sensitization have been investigated most extensively in reflex systems. A reflex is a fairly simple response that occurs in reaction to a specific eliciting stimulus. In the patellar knee-jerk reflex, for example, the lower leg is extended suddenly when an area just below the kneecap is stimulated.

As I noted in Chapter 2, the concept of the reflex was originally formulated by Descartes. Descartes assumed that reflexes have two major features. First, he assumed that the vigor of the elicited response is directly related to the intensity of the eliciting stimulus. In fact, he claimed that the energy required for the reflex response was provided by the eliciting stimulus. Second, Descartes assumed that a reflex response would always occur when its eliciting stimulus was presented. Reflexes were assumed to be automatic reactions to eliciting stimuli.

Descartes was correct in his general conception of the reflex, but he was wrong about the details of its features. Nevertheless, his views continue to dominate how laypersons think about reflexes to this day. Most people think of reflexes as automatic and invariant responses generated by corresponding eliciting stimuli. However, scientists have shown that reflexes are not generated by eliciting stimuli; the energy for a reflex response is not derived from the energy of the eliciting stimulus. In addition, reflexes do not occur in the same way every time an eliciting stimulus is presented. In fact, elicited behavior can show remarkable plasticity. The vigor of an elicited response can be decreased or increased by experience through the mechanisms of habituation and sensitization.

Elicited responses do not occur independently of one another. That would result in disorganized and chaotic behavior. Instead, elicited responses are regulated and organized. I introduced some organizational concepts for elicited behavior in Chapter 2 and noted in passing that response systems are sometimes organized by learning and experience. Habituation and sensitization are the first principles of behavioral organization based on experience that we will consider.

Habituation and sensitization regulate our reflex responses to environmental stimuli. We live in a complex and rich environment that provides many forms of stimulation all the time. Even during an activity as seemingly uneventful as sitting quietly in a chair, we are bombarded with all sorts of visual, auditory, olfactory, tactile, and internal physiological stimuli. All these stimuli can elicit responses on our part.

A pervasive example is the **orienting response.** We orient or turn toward novel visual stimuli (someone new entering the room, for example) and look in the direction of a strange noise. However, if we responded to everything we encountered, we would be wasting much of our effort. Many stimuli are not important enough to warrant orienting toward them. We need to pay attention to someone talking to us, but we need not pay attention to the sounds of a refrigerator humming in the background. Habituation and sensitization serve to regulate our responsivity to environmental events. These processes help us react to stimuli that may be important and ignore events that are probably unimportant.

General Principles of Regulation

Before turning to the specific mechanisms of habituation and sensitization, let us consider in more general terms what it means to regulate something. Something is regulated if its functions are maintained within acceptable limits or within a defined target range. The temperature in a house, for example, is regulated by a thermostat that ensures that the temperature remains within a range that we find comfortable. That is the target range. In the winter, the thermostat may be set to regulate the temperature so that the house remains within 70°–72°F. A driver regulates the speed of a car so that the car does not go too much above or below the posted speed limit. A cook regulates the taste of pasta to make sure it is salty enough but not too salty. In all these instances, regulation serves to keep something within acceptable limits, that is, within a target range.

Physiology is replete with examples of regulation, and in physiological systems the target range is typically referred to as the **homeostatic level.** Perhaps the most obvious example of a homeostatic system is temperature regulation in warm-blooded animals, or endotherms. The body temperature of endotherms is regulated so precisely by physiological and behavioral mechanisms that a deviation from the set point of just 1 degree is interpreted as a sign of illness. Other familiar homeostatic systems include respiration and blood sugar levels. Our respiratory system is designed to limit the buildup of carbon dioxide in the blood. An increase in serum carbon dioxide concentrations above acceptable limits causes drowsiness, coma, and eventual death. Blood sugar concentrations are also maintained within a target range. A drastic drop in serum glucose can result in a coma; too much serum glucose can cause convulsions.

How is regulation generally achieved? To maintain a system within a desired range, forces that push the system in one direction have to be opposed by mechanisms that serve to return the system to the desired or homeostatic level. When the air is cold, a person's shivering and vasoconstriction serve to counteract the cold and maintain homeostatic levels of body temperature. A buildup of carbon dioxide in the blood triggers respiratory reflexes that increase the intake of oxygen. A drop in blood sugar triggers the release of stored glucose from the liver and also induces hunger and eating.

In general, regulation is achieved by the activation of **opponent processes**—processes that counteract or oppose each other. Opponent process concepts have been used in a variety of areas of conditioning and learning. Our first encounter with such processes is in this chapter. Habituation and sensitization are opposing influences that regulate the vigor of elicited behavior.

Effects of the Repeated Presentation of an Eliciting Stimulus

The relationships that we will describe for habituation and sensitization are general characteristics that may be observed with just about any form of elicited behavior. However, for the sake of simplicity, we will illustrate the principles with the orienting response and the **startle response.** The startle response is a sudden movement or flinch caused by a novel stimulus. For example, breaking a balloon behind a man who does not expect it will cause him to suddenly hunch his shoulders and pull in his neck. The sudden movement that characterizes the startle reflex can be easily measured in animals, and this has encouraged numerous studies of habituation and sensitization of the startle reflex in laboratory rats (for example, Davis, 1974; Davis, Hitchcock, & Rosen, 1987).

The rule is that elicited behavior does not occur the same way twice when its eliciting stimulus is repeated. The kinds of changes that can occur are illustrated in Figure 3.1. With repetitions of the eliciting stimulus, responding sometimes declines rapidly in a monotonic fashion. This is illustrated by panel A in Figure 3.1. A sudden but soft sound may cause a person to startle the first few times it occurs, but responding will quickly stop. Similar results are obtained with mild odors. A novel odor—someone's perfume for example—may elicit an orienting response at first, but the response quickly habituates. After a while, the odor will not be apparent.

If the odor is more intense and obnoxious, it is more difficult to get used to it, and the pattern of responding may be akin to what is shown in panel B of Figure 3.1. In this case, responding increases somewhat at first but then declines. Such results are also obtained with the startle reflex if the eliciting stimulus is mildly intense.

Finally, if an eliciting stimulus is very intense, repetitions of the stimulus may result in a sustained increase in responding, as illustrated in panel C of Figure 3.1. If an odor is particularly pungent or irritating for some reason, reactions to it will increase with increased exposure to the odor, and it may never be possible to ignore the odor. Similarly, a sustained increase in the startle response may occur if the eliciting stimulus is a very intense noise. People caught in cross-fire between warring factions never get used to the sound of gun shots.

A decrease in the vigor of elicited behavior of the sort that is illustrated in panel A of Figure 3.1 is called a **habituation effect.** In contrast, an increase in responsivity of sort shown in panel C of Figure 3.1 is called a **sensitization effect.** In panel B of Figure 3.1, a combination of habituation and

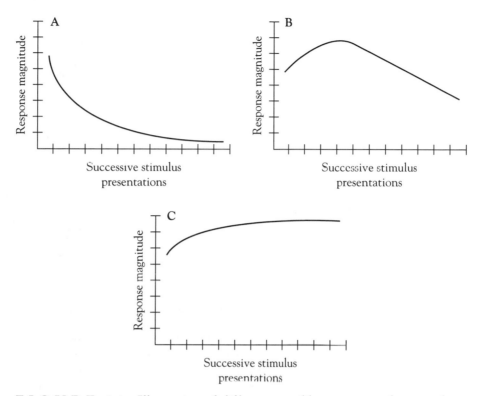

F I G U R E 3.1   Illustration of different possible outcomes of repeated presentations of a stimulus on elicited behavior.
Panel A illustrates the phenomenon of habituation. Panel B illustrates a transient sensitization effect followed by a habituation effect. Panel C illustrates the phenomenon of sensitization. (Hypothetical data.)

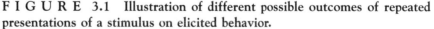

sensitization is illustrated. When both effects occur, the sensitization effect is seen before the habituation effect.

CHARACTERISTICS OF HABITUATION EFFECTS

Numerous factors have been found to influence the course of habituation and sensitization effects.

Effects of stimulus change. Perhaps the most important feature of habituation is that it is specific to the particular stimulus that is repeatedly presented. If the stimulus is altered, there will be a recovery in the response, with the degree of recovery depending on how similar the new stimulus is to the one that had been repeatedly presented. Stimulus specificity is a

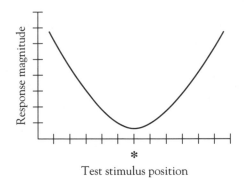

F I G U R E   3.2   Effects of varying the position of a test stimulus on the orienting response after habituation training.
The asterisk indicates the position of the stimulus during habituation training. (Hypothetical data.)

defining feature of habituation (Thompson & Spencer, 1966) and has been used profitably to study information processing in infants (for example, Cohen, 1988; Kaplan, Werner, & Rudy, 1990).

Before they are able to talk, infants cannot tell us in words which stimuli they consider to be similar and which they consider to be different. However, they can provide answers to such questions in their response to test stimuli following habituation. Consider, for example, the following hypothetical experiment. A small green spot of light is repeatedly presented on a screen in front of an infant until the infant stops orienting and looking at the light. Then, the light is again presented in different places on the screen. Let us assume that all of the test stimuli fall on an imaginary horizontal line, with the original habituated stimulus in the middle. How will the baby respond to the various test stimuli? Which test stimuli will the infant consider to be most similar to the habituated stimulus?

The likely outcome is illustrated in Figure 3.2. In this figure, the response to each test stimulus is plotted as a function of how close that test stimulus is to the spot where the light had been presented during habituation training. Notice that the lowest level of responding (most evidence of habituation) is obtained with the stimulus presented exactly where it had occurred during habituation training. The baby also does not respond much to stimuli presented close to the original training position. Thus, the effects of habituation training transfer to other nearby locations. This is called **stimulus generalization of habituation.** Test stimuli that are presented farther and farther from the original training position elicit progressively more responding. This illustrates the stimulus specificity of habituation. The habituated response recovers when the eliciting stimulus is sufficiently different from the training stimulus.

The stimulus specificity of habituation helps to rule out an important

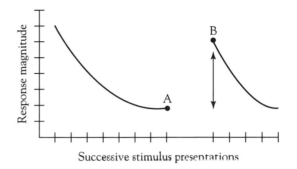

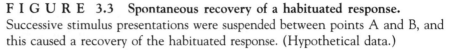

Successive stimulus presentations

FIGURE 3.3   Spontaneous recovery of a habituated response.
Successive stimulus presentations were suspended between points A and B, and
this caused a recovery of the habituated response. (Hypothetical data.)

potential explanation of habituation effects. Responding may decline with
repeated stimulations in a habituation procedure because of fatigue. The
subject simply gets tired of performing the elicited response. Recovery of
responding with a change in the eliciting stimulus rules out such an
explanation. If habituation were due to fatigue, the subject would not
respond to the altered stimulus either.

Effects of time.   Often, habituation effects are temporary. They dissipate or
are lost as time passes without presentation of the eliciting stimulus. A loss
of the habituation effect is evident in a recovery of responding. This is
illustrated in Figure 3.3. Because the response recovery is produced by a
period without stimulation (a period of rest), the phenomenon is called
spontaneous recovery.

Spontaneous recovery is a common feature of habituation (Thompson
& Spencer, 1966). For example, if a child's mother is standing to the child's
right and snaps her fingers a number of times, the child will initially look to
the right, but this orienting response will quickly habituate. However, if the
mother stops the noise for a while and then resumes suddenly, the first snap
of her fingers after the rest period will again elicit the orienting response.

The degree of spontaneous recovery is related to the duration of the
period of rest. Longer periods without repetition of the eliciting stimulus
result in greater recovery of the response. However, in some cases responding
does not recover even with rest periods of several weeks. For example, no
spontaneous recovery is evident in habituation of the novelty response to
taste.

Animals, including people, are cautious about ingesting a food or drink
that has an unfamiliar flavor. This phenomenon is known as **flavor neophobia.** Flavor neophobia probably evolved because things that taste new or
unfamiliar could well be poisonous. With repeated exposure to the new taste,

the neophobic response becomes attenuated. Coffee, for example, often elicits an aversion response in a child who tastes coffee for the first time. However, if the child drinks coffee a number of times without ill effect, his or her neophobic response will become diminished or habituated. Furthermore, the habituation is likely to be long-lasting. Having become accustomed to the flavor of coffee, the child is not likely to show a neophobic response, even after a couple of weeks without coffee. Studies with laboratory rats have shown no spontaneous recovery of flavor neophobia over periods as long as 17 and 24 days (Domjan, 1976; Siegel, 1974).

Habituation effects have been classified by whether or not they exhibit spontaneous recovery. Cases in which substantial spontaneous recovery occurs are called **short-term habituation,** and cases in which significant spontaneous recovery does not occur are called **long-term habituation.** Short-term and long-term habituation are not mutually exclusive phenomena. Sometimes both effects are observed. This is the case if a period of rest produces some recovery in the habituated response, but the recovery is not complete (for example, Leaton, 1976). Factors that promote long-term as contrasted with short-term habituation are not well understood.

Effects of stimulus frequency. The frequency of a stimulus refers to how often the stimulus is presented in a period of time—how often the stimulus occurs per minute, for example. The higher the stimulus frequency, the shorter is the time between stimulations, or the period of rest between repetitions of the stimulus. As we saw in the phenomenon of spontaneous recovery, the duration of rest between stimulations can have a large effect on responding. Because higher stimulus frequencies permit less spontaneous recovery between trials, short-term habituation is greater with higher frequencies of stimulation (Davis, 1970). In contrast, responding does not decline as rapidly if the frequency of stimulation is low.

Effects of stimulus intensity. Habituation is also determined by the intensity of the stimulus. In general, responding declines more slowly if the eliciting stimulus is more intense (Groves, Lee, & Thompson, 1969). For example, laboratory rats are slower to lose their neophobic response to strong flavors than to weak ones (Domjan & Gillan, 1976).

Effects of exposure to a second stimulus. One of the remarkable features of habituation is that it is not determined solely by the eliciting stimulus. The degree of habituation is also influenced by other stimuli the organism experiences. In particular, exposure to a second stimulus can result in recovery of a previously habituated response. This phenomenon is called **dishabituation** (Thompson & Spencer, 1966).

The results of one experiment on dishabituation are summarized in Figure 3.4. Human infants served as subjects and their visual orientation was measured in response to a checkerboard visual stimulus (Kaplan, Werner, &

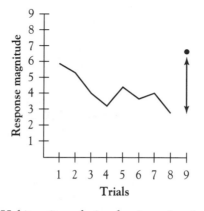

**F I G U R E   3.4   Habituation of visual orientation in infants to a checker-
board stimulus presented on trials 1–8.**
Presentation of a tone with the visual stimulus caused dishabituation of the orientation response on trial 9. (Based on Kaplan, Werner, & Rudy, 1990.)

Rudy, 1990). Repetition of the visual stimulus eight times resulted in a
decline or habituation of the looking response of the infants. After the
eighth trial, a tone (1000 Hz, 75 dB) was presented with the checkerboard
pattern. As Figure 3.4 shows, presentation of the tone caused significant
recovery of the visual orientation response. The response to one stimulus
(the checkerboard pattern) was enhanced by the presentation of a second
stimulus (the tone).

Effects of time after a dishabituating stimulus. The effects of a
dishabituating stimulus are short-lasting. If a period of rest follows
presentation of a dishabituating stimulus, the dishabituation effect will
dissipate and a recovery of the habituated response will not be evident
(Thompson & Spencer, 1966). In the example described above and
summarized in Figure 3.4, the dishabituating stimulus was the tone. If a
period of rest had been provided after presentation of the tone, no recovery
would have occurred in orientation to the habituated visual stimulus.

CHARACTERISTICS OF SENSITIZATION EFFECTS

Sensitization effects are influenced by the same stimulus intensity and time
factors that govern habituation phenomena. In general, greater sensitization
effects (greater increases in responding) occur with more intense eliciting
stimuli (Groves, Lee, & Thompson, 1969).

Like habituation, sensitization effects can be short-term or long-term
(for example, Davis, 1974; Heiligenberg, 1974). **Short-term sensitization**
decays as a result of time without stimulation. Unlike the decay of short-term

habituation, the decay of short-term sensitization has no special name. It is not called spontaneous recovery because responding declines (rather than recovers) as sensitization dissipates. In contrast to short-term sensitization, long-term sensitization effects are evident even after appreciable periods without stimulation.

One important respect in which sensitization is different from habituation is that sensitization effects are not as specific to a particular stimulus as habituation effects. As we noted earlier, habituation produced by repeated exposure to one stimulus will not be evident if the stimulus is altered substantially (see Figure 3.2). In contrast, sensitization is not so stimulus-specific. For example, the reactivity of laboratory rats to auditory cues can be increased or sensitized by exposing the animals to cutaneous pain (Davis, Hitchcock, & Rosen, 1987). Once sensitized by pain, the rats show increased reactivity to a wide range of auditory cues. The experience of illness increases or sensitizes the reactivity of laboratory rats to taste stimuli, and once taste reactivity has been sensitized, the animals show heightened finickiness to a variety of taste stimuli (Domjan, 1977).

Mechanisms of Habituation and Sensitization

So far, I have described the behavioral phenomena of habituation and sensitization. I have not discussed the underlying mechanisms that might produce these behavioral effects. A prominent theory of habituation and sensitization—the *dual-process theory*—was proposed by Groves and Thompson (1970). The theory was based on neurophysiological studies of habituation and sensitization, but it can be described close to the level of a behavioral theory.

The dual-process theory is based on two processes or mechanisms (a habituation process and a sensitization process) that are referred to by the same terms as the habituation and sensitization phenomena I described earlier. However, habituation and sensitization *processes* are distinct from habituation and sensitization *phenomena*. To avoid confusing the terms, it is important to keep in mind that habituation and sensitization *phenomena* are performance effects; they are observable changes in behavior. In contrast, habituation and sensitization *processes* are underlying neural processes or mechanisms that are presumed to be responsible for behavioral habituation and sensitization effects. Processes are underlying mechanisms responsible for the observable behavior changes, but they are not reflected directly in those changes.

THE S-R SYSTEM AND THE STATE SYSTEM

According to the dual-process theory, habituation and sensitization processes are presumed to operate in different parts of the nervous system.

For purposes of the dual-process theory, the nervous system is conceptualized as consisting of two functional components, the S-R system and the state system.

The **S-R system** is the shortest path in the nervous system between an eliciting stimulus and the resulting elicited response. The S-R system corresponds to Descartes's reflex arc. It is the minimal physiological machinery involved in a reflex. Typically, the S-R system consists of three neurons, the **sensory or afferent neuron,** an **interneuron,** and an **efferent or motor neuron.** The eliciting or input stimulus activates the afferent neuron. The afferent neuron in turn activates the interneuron, which in turn activates the efferent neuron. The efferent neuron forms a synapse with the muscles involved in the elicited response and triggers the behavioral response.

The **state system** consists of all neural processes that are not an integral part of the S-R system but influence the responsivity of the S-R system. Spinal reflexes, for example, consist of an afferent neuron that ends in the spinal cord, an interneuron in the spinal cord, and an efferent neuron that extends from the spinal cord to the relevant muscle. That is the S-R system of a spinal reflex. However, the spinal cord also contains neural tracts that ascend to the brain and ones that descend from the brain. These ascending and descending pathways serve to modulate spinal reflexes and make up the state system for spinal reflexes.

Understanding the nervous system as S-R and state components makes the rest of the dual-process theory fairly simple. As I noted earlier, the dual-process theory presumes the existence of separate habituation and sensitization processes. The habituation process is assumed to decrease reflex responsivity, whereas the sensitization process is assumed to enhance reflex responsivity. A critical aspect of the theory concerns the locus of action of the two processes. The habituation process is assumed to take place in the S-R system, whereas the sensitization process is assumed to take place in the state system.

Recall that the habituation and sensitization processes are not directly evident in the behavior of the organism. Rather, observable behavior reflects the net effect of the habituation and sensitization processes. The habituation and sensitization processes serve as opponent mechanisms regulating reflex responsivity. Whenever the habituation process is stronger than the sensitization process, the net effect is a decline in behavioral responsivity. This is illustrated in the left panel of Figure 3.5. The opposite outcome occurs if the sensitization process is stronger than the habituation process. In that event, the net effect of the two processes is an increase in behavioral responsivity. This is illustrated in the right panel of Figure 3.5.

After being activated, both the habituation process and the sensitization process are assumed to decay with time. This temporal decay assumption is needed to explain the short-term nature of some habituation and sensitization effects.

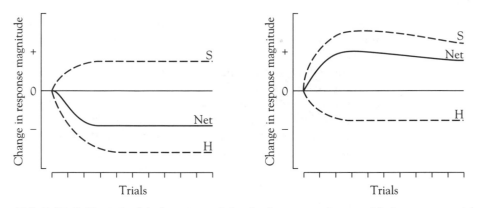

F I G U R E   3.5   Mechanisms of the dual-process theory of habituation and sensitization.

The dashed lines indicate the strength of the habituation (H) and sensitization (S) processes across trials. The solid lines indicate the net effects of these two processes. In the left panel, the habituation process becomes stronger than the sensitization process, and this leads to a progressive decrement in responding. In the right panel, the sensitization process becomes stronger than the habituation process, and this leads to a progressive increment in responding.

IMPLICATIONS OF THE DUAL-PROCESS THEORY

As I noted earlier, the S-R system is, much like Descartes's reflex arc—the minimal or most primitive mechanism of elicited behavior. Therefore, the S-R system is activated every time an eliciting stimulus is presented. Because the habituation process operates in the S-R system, each activation of the S-R system results in some buildup of the habituation process. This makes habituation a universal process of elicited behavior. According to the dual-process theory, the habituation process is activated whenever an eliciting stimulus is presented.

The universality of the habituation process does not mean that a habituation effect, or a decrement in responding, will be observed in all instances of elicited behavior. Whether a habituation effect is observed will depend on whether the habituation process is counteracted by activation of the sensitization process. Whether a habituation effect is observed will also depend on when the eliciting stimulus is presented relative to when it was presented before. If two presentations of a stimulus are separated by a long rest interval, habituation created by the first stimulus presentation will have a chance to decay completely before the stimulus is repeated, and a decrement in responding will not be observed. On the other hand, if the interval between presentations of the eliciting stimulus is too short to permit complete decay of the habituation process, a decrement in responding will occur.

In contrast to the universality of the habituation process, the sensitization process is not assumed to be universal. Sensitization occurs in the state system. The state system modulates responsivity of the S-R system, but it is not essential for the occurrence of elicited behavior. Elicited behavior can occur through the S-R system alone. Therefore, sensitization is not a universal property of elicited behavior.

If the sensitization process is not automatically activated by each presentation of an eliciting stimulus, what activates sensitization? An informal way to think about this is that sensitization represents arousal. Sensitization or arousal occurs if the subject encounters a stimulus that is particularly intense or significant. A person can become aroused by a loud unexpected noise, as well as by hearing a soft voice say that a close friend has recently died in an accident. The state system and the sensitization process are activated by intense or significant stimuli.

The sensitization process can be activated by the same stimulus that is used to elicit the reflex response of interest. This is the case if an intense or significant stimulus is used as the eliciting stimulus. The right panel of Figure 3.5 illustrates such a situation. In that example, the eliciting stimulus produced a substantial degree of sensitization, with the result that the net behavioral effect was an increase in responding.

The sensitization process also can be activated by some event other than the eliciting stimulus. Because the state system is separate from the S-R system, the state system can be activated by stimuli that are not registered in the S-R system of the response we are measuring. This is a critical feature of the dual-process theory and another respect in which sensitization is different from habituation. In contrast to habituation, sensitization is not necessarily produced by the eliciting stimulus of interest.

The fact that the sensitization and habituation processes can be activated by different stimuli permits the dual-process theory to explain a number of key phenomena, including the phenomenon of dishabituation. As I noted earlier (see Figure 3.4), the presentation of a new stimulus can result in recovery of a habituated response. In the example summarized in Figure 3.4, the presentation of a tone caused recovery of the habituated visual orientation response of infants. According to the dual-process theory, this occurs because the new stimulus activates the state system and produces sensitization, which overcomes the previous buildup of habituation. According to this interpretation, dishabituation is produced by the addition of the sensitization process to a behavioral situation rather than the reversal or weakening of the habituation process. Other evidence also supports this interpretation (see Groves & Thompson, 1970).

The dual-process theory is remarkably successful in explaining all short-term habituation and short-term sensitization effects. However, the theory is inconsistent with instances of long-term habituation and long-term sensitization. Theories of long-term habituation and sensitization include concepts of associate learning, which I will discuss in upcoming chapters.

Suggested Readings

GROVES, P. M., & THOMPSON, R. F. (1970). Habituation: A dual-process theory. *Psychological Review, 77*, 419-450.

PEEKE, H.V.S., & PETRINOVICH, L. (Eds.) (1984). *Habituation, sensitization, and behavior.* Orlando, FL: Academic Press.

TIGHE, T.J., & LEATON, R. N. (Eds.) (1976). *Habituation.* Hillsdale, NJ: Erlbaum.

Technical Terms

Afferent neuron
Dishabituation
Efferent neuron
Flavor neophobia
Habituation effect
Homeostatic level
Interneuron
Long-term habituation
Motor neuron
Opponent process
Orienting response

Sensitization effect
Sensory neuron
Short-term habituation
Short-term sensitization
Spontaneous recovery
Startle response
State system
Stimulus generalization of
   habituation
S-R system

CHAPTER FOUR

Pavlovian Excitatory Conditioning

DID YOU KNOW THAT:

- Pavlov never rang a bell in his experiments.
- Pavlov viewed classical conditioning as a technique for the study of the brain.
- Classical conditioning is not limited to glandular and visceral responses.
- The conditioned response is not always like the unconditioned response.
- Different types of conditioned responses develop when different types of conditioned stimuli are used.
- Conditioned stimuli become part of the behavior system activated by the unconditioned stimulus.
- The effectiveness of a conditioned stimulus in classical conditioning depends on the unconditioned stimulus that is used.
- Associative learning is possible in the random control procedure.

In Chapter 3, I described ways in which behavior is changed by experience with individual stimuli. Habituation and sensitization may be considered to be instances of single-stimulus learning. Now let us turn to learning about pairs of stimuli. Such learning is called **associative learning.** Associative learning is different from single-stimulus learning in that the change in behavior that occurs in response to one stimulus depends on how that stimulus was previously presented in relation to a second stimulus. Associative learning represents what we learn about combinations of stimuli. The first form of associative learning I will describe is Pavlovian, or classical conditioning.

Pavlov's Proverbial Bell

The basic elements of Pavlovian or classical conditioning are familiar to most of us. Accounts usually describe a hypothetical experiment in which Professor Pavlov rang a bell just before giving a bit of food powder to his dog subjects. The dogs were loosely held in a harness and were attached to an apparatus that enabled Pavlov to measure how much they salivated. At first, the dogs salivated only when they were given the food powder. However, after several trials of having the bell paired with presentation of food powder, the dogs came to salivate as soon as the bell sounded. Thus, the salivary response, which was only elicited by the food powder initially, also came to be elicited by the bell.

The story of Pavlov conditioning salivation to a bell is useful for introducing some important technical vocabulary. A stimulus like the food powder that elicits the response of interest without prior training is called an **unconditioned stimulus,** or US. Salivation elicited by the food powder is an example of an **unconditioned response,** or UR. The bell is an example of a **conditioned stimulus,** or CS, and the salivation that develops to the bell is called the **conditioned response,** or CR.

Pavlov's proverbial bell illustrates associative learning because salivation to the bell depends on having the bell presented in combination with food powder. Ringing the bell each time the dog is about to receive a bit of food powder presumably results in the dog's making an association of the bell with food. Once the bell has become associated with food, the dog starts to respond to the bell as if it were food. The dog starts to salivate when it hears the bell.

Common Misconceptions about Pavlovian Conditioning

Although Pavlov's proverbial bell is familiar and helpful in introducing technical terms used to describe Pavlovian or classical conditioning, several aspects of this example are misleading. First, Pavlov did not discover classical conditioning by ringing a bell just before presenting food powder. The basic elements of Pavlovian conditioning were well known in Pavlov's laboratory before he turned his attention to the study of classical conditioning (Boakes, 1984).

What Pavlov discovered was not the phenomenon of classical conditioning but the significance of this type of learning. In particular, Pavlov became interested in studying classical conditioning because he regarded classical conditioning to be a particularly powerful technique for the study of the brain. Pavlov was a physiologist, and he pursued investigations of classical conditioning to better understand complex neural functions (Babkin, 1949).

Another misleading implication of the proverbial bell example is that classical conditioning primarily involves the conditioning of a response to a previously ineffective stimulus. In many descriptions, classical conditioning is presented as a mechanism for the learning of new responses. According to this interpretation, classical conditioning is a form of stimulus-response, or **S-R learning.** A more appropriate interpretation is that classical conditioning involves the learning of an association between the conditioned and unconditioned stimulus. According to this view, classical conditioning is a form of stimulus-stimulus, or **S-S learning.** Recent research has shown that classical conditioning usually involves stimulus learning (S-S learning) rather than response learning (S-R learning) (Rescorla, 1988).

The proverbial example of salivary conditioning to a bell also suggests that classical conditioning is involved primarily in the modification of visceral and glandular responses. Skinner elevated this implication to an axiom. He postulated that classical conditioning can only modify glandular and visceral responses (Skinner, 1938). However, subsequent research has shown this to be an unwarranted assumption. Pavlovian conditioning can modify many different types of responses (Turkkan, 1989). In particular, Pavlovian conditioning results in the modification of skeletal responses involved in approaching or moving away from a conditioned stimulus (Wasserman, Franklin, & Hearst, 1974).

In the proverbial bell example, the CR (salivation to the bell) is similar to the UR (salivation to food powder). This has encouraged the assumption that the CR is always similar to the UR. That is another common misconception. Sometimes the form of the CR is opposite to that of the UR (Siegel, 1975). In yet other cases, the form of the CR is entirely different from the form or topography of the UR (Holland, 1984).

Finally, the proverbial bell example has encouraged the view that the CS in a Pavlovian conditioning situation need not have any relevance to the US that is used. The idea is that Pavlov could have selected any stimulus that dogs could detect in place of the bell and salivary conditioning would have proceeded just as rapidly. The assumption that conditioned stimuli can be selected arbitrarily has turned out to be incorrect. Contemporary research has shown that the effectiveness of a CS in a classical conditioning procedure

F I G U R E 4.1   Pigeon in an autoshaping experiment.
A key light is periodically paired with food. As a result, the pigeon starts to
peck the key when it is lit.

depends not only on its detectability but also on its inherent relation to the
US that is employed (for example, LoLordo & Droungas, 1989).

Contemporary Pavlovian Conditioning Preparations

Although classical conditioning was discovered in studies of salivary
conditioning with dogs, dogs are not used in such experiments any longer,
and salivation is rarely the response that is measured. Instead, pigeons, rats,
and rabbits commonly serve as subjects, and several different responses are
used as indices of learning. In some contemporary Pavlovian conditioning
situations, the US is a desirable or appetitive stimulus like food. These
preparations are used to study **appetitive conditioning.** In other situations,
an unpleasant or aversive event is used as the US. Such preparations are used
to study **aversive conditioning.**

APPETITIVE CONDITIONING

Appetitive conditioning is frequently investigated with pigeons and
laboratory rats as subjects. Pigeons that serve in appetitive conditioning
experiments are usually mildly hungry and are tested in a small experimental
chamber called a **Skinner box** (see Figure 4.1). The CS is a light projected
on a plastic disk or response key above the food cup. The response key is
about 2.5 cm in diameter. Pecks at the key are automatically detected and
recorded by an electronic sensing circuit. The conditioning procedure

consists of turning on the key light for a few seconds and then presenting a small amount of food.

After a number of pairings of the key light with food, the pigeons come to approach and peck the key as soon as it is lit (Hearst & Jenkins, 1974; Tomie, Brooks, & Zito, 1989). The conditioned approach and pecking behavior develop even if the key light is located some distance from the food cup (Boakes, 1979). The light becomes a signal for food, and the pigeons come to track the light. Hence, one name for this type of conditioning is **sign-tracking.** Because the procedure results in the pigeons pecking the response key without elaborate intervention by the experimenter, the procedure is also called **autoshaping.**

Laboratory rats are also used in Pavlovian conditioning, with food as the US. Holland (1977) presented a brief tone paired with pellets of food to laboratory rats. As conditioning proceeded, the tone came to elicit a sudden movement of the head, called a head-jerk response. In another group of rats, a light near the top of the experimental chamber served as the CS. As the light was repeatedly paired with food, the rats came to orient toward the ceiling and get up on their hind legs. These results indicate that rats can learn to associate both tones and lights with food, but different CRs develop with the two types of CSs (Holland, 1984).

AVERSIVE CONDITIONING

Laboratory rats are common subjects in studies of aversive conditioning. Aversive conditioning is often carried out with a special procedure known as **conditioned suppression,** a procedure that was developed as a technique for the study of emotional learning and was originally called the *conditioned emotional response procedure,* or CER (Estes & Skinner, 1941).

The CER procedure takes advantage of the fact that animals tend to become motionless or freeze when they are afraid (Bouton & Bolles, 1980). In the conditioned suppression procedure, rats are first trained to press a small bar or response lever to obtain food (see Figure 4.2). Food is provided only some of the times the rats respond, which keeps them pressing the lever steadily. After establishment of lever-pressing, aversive conditioning trials are introduced. On each of these trials, a tone or a light CS is presented for a minute or two and the rats are then given a brief foot-shock. Within a few conditioning trials, presentation of the CS results in suppression of the food-reinforced, lever-press response. The degree of response suppression provides a measure of aversive conditioning of the CS.

Specially bred albino rabbits are also used in studies of aversive conditioning. In these experiments, the blinking of the eye is the response of interest. Eyeblink conditioning was first developed with human subjects (see Kimble, 1961, pp. 55–59). A mild puff of air to one eye served as the US, and a light served as the CS. After a number of pairings of the light with the air puff, the light came to elicit a conditioned eyeblink response. In rabbits, a mild electrical pulse to the skin near one eye serves as the US, and

F I G U R E   4.2   Rat in a conditioned suppression experiment.
Pressing the response lever occasionally produces a pellet of food. Periodically, a tone is presented ending in a brief shock through the grid floor. The rat comes to suppress lever-pressing during the tone.

a brief visual or auditory cue serves as the CS. Pairings of the CS and US result in the rabbit blinking when the CS is presented (Gormezano, Kehoe, & Marshall, 1983).

The Nature of the Conditioned Response

In Pavlov's salivary conditioning experiments, the CR (salivation to a CS) was a glandular visceral response similar in form to the UR (salivation to food powder). These features of conditioned behavior were elevated to axiomatic status during much of the twentieth century. Pavlovian conditioning was considered to be primarily a mechanism for adjusting physiological and glandular responses to the environment through experience (Skinner, 1938), and the CR was assumed to be always similar to the unconditioned response (for example, Mackintosh, 1974). However, the common contemporary preparations used for the study of Pavlovian conditioning described above illustrate that there is no compelling empirical justification for either of these assumptions.

SKELETAL VERSUS GLANDULAR CONDITIONED RESPONSES

In none of the most common contemporary procedures for the study of Pavlovian conditioning is the measured CR a glandular or visceral response. In sign-tracking or autoshaping, the CR is pecking a key light. This response involves skeletal muscles, not the smooth musculature involved in visceral responses. Skeletal responses are also involved in the freezing response that is the basis for conditioned suppression. The head-jerk and rearing responses observed in Pavlovian food conditioning in rats, as well as the eyeblink response of rabbits, also involve skeletal rather than visceral responses.

The argument can be made that the responses measured in contemporary Pavlovian conditioning procedures are only indirect reflections of what is actually being conditioned and that the "true" conditioned response is in fact a visceral or glandular response. Such an argument has some validity in the case of the conditioned suppression procedure; various physiological manifestations of fear and aversion no doubt become conditioned in the CER procedure. The response suppression that comes to be elicited by the CS may be mediated by these visceral CRs. However, it is less obvious what visceral CRs might give rise to the skeletal responses involved in conditioned sign-tracking in pigeons, the conditioned head-jerk and rearing responses of rats, or the conditioned eyeblink responding of rabbits. A more parsimonious characterization of the empirical evidence is that Pavlovian conditioning can result in the modification of skeletal responses.

SIMILARITY OF CONDITIONED AND UNCONDITIONED RESPONSES

What implications do the common contemporary Pavlovian conditioning preparations have for the traditional assumption that the CR is similar in topography to the response elicited by the US? Here, the evidence is mixed. In some conditioning preparations, the CR does resemble the UR. This is the case, for example, in eyeblink conditioning. In eyeblink conditioning, both the conditioned and the unconditioned responses involve blinking. However, in other cases the conditioned and unconditioned responses are distinctively different.

In the conditioned suppression procedure, the US is a brief mild shock to the grid floor on which the rat is standing. Because the rat detects the shock through its foot pads, the shock elicits sudden and vigorous jumping. This unconditioned response of vigorous jumping contrasts dramatically with the lack of movement and response suppression that develops as the CR in this situation.

THE BEHAVIOR SYSTEM APPROACH

If the CR will not always be similar to the UR, is it possible to predict what kind of behavior will develop with Pavlovian conditioning? This question remains a major puzzle (for example, Stewart & Eikelboom, 1987). Although a definitive answer is not yet available, a promising approach for analyzing the topography of behavioral conditioned responses has been developed in recent years based on the idea of behavior systems.

I introduced the concept of **behavior systems** in Chapter 2. The concept is relevant to the present discussion because presentations of a US in a

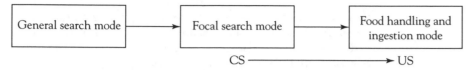

FIGURE 4.3   Behavior systems and Pavlovian conditioning.
Conditioning procedures with food as the US involve the feeding system. As a result of pairings of the CS with food, the CS becomes incorporated into the feeding system and comes to elicit food-related responses.

Pavlovian conditioning procedure activate the behavior system relevant to that US. Presentations of food to a hungry animal activate the feeding system, and presentations of shock activate the defensive behavior system. The CR that develops depends on how the CS becomes incorporated into the behavior system activated by the US.

The feeding system involves a sequence of response modes: general search, focal search, and ingestive consummatory behavior (see Figure 4.3). If a CS is presented before each portion of food the animal receives, the CS will become incorporated into one of the response modes of the feeding behavior system, and that in turn will determine what type of CR the subject will perform (Timberlake & Lucas, 1989). If the CS becomes incorporated into the focal search mode, the CR will consist of focal search responses such as approach and sign-tracking (Wasserman, Franklin, & Hearst, 1974). In contrast, if the CS becomes incorporated into the ingestive, consummatory response mode, the CR will involve handling and chewing the CS (Boakes, Poli, Lockwood, & Goodall, 1978).

In aversive conditioning, the nature of the CR is determined by the defensive behavior system (Fanselow & Lester, 1988). Foot-shock used in studies of conditioned suppression is an external source of pain, much like being bitten by a predator, and the response to shock is similar to the response to being bitten. One of the predators rodents have to cope with are snakes. When a rat is bitten by a snake, it leaps into the air. Similarly, rats jump when they receive brief foot-shock.

The rat's defensive response to an impending or possible attack is different from its response to the actual attack. If a rat sees or smells a snake that is about to strike, the rat freezes. In the conditioned suppression procedure, the CS signals impending attack. Therefore, the CS comes to elicit the freezing defensive behavior (Fanselow, 1989).

The Contents of Pavlovian Associations

As I noted earlier, a common belief about Pavlovian conditioning is that it involves primarily the learning of a CR to a CS. In many cases, however,

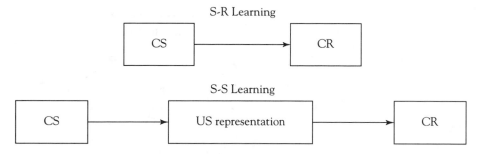

F I G U R E 4.4 Distinction between S-R and S-S learning.
In S-R learning, a direct connection or association is established between the
CS and the CR. In S-S learning, the CS activates a representation of the US,
which in turn leads to the CR.

Pavlovian conditioning appears to involve stimulus-stimulus (S-S) learning
rather than stimulus-response (S-R) learning. Whether Pavlovian conditioning results in an S-S or an S-R association is related to the contents of
the learning. In the present section, I will discuss how investigators have
distinguished between S-S and S-R learning.

According to the S-S learning mechanism, classical conditioning leads
to the formation of an association between the CS and a US. As a result of
this association, presentation of the CS activates a neural representation of
the US (see Figure 4.4). Expressed informally, this means that upon
encountering the CS, the subject will be reminded of the US. What the
subject will do when it is stimulated to "think" about the US will depend
on its motivation to respond to the US.

EFFECTS OF US DEVALUATION

A powerful technique for differentiating between S-R and S-S mechanisms
was popularized by Robert Rescorla (1973) and is basically a test of
performance. The test involves evaluating the vigor of conditioned
responding after the subject's motivation to respond to the US has been
changed. In one type of experiment, motivation to respond to the US is
reduced. This manipulation is called **US devaluation.**

Consider, for example, a study of sexual Pavlovian conditioning that was
conducted with sexually motivated male quail (Holloway & Domjan, 1993).
Brief exposure to a visual stimulus was paired with access to a female bird
once a day. Initially, the visual CS did not elicit any significant behavior.
However, the subjects always readily copulated with the female that was
presented at the end of each conditioning trial. After ten of these
conditioning trials, the CS came to elicit a strong approach response.

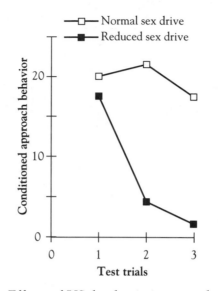

FIGURE 4.5. **Effects of US devaluation on sexual approach conditioned behavior.**
Three test sessions were conducted at 1-week intervals after two groups of quail had acquired a conditioned approach response. During the test phase, the sexual motivation of one group of birds was reduced. This US devaluation procedure resulted in a decrease in their conditioned responding. (Based on Holloway & Domjan, 1993.)

Regardless of where they were in the test arena, the subjects rapidly approached when the visual CS was presented.

According to the S-R learning mechanism, conditioned responding reflects the establishment of a direct connection between the CS and the CR. If such a direct connection has been established, then changing the animal's motivation to perform the UR should not influence its conditioned responding. An S-R interpretation predicts that once the quail learns the sexual conditioned approach response, presentation of the CS will elicit the CR, even if the quail lose their sexual motivation.

Holloway and Domjan tested this prediction by reducing the sex drive of one group of birds. This was done by changing the light cycle in the laboratory to mimic winter conditions when the birds do not breed rather than summer conditions when they are reproductively active. The results of the experiment are summarized in Figure 4.5. Contrary to predictions of the S-R mechanism, a reduction in sexual motivation reduced conditioned responding to the visual CS.

The results summarized in Figure 4.5 are consistent with an S-S learning interpretation. With S-S learning, subjects do not learn a specific CR. Rather, they learn an association between the CS and the US. Presentation of the CS activates a representation of the US. That in turn leads to conditioned responding if the subjects are motivated to respond to the US. In this experiment, the opportunity to copulate with a female was the US. When the males were not sexually motivated, they did not copulate when the female was presented. Reduced sexual motivation also reduced responding to the visual CS that had become associated with presentation of a female.

EFFECTS OF US INFLATION

In the above example, motivation to respond to the US was reduced in the test for S-S learning, and this resulted in a decrease in conditioned responding. Motivation to respond to the US can also be increased. That is called **US inflation,** and it results in increased conditioned responding.

In a particularly interesting application of the US inflation method, laboratory rats served as subjects, and the US was the taste of salt (Rescorla & Freberg, 1978, Experiment 3; see also Fudim, 1978). The preference of rats for salt can be greatly increased by injecting them with a drug (formalin) that creates a physiological sodium deficiency. Because inducing a sodium deficiency greatly increases unconditioned responses to salt, this is a powerful US inflation procedure. The question addressed by the experiment was whether US inflation would also increase responding to a CS that had become associated with salt.

Two groups of subjects served in the experiment. Conditioning was carried out in the absence of sodium deficiency. A weak bitter taste (created by a small amount of quinine mixed in water) served as the CS. For the experimental group, the bitter flavor was paired with the taste of salt by adding the quinine to a mixture of salt and water. For the control group, the bitter flavor and the taste of salt were presented on alternate days. After these procedures, US inflation was created by inducing sodium deficiency in both groups. The subjects were then tested for their response to the bitter flavor presented alone.

During the test, subjects in the experimental group drank much more of the quinine-flavored water than subjects in the control group. This is a remarkable result because ordinarily, rats (and people) hate to drink quinine. In this case, the taste of quinine had become associated with salt. After conditioning, sodium deficiency increased the value of salt, and that in turn increased their response to the salt-associated quinine flavor.

Are All Conditioned Stimuli Equally Conditionable?

The last traditional assumption about Pavlovian conditioning to consider here is that a stimulus (a brief tone, for example) that is effective as a CS in one conditioning situation will be equally effective as a CS in

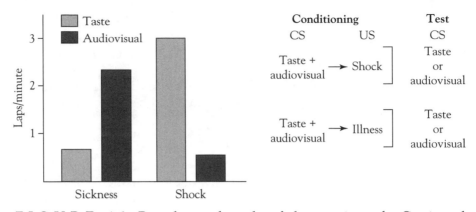

F I G U R E   4.6   Procedure and results of the experiment by Garcia and Koelling (1966) demonstrating selective associations in aversion learning. (Graph only: based on Garcia & Koelling, 1966.)

other conditioning situations. This is known as the **equipotentiality assumption.**

Investigators have known for a long time that subjects do not learn about all conditioned stimuli equally rapidly. Pavlov (1927), for example, observed that a low-intensity CS becomes conditioned more slowly than a high-intensity CS. However, such differences do not contradict the equipotentiality assumption because a low-intensity CS is likely to be difficult to condition no matter what US is used.

The first clear evidence against the equipotentiality assumption was obtained in studies of aversion conditioning. The conditioned suppression phenomenon illustrates one type of aversion conditioning. Here, a tone or a visual stimulus is paired with shock, with the result that the tone or light acquires aversive properties. Another type of aversion conditioning is **taste aversion learning**. In this case, a novel taste is followed by an unpleasant illness (a mild case of food poisoning, for example), and the subject learns an aversion to the novel taste as a result.

The conditioned suppression and taste aversion learning phenomena demonstrate that audiovisual cues and taste cues are both highly effective as conditioned stimuli. Interestingly, however, they are effective only in combination with their own particular US (see Figure 4.6). Rats do not easily learn an aversion to an auditory or visual cue paired with illness, and they do not easily learn an aversion to a taste cue paired with shock (Garcia & Koelling, 1966; Domjan & Wilson, 1972). Such results illustrate the phenomenon of **selective association.** The effectiveness of a CS in a Pavlovian conditioning procedure depends selectively on the US that is used (LoLordo & Droungas, 1989).

Evidence consistent with selective aversion learning has been also obtained with human subjects. People who experience some form of gastrointestinal illness are more likely to learn an aversion to a novel food eaten just before becoming sick than they are to learn an aversion to other types of stimuli they may have encountered. However, people do not report acquiring a food aversion if they hurt themselves in a physical accident or if they develop an irritating skin rash (Logue, Ophir, & Strauss, 1981; Pelchat & Rozin, 1982).

Since the initial demonstrations of selective association in aversion learning, such effects have been found in other forms of learning as well. For example, Shapiro, Jacobs, and LoLordo (1980) found that pigeons are more likely to associate a visual stimulus than an auditory stimulus with food. However, when the birds are conditioned with shock, the auditory cue is more likely to become conditioned than the visual cue.

In identifying selective associations, it is important to keep in mind that instances of selective learning are not absolute. For example, the fact that taste stimuli are more easily associated with gastrointestinal illness than are audiovisual cues does not mean that aversions to nongustatory cues cannot be established with illness. Nongustatory cues can become associated with illness, but such learning is more difficult and requires special procedures (for example, Best, Batson, Meachum, Brown, & Ringer, 1985). Selective associations are instances in which the rate of learning depends on the combination of conditioned and unconditioned stimuli that is used, as opposed to the individual or independent features of the CS and US.

Although selective associations are well established, why such effects occur remains open to speculation. One factor that probably contributes to selective associations is the similarity of conditioned and unconditioned stimuli. Evidence indicates that similarity between conditioned and unconditioned stimuli facilitates the establishment of associations (Rescorla & Gillan, 1980; Testa, 1974). However, the concept of similarity cannot explain why pigeons associate auditory cues with shock more readily than they associate visual stimuli with shock. It is not obvious how an auditory cue might be more similar than a visual cue when compared with shock.

The Control Problem in Pavlovian Conditioning

The critical feature of Pavlovian conditioning is that it involves the formation of an association between a CS and a US. Before any change in behavior can be attributed to Pavlovian conditioning, the establishment of an association between the CS and the US must be demonstrated.

To promote the development of an association, the conditioned and unconditioned stimuli are presented in combination with one another in Pavlovian procedures. It is particularly effective, for example, to present the

CS just before the presentation of the US on each conditioning trial. In addition, a number of conditioning trials are usually needed to get a learning effect. Thus, a Pavlovian conditioning procedure involves repeated presentations of the conditioned and unconditioned stimuli. As we saw in Chapter 3, repeated presentations of stimuli can result in habituation and sensitization effects. Therefore, habituation and sensitization effects can occur during the course of Pavlovian conditioning.

Habituation and sensitization effects of repeated CS and US presentations do not depend on the formation of an association between the CS and the US and therefore do not constitute Pavlovian conditioning. Before a change in behavior can be interpreted as an instance of Pavlovian conditioning, it has to be distinguished from habituation and sensitization effects of repeated CS and US presentations.

Habituation effects are typically of little concern because habituation results in decreased responding, whereas Pavlovian conditioning involves an increase in responding to the CS. In contrast, sensitization effects are of potential significance. Increased responding to the CS could be due to sensitization resulting from CS exposures, sensitization resulting from presentation of the US, or both. What control procedures could be used to rule out such sensitization effects in studies of Pavlovian conditioning?

A universally applicable and acceptable solution to the control problem in Pavlovian conditioning has not been developed. Instead, various control procedures have been used, each with its advantages and disadvantages. In one procedure, CS sensitization effects are evaluated by repeatedly presenting the CS by itself. Such a procedure, called the CS-*alone control,* is inadequate because it does not take into account possible increased responding to the CS caused by sensitization effects of the US. Another control procedure involves repeatedly presenting the US by itself (the US-*alone control*) to measure US-induced sensitization. But, the US-alone control does not consider possible sensitization effects of CS presentations.

About 30 years ago, Rescorla proposed an ingenious solution, the **random control procedure,** that appeared to solve the problems of the CS-alone and US-alone controls (Rescorla, 1967). In the random control procedure, both the conditioned and unconditioned stimuli are presented repeatedly, but they occur at random times in relation to each other. The random timing of CS and US presentations is designed to prevent the formation of an association between them but permits the development of sensitized responding to the CS.

The random control became popular soon after its introduction, but as investigators began to examine it in detail, they discovered some serious difficulties (Papini & Bitterman, 1990). Studies demonstrated that the random control is not neutral from the standpoint of associative learning. Associative learning can develop in a random control procedure in two ways. First, random CS and US presentations permit occasional instances in which the CS is presented in conjunction with the US. Random procedures can

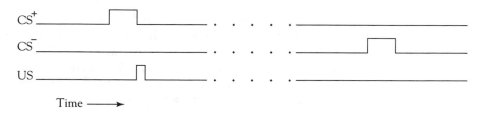

Time ———▶

F I G U R E 4.7 Diagram of the discriminative control procedure for Pavlovian conditioning.
Two conditioned stimuli are used, CS^+ and CS^-. The CS^+ is paired with the US, whereas the CS^- is presented alone. Stronger conditioned responding to CS^+ than to CS^- is evidence of associative learning rather than some form of sensitization.

result in nonrandom patterns in the short run. Whether the flip of a coin results in heads or tails is entirely random, for example, but flipping a coin just five times may yield five heads in a row. In an analogous fashion, random presentations of a CS and a US can result in occasional pairings of the CS and US. If such unintentional CS-US pairings occur early in training, conditioned responding may develop. Associative learning can result from chance pairings of the CS and US early in training (Benedict & Ayres, 1972).

Associative learning can also result from occasions when the US is presented without the CS in the random control procedure. In these instances, the US is being presented in the presence of the contextual background cues of the experimental situation. The background contextual cues of an experimental situation were ignored through much of the early development of Pavlovian conditioning. However, more recent research has shown that the repeated presentation of a US in the absence of an explicit CS can result in the conditioning of cues of the background or environmental context in which the US presentations occur (Balsam & Tomie, 1985; Kremer, 1974).

The random control procedure can result in the conditioning of background cues, and this makes the random procedure ineffective as a control for Pavlovian conditioning. Conditioned contextual cues provide an active source of interference for the conditioning of explicit conditioned stimuli. Organisms are less likely to associate a CS with food, for example, if the CS occurs in the presence of conditioned background stimuli (Tomie, Murphy, Fath, & Jackson, 1980). Because it permits the conditioning of background cues, the random control does not provide a nonassociative baseline for demonstrations of Pavlovian conditioning.

Although no entirely satisfactory control procedure for Pavlovian conditioning is available, a **discrimination control** procedure is reasonably effective. Figure 4.7 illustrates the discrimination control procedure. Two conditioned stimuli are used. One may be a brief tone, and the other may be a brief presentation of light. On half the trials, one of the conditioned stimuli (the CS$^+$), is presented and paired with the US. On the remaining trials, the other stimulus (the CS$^-$) is presented alone. CS$^+$ and CS$^-$ trials are alternated randomly. For half the subjects, the tone serves as the CS$^+$, and the light serves as the CS$^-$. For the remaining subjects, these stimulus assignments are reversed.

With a discrimination control procedure, evidence for associative learning is provided by greater responding to the CS$^+$ than to the CS$^-$. Such differential responding to the CS$^+$ and the CS$^-$ cannot be due to sensitization effects. Sensitization effects of CS or US presentations would elevate responding to both the CS$^+$ and the CS$^-$ equally.

Suggested Readings

HOLLAND, P. C. (1984). Origins of behavior in Pavlovian conditioning. In G. H. Bower (Ed.), *The psychology of learning and motivation* (Vol. 18, pp. 129–174). Orlando, FL: Academic Press.

LOLORDO, V. M., & DROUNGAS, A. (1989). Selective associations and adaptive specializations: Taste aversions and phobias. In S. B. Klein & R. R. Mowrer (Eds.), *Contemporary learning theories: Instrumental conditioning and the impact of biological constraints on learning* (pp. 145–179). Hillsdale, NJ: Erlbaum.

PAPINI, M. R., & BITTERMAN, M. E. (1990). The role of contingency in classical conditioning. *Psychological Review, 97,* 396–403.

RESCORLA, R. A. (1988). Pavlovian conditioning: It's not what you think it is. *American Psychologist, 43,* 151–160.

Technical Terms

Appetitive conditioning	S-R learning
Associative learning	S-S learning
Autoshaping	Selective association
Aversive conditioning	Sign-tracking
Behavior system	Skinner box
Conditioned response	Taste aversion learning
Conditioned stimulus	Unconditioned stimulus
Conditioned suppression	Unconditioned response
Discrimination control procedure	US devaluation
Equipotentiality assumption	US inflation
Random control procedure	

CHAPTER FIVE

Stimulus Relations in Pavlovian Conditioning

DID YOU KNOW THAT:

- Delaying the US a bit after presentation of the CS produces stronger evidence of conditioning than presenting the CS and US at the same time.
- A gap of just half a second can seriously disrupt some forms of excitatory conditioning.
- Taste aversions can be learned with a delay of several hours between the conditioned and unconditioned stimuli.
- Pavlovian conditioning depends not only on the temporal relation between the CS and the US but also on signal relations.
- Pavlov considered the conditioning of inhibition to be just as important as the conditioning of excitation.
- Extinction reduces responding but not through inhibitory conditioning.
- Inhibitory conditioning reflects the learning of a higher-order relation in which one CS signals that a second CS will not be paired with the US.
- The opposite of conditioned inhibition is facilitation or positive occasion setting—not conditioned excitation.
- In a facilitation procedure, one CS signals that a second CS will be paired with the US.

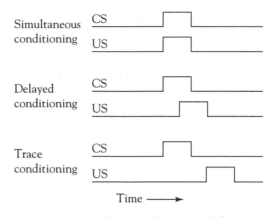

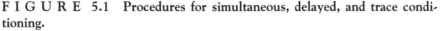

F I G U R E 5.1 **Procedures for simultaneous, delayed, and trace conditioning.**

In Chapter 4, I introduced Pavlovian conditioning as a type of learning that involves establishing an association between two stimuli, the conditioned and the unconditioned stimulus. For two stimuli or events to become associated with one another, they have to be related to each other in some way. In the present chapter, I will describe various relations that can exist between a conditioned and an unconditioned stimulus. I will also describe how different stimulus relations determine what is learned in Pavlovian conditioning.

Temporal Relation between CS and US

The first and historically most prominent relation in Pavlovian conditioning is the timing of the CS relative to the US, that is, the temporal relation between them.

SIMULTANEOUS CONDITIONING

One temporal arrangement between the CS and the US is to present them at the same time. Such a procedure is called **simultaneous conditioning** and involves **temporal contiguity** between the CS and the US (see Figure 5.1). Aristotle claimed that temporal contiguity is the most effective temporal relation for associative learning. According to Aristotle, two events have to occur at the same time to become associated. In many cases, however, simultaneous presentation of the CS and US does not yield strong evidence of learning (Bitterman, 1964; Smith, Coleman, & Gormezano, 1969).

DELAYED CONDITIONING

The best evidence for associative learning usually comes from procedures in which the CS is presented slightly before the US (Schneiderman & Gormezano, 1964). Such a procedure is called **delayed conditioning,** because the US is delayed after the presentation of the CS. An example of a delayed conditioning procedure is shown in the middle panel of Figure 5.1. Note that the CS remains present until the US occurs. There is no gap between the CS and the US.

TRACE CONDITIONING

Introducing a gap between the CS and the US changes a delayed conditioning procedure into a **trace conditioning** procedure. A trace conditioning procedure is presented in Figure 5.1 for contrast with the delayed conditioning procedure. The gap between the CS and the US is called the **trace interval.**

Introducing a gap, or trace interval, between the CS and the US can reduce drastically the degree of conditioned responding that develops. Kamin (1965), for example, compared fear conditioning in two groups of laboratory rats using the conditioned suppression procedure. One group received a delayed conditioning procedure in which a 3-minute tone CS ended in a brief foot-shock, without a gap between the tone and shock. For the second group of subjects, the tone also started 3 minutes before each presentation of shock but ended half a second before the shock. Thus, the second group received a trace conditioning procedure with just a half-second gap, or trace interval. The trace conditioning group showed much less conditioned suppression than the delayed conditioning group.

Kamin's results indicate that temporal contiguity is important for Pavlovian conditioning but not exactly in the way that Aristotle may have had in mind. The CS and the US do not have to be presented simultaneously. In fact, having the CS start before the US is usually helpful. However, for best results, the CS should remain on until the US occurs. There should not be a gap between the CS and the US.

EFFECTS OF THE CS-US INTERVAL

Another temporal relation that is critical for associative learning is the amount of time that passes between the introduction of the CS and the introduction of the US. The interval between the onset of the CS and the onset of the US is called the **CS-US interval** or **interstimulus interval**.

As I noted earlier, learning is usually not evident with simultaneous conditioning, which involves a CS-US interval of zero. More evidence of learning is seen with delayed conditioning procedures in which the CS-US interval is greater than zero. However, the benefits of delaying the US after

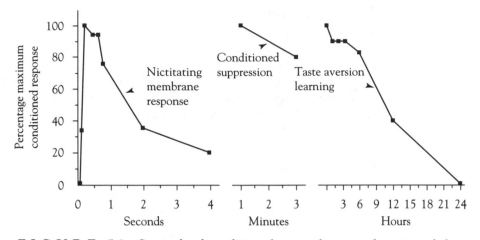

FIGURE 5.2 **Strength of conditioned responding as a function of the CS-US interval in conditioning the nictitating membrane response of rabbits (based on Schneiderman & Gormezano, 1964; Smith, Coleman, & Gormezano, 1969), conditioned suppression (based on Kamin, 1965), and taste aversion learning (based on Smith & Roll, 1967).**

the start of the CS are limited. As the CS-US interval becomes longer and longer, evidence of learning declines. How rapidly responding declines with increases in the CS-US interval depends on the response system that is being conditioned.

Figure 5.2 illustrates the effects of the CS-US interval in three different conditioning preparations. The left panel represents data from conditioning of the nictitating membrane response of rabbits. The nictitating membrane response is a kind of eyeblink response. As with the eyeblink, the nictitating membrane response is elicited unconditionally by a puff of air to the eye. Notice that in conditioning the nictitating membrane response, the best results are obtained with a CS-US interval of .2–.5 seconds. If the CS-US interval is shorter, less conditioned responding develops. In addition, conditioned responding drops off quickly as the CS-US interval is extended past a half a second. Little, if any, learning is evident if the CS-US interval is more than 2 seconds.

Conditioned suppression represents an intermediate case. Here, strong learning can occur with CS-US intervals in the range of 2–3 minutes.

Learning over the longest CS-US intervals is seen in taste aversion learning. A taste aversion is learned if the ingestion of a novel-flavored food (or drink) results in some form of illness or interoceptive distress (Braveman & Bronstein, 1985). The novel flavor is the CS, and the US is provided by the illness experience.

A taste aversion can be learned even if the illness experience is delayed several hours after ingestion of the novel flavor. This phenomenon was first documented by John Garcia and his associates (Garcia, Ervin, & Koelling, 1966) and is called **long-delay learning** because learning occurs with CS-US intervals that are a great deal longer than intervals that will support eyeblink conditioning or conditioned suppression. However, as is illustrated in Figure 5.2, even with flavor-aversion learning, there is an inverse relation between conditioned responding and the CS-US interval.

Signal Relation between CS and US

Although a close temporal relation between the CS and US is required for successful Pavlovian conditioning in most response systems, adequate temporal pairing is not sufficient for the formation of a CS-US association. Another important factor is the signal relation or informational relation between the CS and the US. In general, conditioned responding develops more rapidly with conditioning procedures in which the CS serves as a good signal for, or provides reliable information about, the occurrence of the US.

In the typical delayed conditioning procedure, each conditioning trial consists of the presentation of the CS, followed shortly by the presentation of the US. In addition, the US does not occur without being preceded by the CS. In such a procedure, occurrences of the US can be predicted perfectly from occurrences of the CS. The CS signals occurrences of the US perfectly, and an association between the CS and US develops quickly.

THE BLOCKING EFFECT

How might the signal relation between the CS and US be disrupted? One way is to present the CS along with another cue that already predicts the US. In this case, the CS will be redundant, and little conditioned responding will develop. This idea was first developed experimentally by Kamin in what has come to be known as the **blocking effect** (Kamin, 1969).

Although Kamin studied the blocking effect using the conditioned suppression procedure with rat subjects, the phenomenon may be more effectively illustrated with a hypothetical example of taste aversion learning. Let us assume that a man is allergic to shrimp and gets slightly ill every time he eats some. Because of these experiences, he acquires an aversion to the flavor of shrimp. However, he continues to eat shrimp on special occasions when he doesn't want to offend his host. On one such occasion, he is served shrimp with a steamed vegetable he doesn't remember eating before. To be polite, he eats some of the vegetable, as well as some of the shrimp. The vegetable tastes pretty good, but he ends up feeling slightly ill after the meal.

To what will the man attribute his illness, the shrimp or the new vegetable? Given a history of bad reactions to shrimp, he is likely to attribute

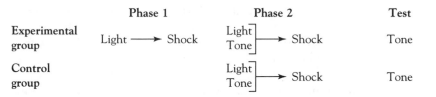

F I G U R E 5.3 Diagram of the blocking procedure in a conditioned suppression experiment.
During Phase 1, a light CS is conditioned with foot-shock in the Experimental group until light produces maximum conditioned suppression. The Control group does not receive a conditioning procedure in Phase 1. In Phase 2, both groups receive conditioning trials in which the light CS is presented together with a novel tone CS, and the light-tone compound is paired with shock. Finally, during the Test phase, responding is measured to the tone presented alone. Less conditioned suppression develops to the tone in the Experimental group than in the Control group.

his illness to the shrimp and may not acquire an aversion to the vegetable. In this situation, the presence of a previously conditioned flavor (shrimp) blocks the conditioning of a novel flavor (the vegetable), even though the novel flavor was just as closely paired with the illness US.

As the above example illustrates, the blocking effect shows that what subjects learn about one CS is influenced by the presence of other cues that were previously conditioned with the same US. The CSs Kamin used were a light and a tone (see Figure 5.3). For the blocking group, the light CS was first conditioned by pairing it with foot-shock a sufficient number of times to produce asymptotic conditioned suppression to the light. In the next phase of the experiment, the tone and light CSs were presented simultaneously, immediately before the shock US. A control group received the same pairings of the tone-light compound with shock as the blocking group, but for the control subjects the light had not been conditioned earlier. For the control subjects, the light and tone were both novel. The question addressed in the experiment was on how much fear became conditioned to the novel tone CS. Because of the prior conditioning of the light, less conditioned suppression developed to the tone in the blocking group than in the control group.

The blocking phenomenon is important because it illustrates that temporal contiguity between a CS and a US is not sufficient for successful associative learning. The temporal relation between the novel tone CS and the US was identical in the blocking and in the control groups. Nevertheless, strong conditioned suppression developed only if the tone was not presented with a light CS that had been previously conditioned. The prior conditioning of the light reduced the effectiveness of the tone as a signal for shock.

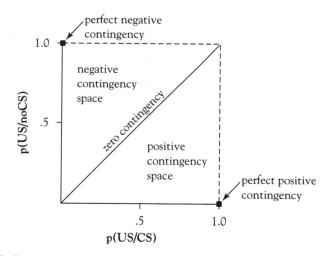

F I G U R E 5.4 Contingency between a CS and a US.
Contingency is determined by the probability of the US, given that the CS has occurred (represented on the horizontal axis) and the probability of the US, given that the CS has not occurred (represented on the vertical axis). When the two probabilities are equal (the 45° line), the CS/US contingency is zero.

CS/US CONTINGENCY

One way to characterize the signal relation between CS and US is in terms of the **contingency** between the CS and the US. The contingency between two events refers to the extent to which those events are linked, or covary. The CS/US contingency is defined in terms of two probabilities (see Figure 5.4). One of these is the probability of occurrence of the US, given that the CS has been presented (p[US/CS]); the other is the probability of US occurrence in the absence of the CS (p[US/noCS]). A situation in which the US always occurs with the CS and never by itself illustrates a perfect positive contingency between the CS and the US. In contrast, a situation in which the US always occurs when the CS is absent and never occurs paired with the CS illustrates a perfect negative contingency between the CS and the US. Finally, if the US occurs equally often with the CS and without the CS, the CS/US contingency is said to be zero.

In a positive contingency, the CS is a reliable signal for the occurrence of the US. In contrast, with a zero contingency, the CS provides no useful information about whether the US will or will not occur.

When it was first introduced, the CS/US contingency was considered to be a primary variable determining the extent of Pavlovian conditioning (Rescorla, 1967). However, this idea was soon abandoned (Rescorla, 1972). Contemporary analyses of contingency effects have focused on the background cues that are present in any situation in which an organism encounters repeated presentations of discrete conditioned and unconditioned stimuli. Procedures involving a zero CS/US contingency involve presentations of the US by itself, presentations of the CS by itself, and occasional presentations of the CS together with the US. Presentations of the US alone can result in conditioning of the background or contextual cues in which the experiment is conducted. The presence of those conditioned background contextual cues can then block the future conditioning of the explicit CS on those few occasions when the CS is paired with the US (Tomie et al., 1980) or disrupt performance of conditioned responding through other means (Miller & Matzel, 1989).

Higher-Order Relations in Pavlovian Conditioning: Conditioned Inhibition

In the examples of Pavlovian conditioning considered thus far, the focus of interest has been on how a CS is directly related to a US. Now let us turn to more complex stimulus relations in Pavlovian conditioning. In higher-order stimulus relations, the focus of interest is not on how a CS signals a US but on how one CS can signal whether or not a second CS will be paired with the US. First I will discuss conditioned inhibition or negative occasion setting. Then I will turn to facilitation, or positive occasion setting.

INHIBITORY CONDITIONING PROCEDURES

Conditioned inhibition was the first kind of higher-order signal relation that was discovered and investigated. Concepts of inhibition are prominent in various areas of physiology. As a physiologist, Pavlov was interested in not only processes that activated behavior but also processes that were responsible for the inhibition of responding. This led him to investigate conditioned inhibition. He considered the conditioning of inhibition to be just as important as the conditioning of excitation (Pavlov, 1927).

In excitatory conditioning procedures, the CS becomes a signal for the impending presentation of the US. In contrast, in inhibitory conditioning, the CS of interest becomes a signal for the absence of the US. Ordinarily, the absence of something has no particular psychological significance. For successful inhibitory conditioning, however, the absence of the US has to be a significant event. How can the absence of something be made important?

If a young woman's uncle tells her that he is not giving her $100 today, she is not likely to be disappointed if she didn't expect to get the money in the first place. However, if she is graduating from college and her uncle had promised to give her $100 when she graduated, she will be upset if he decides against the generous gift. The absence of something is psychologically significant if for some reason the event is expected to occur.

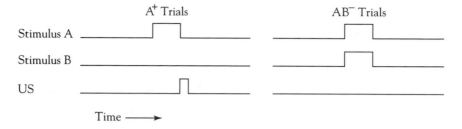

F I G U R E 5.5 The standard procedure for conditioned inhibition. On A^+ trials, stimulus A is paired with the US. On AB^-, stimulus B is presented with stimulus A and the US is omitted. The procedure is effective in conditioning inhibitory properties to stimulus B.

Standard conditioned inhibition procedure. As in the above example, in Pavlovian conditioning, the absence of the US is significant if the US fails to occur when it is expected. This general principle is the basis of the standard Pavlovian conditioned inhibition procedure. The procedure involves two different conditioned stimuli (A and B) and one unconditioned stimulus (see Figure 5.5). For example, stimulus A might be a tone, stimulus B might be a light, and the US might be a few pellets of food. On some trials, stimulus A is presented by itself and is paired with the US. These trials may be represented as A^+ (A plus). Because of the A^+ trials, the subject comes to expect the US when it encounters stimulus A. This sets the stage for inhibitory conditioning. On inhibitory conditioning trials, stimulus B is presented with stimulus A (forming the compound stimulus AB), but the US does not occur. These trials may be represented as AB^- (AB minus). Because of the presence of stimulus A on the AB trials, stimulus B is encountered in the context of the expectancy of the US. This makes the absence of the US psychologically significant and serves to condition inhibitory properties to stimulus B.

Differential inhibition. The standard inhibitory conditioning procedure (A^+, AB^-) is especially effective in making B a conditioned inhibitor, but there are other successful inhibitory conditioning procedures as well. In the **differential inhibition** procedure, for example, two conditioned stimuli, A and B, are again used, along with a US (see Figure 5.6). On some trials, A is paired with the US (A^+). On other trials, B is presented without the US (B^-). A^+ trials are randomly alternated with B^- trials, and stimulus B becomes a conditioned inhibitor.

Notice that unlike the standard inhibitory conditioning procedure, the differential inhibition procedure does not involve presenting B with an explicit excitatory CS. What then provides the excitatory context for

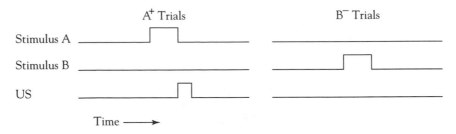

F I G U R E 5.6 The differential inhibition procedure.
On A⁺ trials, stimulus A is paired with the US. On B⁻ trials, stimulus B is presented and the US is omitted. A⁺ trials are randomly alternated with B⁻ trials, and stimulus B acquires inhibitory properties.

inhibitory conditioning? The answer appears to be that the background contextual cues of the situation in which the experiment is conducted become associated with the US on the A⁺ trials (LoLordo & Fairless, 1985). This contextual conditioning is not substantial. Most of the excitatory conditioning that occurs on A⁺ trials involves the conditioning of stimulus A, but a sufficient degree of excitation also becomes conditioned to the background cues to enable the background cues to provide an excitatory context for the B⁻ trials. The absence of the US in this excitatory context makes B a conditioned inhibitory stimulus.

BEHAVIORAL MANIFESTATIONS OF CONDITIONED INHIBITION

The behavioral manifestations of excitatory conditioning are fairly obvious. Subjects come to make a new response, the CR, to the CS. What happens in the case of conditioned inhibition? A conditioned inhibitory stimulus has behavioral effects that are opposite the behavioral effects of a conditioned excitatory stimulus. Thus, a conditioned inhibitory stimulus suppresses or inhibits conditioned responding. Unfortunately, suppression of responding is evident only under special circumstances.

Consider for example, the eyeblink response of rabbits. Rabbits blink very infrequently, perhaps once or twice an hour. A conditioned inhibitory stimulus (CS⁻) presumably suppresses blinking. Since rabbits hardly ever blink under ordinary circumstances, how can we tell when a CS⁻ actively inhibits their blinking?

Inhibition of blinking would be easy to determine if the baseline rate of blinking were elevated. If rabbits blinked once per second and we presented a conditioned inhibitory stimulus (CS⁻), blinking should decline substantially below the once-per-second rate. Thus, the problem of measuring conditioned inhibition can be solved in principle by elevating the baseline rate of responding.

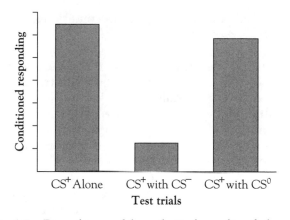

F I G U R E 5.7 Procedure and hypothetical results of the summation test of conditioned inhibition.

On some trials, a conditioned excitatory stimulus (CS⁺) is presented alone and a high level of conditioned responding is observed. On other trials, CS⁺ is presented with a conditioned inhibitory stimulus (CS⁻) or a neutral stimulus (CS°). The fact that CS⁻ disrupts responding to CS⁺ much more than CS° is evidence of the conditioned inhibitory properties of CS⁻.

Summation test. How can the baseline rate of responding be elevated? Perhaps the simplest way is to condition another stimulus as a conditioned excitatory cue (CS⁺). Substantial responding should be evident when the CS⁺ is presented by itself. Using this as a baseline, we can test the effects of a conditioned inhibitory stimulus (CS⁻) by presenting it at the same time as the CS⁺. Such a test sequence is called the **summation test** for conditioned inhibition.

Figure 5.7 presents hypothetical results of a summation test. Notice that considerable responding is observed when CS⁺ is presented by itself. Adding a conditioned inhibitory stimulus (CS⁻) to CS⁺ results in much less responding than when the CS⁺ is presented alone. This should be the outcome if CS⁻ has acquired conditioned inhibitory properties. However, presentation of CS⁻ might disrupt responding simply by distracting the subject from the CS⁺. That possibility is evaluated in the summation test by determining what happens to responding to the CS⁺ when a neutral stimulus without a history of either excitatory or inhibitory training is presented. Such a neutral stimulus is represented by CS° in Figure 5.7.

In the results depicted in Figure 5.7, CS° disrupts responding to CS⁺ a bit. This reflects the distracting effects of adding any stimulus to CS⁺. The disruption is much greater, however, when CS⁻ is presented with CS⁺. That outcome proves that CS⁻ has conditioned inhibitory properties (Reberg & Black, 1969).

Retardation-of-acquisition test. The summation test is a performance-based test of inhibition. It is based on the assumption that the performance of excitatory conditioned behavior will be suppressed by a conditioned inhibitory stimulus. A second popular approach to the measurement of conditioned inhibition is an acquisition test. This test is based on the assumption that conditioned inhibitory properties will interfere with the conditioning of excitatory properties to a stimulus. Hence, this is called the **retardation-of-acquisition test.**

The retardation-of-acquisition test involves comparing the rate of excitatory conditioning of two groups of subjects. The same CS (a tone, for example) is used for both groups. For the experimental group, the tone is first trained in an inhibitory conditioning procedure. For the comparison group, a control procedure is used that leaves the tone relatively neutral. For example, the tone may be presented alone as often as it occurs in inhibitory training for the experimental group. Then, for both groups the tone is paired with the US, and the development of excitatory responding to the tone is observed. If inhibitory conditioning was successful in the first stage of the experiment, excitatory conditioned responding should develop more slowly in the experimental group than in the control group in the second stage.

STIMULUS RELATIONS IN CONDITIONED INHIBITION

The relationship between CS⁻ and the US in an inhibitory conditioning procedure may be characterized in one of two ways. One characterization emphasizes a direct relation between CS⁻ and the US; the other emphasizes an indirect, or higher-order relation.

B–noUS relation versus B(A–noUS) relation. In all of the procedures that are effective in producing conditioned inhibition, the US occurs on some occasions, but it is never paired with CS⁻. In the standard Pavlovian inhibition procedure, for example, the US occurs when stimulus A is presented alone (A⁺) but does not occur when A is presented with stimulus B in the AB⁻ compound and B acquires inhibitory properties.

The inhibitory conditioning of stimulus B may be characterized in terms of a direct relation between stimulus B and the US, that is, stimulus B becomes a signal for the absence of the US. This direct relation may be represented as a B–noUS association. Alternatively, the conditioned inhibitory stimulus may be characterized as related to the US only indirectly. According to this view, the critical feature of inhibitory conditioning procedures is that they enable the CS^- to provide information about how another stimulus is related to the US.

Consider, for example, the standard inhibitory conditioning procedure: A^+ on some trials and AB^- on other trials. In this procedure, B provides perfect information about whether or not stimulus A will be paired with the US on a particular trial. If stimulus B is present, A will not be paired with the US. In contrast, if stimulus B is absent, A will be paired with the US. This is said to be a **higher-order stimulus relation** because in this relation, B does not signal directly whether the US will (or will not) be presented. Rather, B signals whether A will (or will not) be paired with the US. The higher-order relation may be represented as B(A–noUS).

Extinction versus conditioned inhibition. How can we tell whether inhibitory conditioning results in a direct B–noUS association or a higher-order B(A–noUS) association? One possible strategy for answering this question involves comparing inhibitory conditioning to procedures in which only a B–noUS association could develop. One such procedure is **extinction,** which will be described in greater detail in Chapter 9. For the present discussion, it is sufficient to comment that in an extinction procedure a CS is repeatedly presented without the US. Thus, an extinction procedure is one that might result in a CS–noUS association. However, given the simplicity of an extinction procedure, it could not result in a higher-order relation B(A–noUS) association.

Does an extinguished stimulus have the same behavioral effects as a conditioned inhibitory stimulus? Is an extinguished stimulus slower to acquire conditioned excitatory properties than a neutral stimulus in a retardation-of-acquisition test? And does an extinguished stimulus suppress responding elicited by an excitatory CS in a summation test?

Studies have demonstrated that extensive extinction can produce resistance to subsequent excitatory conditioning (Bouton, 1986). An extinguished stimulus is retarded in its subsequent acquisition of conditioned excitatory properties if the stimulus is presented in a context that reactivates memories of the extinction procedure (Bouton & Swartzentruber, 1989). Thus, an extinguished stimulus can pass the retardation-of-acquisition test of inhibition. However, even after extensive extinction training, an extinguished stimulus does not pass a summation test of inhibition (Reberg, 1972). Only stimuli that have been used in one of the inhibitory conditioning procedures I have described are effective in suppressing responding in a summation test of conditioned inhibition. These results suggest that an important aspect of inhibitory conditioning involves the opportunity to learn a higher-order relation in which the conditioned inhibitor provides information about occasions when another CS is paired with the US.

	Trials with the US	Trials without the US
Conditioned inhibition	A ⟶ US	AB ⟶ no US
Conditioned facilitation	AB ⟶ US	A ⟶ no US

F I G U R E 5.8 Comparison of the types of trials that occur in procedures for conditioned inhibition and conditioned facilitation.
A and B represent two different conditioned stimuli.

Higher-Order Relations in Pavlovian Conditioning: Conditioned Facilitation

A conditioned facilitation procedure is similar to inhibitory conditioning procedures in that it involves one US and two CSs. As in inhibitory conditioning, the stimuli are arranged in such a way that the occasions when one CS (A) is paired with the US are perfectly predicted by a second CS (B). The difference between **facilitation** and inhibition is illustrated in Figure 5.8.

In conditioned inhibition procedures, stimulus B is presented on trials when stimulus A is not followed by the US (AB–noUS or AB⁻), and B is omitted when A is paired with the US (A–US or A⁺). This arrangement is reversed in a facilitation procedure. In a facilitation procedure, stimulus B is presented on trials when A is reinforced (AB–US or AB⁺), and B is omitted on trials when A is not reinforced (A–noUS or A⁻). The outcome is that the subject responds on trials when A and B are presented together but does not respond when A is presented alone (Holland, 1992).

STIMULUS RELATIONS IN CONDITIONED FACILITATION

What kind of associations might produce responding in a facilitation procedure? As in the case with inhibitory conditioning, there are two possibilities, one involving a direct relation of stimulus B with the US and the other involving an indirect, or higher-order relation.

In a facilitation procedure, AB⁺ trials are intermixed with A⁻ trials. The US is only presented on trials when stimulus B occurs. This allows for the acquisition of a direct relation between stimulus B and the US (a B–US association).

A facilitation procedure also contains a higher-order relation. Stimulus B provides perfectly accurate information about the occasions when stimulus A will be paired with the US. Stimulus A will end with the US on trials when stimulus B is presented (AB⁺) but will not end with the US on trials when stimulus B is absent (A⁻). Therefore, a facilitation procedure may result in

Trials with the US   **Trials without the US**

Noise present   Noise absent

Light ⟶ Food   Light ⟶ No food

F I G U R E 5.9   Outline of facilitation experiment by Rescorla, Durlach, & Grau, 1985.

---

the learning of a higher-order relation in which B comes to signal the pairing of stimulus A with the US. This higher-order relation may be represented as B(A–US). Because stimulus B signals the occasions when A is paired with the US, the facilitation procedure is also called **occasion setting** (for example, Holland, 1986).

DISTINGUISHING BETWEEN B–US AND B(A–US) RELATIONS

Conditioned response topographies. How can we decide whether subjects learn a B–US relation or a B(A–US) relation in a facilitation procedure? One approach is to determine whether the subjects are directing their conditioned responding to stimulus A or to stimulus B. This approach has been used extensively in studies of facilitation in appetitive conditioning (Holland, 1992).

In one experiment (Rescorla, Durlach, & Grau, 1985), pigeons served as subjects, a noise like static on the radio served as stimulus B, and a key light served as stimulus A. When noise and key light stimuli are paired with food, different CRs result. A key light associated with food elicits conditioned pecking behavior. In contrast, a noise stimulus paired with food elicits increased locomotion but no pecking at the response key. Thus, any key pecks observed in this experiment can only be interpreted as conditioned behavior directed toward the key light, not as conditioned behavior directed toward the noise CS.

The procedure for the experiment is summarized in Figure 5.9. The key light was paired with food in the presence of the noise stimulus (AB–US). When the noise was absent, the key light did not end in food (A–noUS). The pigeons came to peck the key light when the noise was present and did not peck when the noise was off. This outcome cannot be explained in terms of a direct association between stimulus B (the noise), and the US (a B–US association) because pigeons do not peck a noise stimulus associated with food. The results also cannot be explained in terms of a simple association between the stimulus A (the key light), and food (an A–US association) because such an association would have produced pecking of the key light whether or not the noise was present. The fact that the birds pecked the key light only when the noise was present suggests that the pigeons learned a

B(A–US) relation in which the noise set the occasion for responding to the key light.

Effects of extinction of stimulus B. An alternative strategy for distinguishing between B–US and B(A–US) relations in a facilitation procedure involves testing the effects of extinguishing stimulus B. As was the case with conditioned inhibition, an extinction procedure turns out to be a powerful diagnostic tool. Extinction of B involves repeatedly presenting stimulus B by itself. This experience is contrary to a B–US relation and should reduce responding that depends on the B–US relation. However, repeating presentations of stimulus B by itself is not contrary to a B(A–US) relation. Therefore, extinction of stimulus B should not disrupt responding mediated by the B(A–US) relation. Results consistent with this prediction have been obtained repeatedly (for example, Holland, 1989; Rescorla, 1985; Ross, 1983). Simple extinction of stimulus B does not weaken the ability of stimulus B to facilitate responding to A following training on a facilitation procedure.

Finally, I should point out that subjects do not invariably learn a B(A–US) relation as a result of a facilitation procedure. Sometimes, procedures involving a mixture of AB–US trials and A–noUS trials result in the learning of only a B–US relation. In other cases, subjects learn both a B–US relation and a higher-order B(A–US) relation. A number of factors beyond the scope of the present discussion determine whether a particular procedure favors the acquisition of a B–US relation or a B(A–US) relation (Holland, 1992).

Suggested Readings

DOMJAN, M. (1985). Cue-consequence specificity and long-delay learning revisited. *Annals of the New York Academy of Sciences, 443,* 54–66.

GORMEZANO, I., KEHOE, E. J., & MARSHALL, B. S. (1983). Twenty years of classical conditioning research with the rabbit. In J. M. Sprague & A. N. Epstein (Eds.), *Progress in psychobiology and physiological psychology* (Vol. 10, pp. 197–275). Orlando, FL: Academic Press.

HOLLAND, P. C. (1992). Occasion setting in Pavlovian conditioning. In G. Bower (Ed.), *The psychology of learning and motivation* (Vol. 28, pp. 69–125). Orlando, FL: Academic Press.

KAMIN, L. J. (1969). Predictability, surprise, and attention, and conditioning. In B. A. Campbell and R. M. Church (Eds.), *Punishment and aversive behavior* (pp. 279–296). New York: Appleton-Century-Crofts.

PAPINI, M. R., & BITTERMAN, M. E. (1990). The role of contingency in classical conditioning. *Psychological Review, 97,* 396–403.

Technical Terms

Blocking effect
Conditioned inhibition
Contingency
CS-US interval
Delayed conditioning
Differential inhibition
Extinction
Facilitation
Higher-order stimulus relation

Interstimulus interval
Long-delay learning
Occasion setting
Retardation-of-acquisition test
Simultaneous conditioning
Summation test
Temporal contiguity
Trace conditioning

CHAPTER SIX

Instrumental and Operant Conditioning

DID YOU KNOW THAT:

- Learning a new instrumental response often involves learning a new combination of familiar response components.
- Variability in behavior can be an advantage in the learning of new responses.
- The deleterious effects of reinforcement delay can be overcome by presenting a marking stimulus immediately after the instrumental response.
- Thorndike's Law of Effect does not involve an association between the instrumental response and the reinforcer.
- Instrumental conditioning allows for the learning of three binary associations and one higher-order association.
- Pavlovian associations in instrumental conditioning can interfere with the instrumental response.

The various environmental manipulations that I have described so far (habituation, sensitization, and Pavlovian conditioning procedures) all involve presentations of different types of stimuli according to various arrangements. The procedures produce changes in behavior, as well as increases and decreases in responding, as a result of the stimulus presentations. An important feature of habituation, sensitization, and Pavlovian conditioning procedures is that they are defined independently of the actions of the organism. What the subjects do as a result of the procedures does not influence the scheduled presentation of stimuli.

In a sense, studies of habituation, sensitization, and Pavlovian conditioning represent how organisms learn about events that are beyond their control. Adjustments to uncontrollable events are important because many aspects of the environment are beyond our control. When a class is scheduled, how long it takes to toast bread, how far it is between city blocks, and when the local post office is open are but a few examples. By learning about uncontrollable events, we can adjust and respond to them more effectively. However, not all learning involves situations in which events are beyond the control of the organism. Another important category of learning involves situations in which the presentation of a US depends on the subject's behavior. Such cases involve *instrumental* or *operant conditioning*.

Instrumental conditioning procedures involve the periodic presentation of a significant stimulus or event. However, whether or not the event occurs depends on the behavior of the organism. Common examples of instrumental behavior involve turning a doorknob to open a door, putting ingredients together to make lemonade, changing the television channel to find a particular show, and saying "Hello" to someone to get a greeting in return. In all of these cases, a particular response is required to obtain a specific stimulus or consequence. Because the response is instrumental in producing the stimulus, the response is referred to as **instrumental behavior.** The consequent stimulus (the open door, the tasty lemonade, the television show, and the reciprocal greeting) is referred to as the **reinforcer.**

Sometimes, instrumental behavior is also called **operant behavior.** This is the case if the response is defined in terms of a particular operation, or manipulation of the environment. For example, we may define an operant response as turning a doorknob far enough to open a door. Given this definition, it does not matter what muscle movements are used to turn the door knob, provided the knob gets turned far enough to open the door. The knob could be turned with a person's right hand, left hand, fingertips, or with a full grip of the knob. Such variations in response topography are ignored with operant responses.

A common example of operant behavior in animal research involves a laboratory rat pressing a response lever in a small experimental chamber (see Figure 6.1). (We previously encountered this example in discussions of conditioned suppression in Chapter 4.) Whether or not a lever-press response has occurred can be determined by placing a microswitch under the

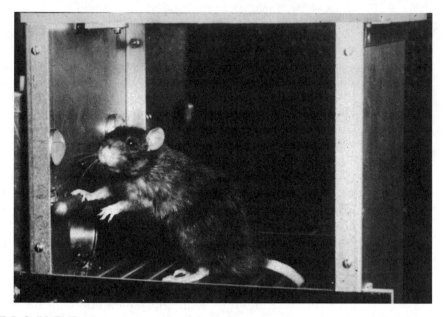

**F I G U R E 6.1   A common laboratory preparation for the study of oper-
ant behavior.** (Omikron/Photo Researchers)

lever. A press of a lever with enough force to activate the microswitch is
counted as a response. Lever-presses that are too weak to activate the switch
are ignored. In this case, the lever-press response "operates" on the
environment by activating the microswitch.

Another common example of operant behavior in animal research is a
pigeon pecking a circular disk or response key on a wall (see Figure 4.1). A
microswitch behind the response key is used to detect instances of the
key-peck response.

The Traditions of Thorndike and Skinner

The intellectual traditions of classical conditioning were set by one
dominant figure, Ivan Pavlov. In contrast, the intellectual traditions of
instrumental and operant conditioning have their roots in the work of two
American giants of twentieth-century psychology, Edward L. Thorndike and
B. F. Skinner (see Figures 6.2 and 6.3). The empirical methods, as well as the
theoretical perspectives of these two scientists, were strikingly different, but
the traditions started by each of them have endured to this day. I will first
discuss the distinctive experimental methods used by Thorndike and
Skinner, and then note some differences in their theoretical perspectives.

F I G U R E 6.2 Edward L. Thorndike (1874–1949).
(Archives of the History of American Psychology)

METHODOLOGICAL CONSIDERATIONS

Thorndike was interested in studying animal intelligence. To do this, he designed a number of escape tasks for young cats in a project that would become his Ph.D. dissertation at Columbia (Thorndike, 1898). Each task involved a box of some kind, a **puzzle box.** A different type of response was required to get released from each box. The puzzle was to figure out how to get out of the box.

Thorndike would put a kitten into a puzzle box several times and measure how long the kitten took to escape and obtain a piece of fish. In some puzzle boxes, the kittens had to make just one type of response (turning a latch, for example) to get out. In others, several actions were required, and these had to be performed in a particular order. Thorndike found that with repeated trials in a particular box, the kittens got quicker and quicker at escaping. Their escape latencies decreased.

The discrete-trial method. Thorndike's experiments illustrate the **discrete-trial method** in the study of instrumental behavior. In this method,

F I G U R E 6.3   B. F. Skinner (1904–1990). (Bettman Archive)

the subject has the opportunity to perform the instrumental response only at certain times (during discrete trials), as determined by the experimenter. In the case of Thorndike's experiments, the kittens could only perform the instrumental escape response when they were placed in a puzzle box. When they made the required response, they were released from the box, and the next trial did not begin until Thorndike chose to put them back in.

The discrete trial method was subsequently adopted by investigators who used mazes of various sorts to study instrumental conditioning. Mazes are most commonly used with laboratory rats and were introduced into the investigative artillery of scientists by Willard Small, who built a maze in an effort to mimic the tunnel-like structures of the underground burrows in which rats live (Small, 1899, 1900).

A common type of maze is a **straight-alley runway** (see Figure 6.4). In

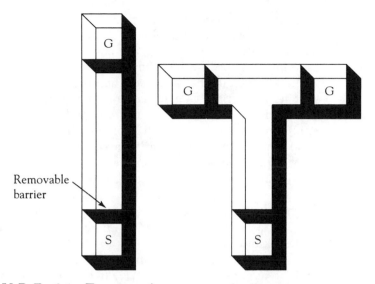

F I G U R E 6.4 **Top view of a runway and a T-maze.**
S is the start box; G is the goal box. (Domjan & Burkhard, 1993.)

a straight-alley runway, subjects are first placed in a start box. The start box door is then lifted to start a trial, and the subjects are given the opportunity to go to the other end of the runway. When the subjects reach the box, they are given a small piece of food. After eating the food, they are removed from the goal box until it is time to run the next trial. The speed of running from the start box to the goal box is measured. As subjects learn, they become faster at getting from the start box to the goal box. Learning results in increased speed of running.

The discrete trial method requires handling the subject a great deal. The experimenter has to pick up the rat, place it in the start box, wait for it to reach the goal box, remove it from the goal box, and then put it in a holding area for the intertrial interval. In addition, how long the subject has to wait between trials is determined by the experimenter.

The free-operant method. The major alternative to the discrete trial method for the study of instrumental behavior is the **free operant method,** which was developed by Skinner (1938). Skinner made numerous methodological and conceptual contributions to the study of behavior, and these two types of contributions were often interrelated. The free-operant method is a case in point.

Skinner's development of the free-operant method started with his interest in designing an automated maze for rats—a maze in which the subjects would automatically return to the start box after each trial. Such an apparatus would have the obvious advantage that the rat would have to be handled only at the start and the end of a training session, freeing up the experimenter to do other things in the meanwhile. An automated maze would also permit the rat rather than the experimenter to decide when to start its next trial. That would enable the investigation of not only how rapidly the rat completed an instrumental response but how frequently it elected to engage in the instrumental behavior. Thus, an automated maze promised to provide information about motivated behavior that could not be obtained as easily with the discrete-trial method.

Skinner tried several approaches to automating the discrete-trial maze procedure. Each approach incorporated some improvements on the previous design, but as the work progressed the apparatus became less and less maze-like (Skinner, 1956). His efforts culminated in what has come be to known as the **Skinner box.**

We encountered the Skinner box in discussing the definition of an operant response (see Figure 6.1). It is a small rectangular chamber with three plain walls. The fourth wall has a small lever that the rat can press over and over again, and there is a food cup nearby, into which small pieces of food can be dropped by an automatic dispenser. Each lever-press response is electronically detected by the closure of a microswitch, and the apparatus can be programmed so that a piece of food is delivered each time the rat presses the lever.

In the Skinner box, the response of interest is defined in terms of the closure of a microswitch. The apparatus ignores whether the rat presses the lever with one paw or the other, or with its tail. Therefore, the Skinner box is designed to study operant behavior. Furthermore, the operant response can occur at any time. The interval between successive responses is determined by the subject rather than by the experimenter. The method is called the free-operant method because the operant response can be made at any time.

The primary conceptual advantage of the free-operant method is that it allows the subject to initiate the instrumental response. Skinner focused on this aspect of the rat's behavior. How often a subject elects to initiate the instrumental behavior can be quantified in terms of the frequency of the response in a given period of time, or the **rate of responding.** Rate of responding has come to serve as the primary measure of operant behavior.

The Establishment of an Instrumental or Operant Response

People often think about instrumental or operant conditioning as a technique for training new responses. In what sense are the responses new? Does instrumental conditioning always establish entirely new responses? Does it combine familiar responses in new ways? Or does it establish a familiar response in a new situation?

LEARNING WHERE AND WHAT TO RUN FOR

Consider, for example, a hungry rat learning to run from one end of a runway to the other for a piece of food. An experimentally naive rat is slow to run the length of the runway at first. But, this is not because it enters the experiment without the motor skill of running. Rats do not have to be taught to run. What they have to be taught is where to run and what to run for. In the straight-alley runway, the instrumental conditioning procedure provides the stimulus control and the motivation for the running response. It does not establish the running response in the subject's repertoire.

COMBINING FAMILIAR RESPONSES IN NEW WAYS

Pressing a response lever as an instrumental response is a bit different from running. An experimentally naive rat probably has never encountered a response lever before and has never performed a lever-press response. In this case, the required instrumental response is missing from the subject's repertoire at first. Unlike the running response, the lever-press response has to be learned in the experimental situation. But, does it have to be learned from scratch? Hardly.

An untrained rat is not as naive about pressing a lever as one might think. Lever-pressing consists of a number of response components: getting up on hind legs and raising one or both front paws, extending a paw forward over the lever, and then bringing the paw down with sufficient force to press the lever. Rats are likely to have performed responses much like these at various times while exploring their cages, exploring each other, or handling pellets of food. What they have to learn in the operant conditioning situation is how the various response components go together to depress the lever and produce food.

Pressing a lever is a new response only in the sense that it involves a new combination of response components that already exist in the subject's repertoire. In this case, instrumental conditioning involves the construction or synthesis of a new behavioral unit from preexisting response components (Schwartz, 1981).

SHAPING NEW RESPONSES

Can instrumental conditioning also be used to condition entirely new responses, that is, responses that the subject would never perform without instrumental conditioning? Most certainly. Instrumental conditioning is used to teach a police dog to climb a 15-foot vertical barrier, a sprinter to run a mile in 4 minutes, and a golf pro to drive a ball 200 yards in one stroke. Such responses are remarkable because they are unlike anything the subjects are likely to do without special training.

In an instrumental conditioning procedure, the subject has to perform the required response before the reinforcer is delivered. Given this restriction, how can instrumental procedures be used to condition responses that never occur on their own? The learning of entirely new responses is possible because of the variability of behavior. Variability is perhaps the most obvious feature of behavior. Organisms rarely do the same thing twice in exactly the same fashion. Response variability is usually considered a curse because it makes predicting and controlling behavior difficult. However, for learning new responses, variability is a blessing.

The delivery of a reinforcer (reinforcement) does not result in the exact repetition of the response that produced the reinforcer the first time. If a rat, for example, is reinforced for pressing a response lever with a force of 2 grams, it will not always press the lever with a force of 2 grams. Sometimes it will press with less force; other times it will press with more force.

The left panel in Figure 6.5 shows what the distribution of responses might look like if lever-pressing is reinforced only when the lever is depressed with a force greater than 2 grams. Notice that many, but not all, of the lever-presses exceed the 2-gram criterion. A few of the responses exceed as much as 3 grams, but none of the responses exceed 4 grams.

Because the variability in behavior includes responses as forceful as 3 grams, we can change the response criterion so that reinforcement is only provided if the rat presses the lever with a force exceeding 3 grams. After several sessions on this new force requirement, the distribution of lever-presses will look something like what is represented in the middle panel of Figure 6.5.

Responding remains variable after the shift in the response requirement. Increasing the force requirement results in a shift of the force distribution to the right so that now the majority of the lever-presses exceed 3 grams. One consequence of this shift is that now the rat occasionally presses the lever with a force exceeding 4 grams. These responses are entirely new. They did not occur originally.

Since we now have responses exceeding 4 grams, we can increase the response requirement again. We can now set the procedure so that reinforcement is only given for lever-presses that exceed 4 grams. This will result in a further shift of the force distribution to yet higher values, as shown in the right panel of Figure 6.5. Now, most of the responses exceed 4 grams, and sometimes the rat presses the lever with a force exceeding 5 grams. Responses with such force are very different from what the rat started out doing.

The procedure described for increasing the force of lever-pressing in a rat is called **shaping.** Shaping is used when the researcher is interested in conditioning instrumental responses that are not in the subject's existing behavioral repertoire. New behavior is shaped by imposing a series of response criteria. The response criteria take the subject from its starting behavioral repertoire to the desired target response (for example, Deich, Allan, & Zeigler, 1988; Galbicka, 1988).

In setting up a shaping procedure, the desired final performance must be defined clearly. This sets the goal or end point of the shaping procedure.

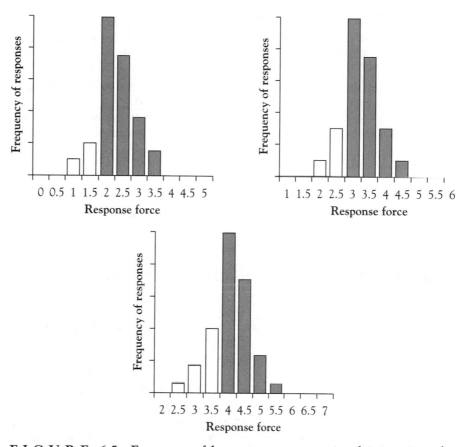

F I G U R E 6.5 Frequency of lever-press responses involving various degrees of force.
In the left panel, only responses greater than 2 grams in force resulted in delivery of the reinforcer. In the middle panel, only responses greater than 3 grams in force were reinforced. In the right panel, only responses greater than 4 grams in force were reinforced. (Hypothetical data.)

Next, the existing behavioral repertoire of the subject has to be clearly described to identify the starting point. Finally, a sequence of training steps must be designed that start with the existing behavior of the subject and end with the final target response. The sequence of training steps involves successive approximations to the final target response. Therefore, shaping is typically defined as *the reinforcement of successive approximations*.

Shaping is useful not only in training entirely new responses but also in training new combinations of existing response components. Riding a bicycle, for example, involves three rather large response components—

steering, pedaling, and maintaining balance. Children learning to ride usually start by learning to pedal. Pedaling is a new response. It is unlike anything a child is likely to have done before getting on a bicycle. To enable the child to learn to pedal without having to balance, parents usually start by giving a child a tricycle or a bicycle with training wheels. Pedaling involves fairly familiar leg movements and is therefore learned quickly. While learning to pedal, the child is not likely to pay much attention to steering and will need help to avoid riding into a bush or off the sidewalk.

Once the child has learned to pedal, pedaling may be combined with steering. Only after the child has learned to combine pedaling with steering can the balance component be added. This component is the hardest part of learning to ride a bicycle. That is why parents often wait until a child is proficient in riding a bicycle with training wheels before letting the child ride without them.

The Importance of Immediate Reinforcement

Instrumental conditioning is basically a response selection process. The response (or unique combination of response components) that results in the delivery of the reinforcer is selected from the diversity of actions the subject performs in the conditioning situation. It is critical to this response selection process that the reinforcer be delivered immediately after the desired or target response. If the reinforcer is delayed, other activities are bound to occur between the target response and the reinforcer, and one of those other activities may be reinforced instead of the target response (see Figure 6.6).

Delivering a primary reinforcer immediately after the target response is not always practical. The opportunity to go to a playground serves as an effective reinforcer for children in elementary school. However, it would be disruptive to allow children to go outside each time they finish a math problem. A more practical approach is to give a coin or token for each problem completed, and then allow those tokens to be exchanged for the opportunity to go to the playground. With such a procedure, the primary reinforcer (access to the playground) is delayed after the instrumental response. But, the instrumental response is immediately followed by a stimulus (the token) that is associated with the primary reinforcer.

A stimulus that is associated with a primary reinforcer is called a **conditioned** or **secondary reinforcer.** The delivery of a conditioned reinforcer immediately after the instrumental response overcomes the ineffectiveness of delayed reinforcement as an instrumental conditioning procedure (for example, Winter & Perkins, 1982).

The ineffectiveness of delayed reinforcement can be also overcome by presenting a **marking stimulus** immediately after the target instrumental response. A marking stimulus is not a conditioned reinforcer and does not provide information about a future opportunity to obtain primary reinforce-

$$R_1 \quad R_2 \quad R_3 \quad R_4 \quad R_x \quad S^* \qquad\qquad R_1 \quad R_2 \quad R_x \quad R_3 \quad R_4 \quad S^*$$
Immediate reinforcement   Delayed reinforcement

F I G U R E   6.6   Diagram of immediate and delayed reinforcement of the target response R_x.
R_1, R_2, R_3, . . . represent different activities of the organism. S^* represents delivery of the reinforcer; when reinforcement is delayed after R_x, other responses occur closer to the reinforcer.

___

ment. Rather, it is a brief visual or auditory cue that distinguishes the target instrumental response from the other activities the subject is likely to perform during a delay interval. In this way, the marking stimulus makes the instrumental response more memorable and helps to overcome the deleterious effect of the reinforcer delay (Lieberman, McIntosh, & Thomas, 1979; Thomas & Lieberman, 1990).

Event Relations in Instrumental Conditioning

Methodologically, the most obvious events in instrumental conditioning are the instrumental response and the reinforcer. The response may be represented as R and the reinforcer as S^*. The relation between the response and reinforcer may be represented as $R-S^*$. However, there is more to an instrumental conditioning situation than just the response and the reinforcer. Starting with the earliest theorizing, investigators were aware that more than just the response and the reinforcer have to be considered in analyses of instrumental learning.

Thorndike pointed out that subjects experience a unique set of stimuli whenever they perform an instrumental response. In Thorndike's experiments, these stimuli were provided by the puzzle box in which the subjects were placed at the start of a training trial and the particular latch they had to manipulate to get out.

We don't know whether Thorndike's subjects focused on the visual features of the puzzle box, the tactile cues of the surfaces they touched, or both. But, that does not matter for the theoretical analysis. Regardless of which stimuli a subject paid attention to, once it was assigned to a puzzle box, it experienced a unique set of stimuli whenever it performed the required escape response. The stimuli a subject experiences whenever it performs a required instrumental response may be represented by S.

The above considerations suggest that an instrumental conditioning situation is made up of not just the response R and the reinforcer S^*, but also

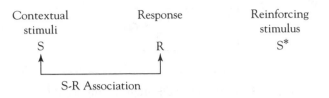

Contextual stimuli	Response	Reinforcing stimulus
S	R	S*

S-R Association

F I G U R E   6.7 **Diagram of the S-R association in instrumental conditioning.**

the set of stimuli S in the presence of which the instrumental response occurs. The three components, S, R, and S*, allow for the establishment of several event relations in instrumental conditioning in addition to the **R-S* association.**

THE S-R ASSOCIATION: THORNDIKE'S LAW OF EFFECT

Thorndike proposed that during the course of instrumental conditioning an association comes to be established between the response R and the environmental stimulus S (see Figure 6.7). In fact, Thorndike considered this **S-R association** to be solely responsible for instrumental behavior and made S-R learning a critical part of his law of instrumental learning—the **Law of Effect.** The Law of Effect states that instrumental learning involves the formation of an association between the instrumental response R and the stimulus S, in the presence of which the response is performed. The reinforcer delivered after the response serves to strengthen or "stamp in" the S-R association but is not an element of that association.

According to the Law of Effect, instrumental learning does not involve learning to associate the reinforcer with the response. It does not involve the establishment of an R-S* association or learning about the reinforcer. Rather, instrumental conditioning only results in the establishment of an S-R association. The reinforcer S* is important only as a catalyst for the learning of the S-R association.

Assuming that organisms do not learn about the reinforcer in instrumental conditioning may seem counterintuitive. However, the Law of Effect was consistent with other theorizing at the start of the twentieth century. The Law of Effect is an adaptation of the Pavlovian concept of the conditioned response to instrumental learning. A Pavlovian CR is a response to a particular stimulus, the CS. In an analogous fashion, the Law of Effect considers the instrumental response R to be a response to a particular set of stimuli S. Pavlovian conditioning was assumed to result in the establishment of a CS-CR association. Thorndike assumed that instrumental conditioning results in the establishment of an analogous S-R association.

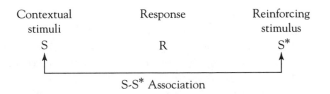

FIGURE 6.8 Diagram of the S-S* association in instrumental conditioning.

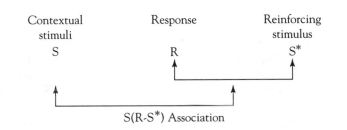

FIGURE 6.9 Diagram of the S(R-S*) association in instrumental conditioning.

S-S* AND S(R-S*) RELATIONS

Another event relation in instrumental conditioning that has received considerable theoretical and empirical attention is the relation between the antecedent stimuli S and the reinforcer S* (see Figure 6.8). Because the instrumental response R results in delivery of the reinforcer S* in the presence of S, S is paired with S* and this is assumed to result in the learning of an **S-S* association** (Hull, 1930, 1931). This S-S* association is much like a Pavlovian CS-US association and presumably has the same behavioral consequences. The establishment of the S-S* association presumably results in Pavlovian conditioned responses being elicited by S.

The event relations considered thus far—R-S*, S-R, and S-S*—are binary, or direct associations between pairs of elements of the instrumental conditioning situation. Another way that S, R, and S* may become related in instrumental conditioning is through a higher-order relation that may be represented as S(R-S*) (see Figure 6.9). The first theoretician to recognize the S(R-S*) relation was Skinner (1938).

Skinner emphasized that in instrumental conditioning the reinforcer S* is presented contingent on the prior occurrence of the response R, not contingent on the prior occurrence of S. However, the R-S* contingency is in effect only in the presence of S. Based on these considerations, he suggested that a higher-order relation becomes established in which S signals the existence of the R-S* contingency or sets the occasion for the R-S* association. Skinner referred to this as a "three-term contingency." The three-term contingency may be represented as S(R-S*). The S(R-S*) relation in instrumental conditioning is analogous to the higher-order B(A–US) relation in Pavlovian conditioning discussed in Chapter 5.

Two-Factor and Three-Factor Theories of Instrumental Learning

Experimental investigations of the associative structure of instrumental conditioning have provided evidence for all of the event relations identified so far—R-S*, S-R, S-S*, and S(R-S*). Thorndike was the first to identify and emphasize the importance of the S-R association in instrumental conditioning. This association and the mechanisms of the Law of Effect were subsequently used in the more elaborate neobehaviorist theories (for example, Amsel, 1958; Hull, 1930, 1931; Spence, 1956). These theories, as well as subsequent so-called **two-factor theories of learning** (see Rescorla & Solomon, 1967), also emphasized the importance of the S-S* association that may develop in instrumental conditioning.

Until recently, two-factor theories have predominated associative analyses of instrumental learning. Some two-factor theories were based on the S-R and the S-S* associations (for example, Spence, 1956). Others were based on the R-S* and the S-S* associations (for example, Bolles, 1972). More recently, investigators have returned to Skinner's higher-order S(R-S*) relation as a critical component of instrumental learning (for example, Colwill & Rescorla, 1990).

NEUROPHYSIOLOGICAL IMPLICATIONS

The complexity of the associative structure of instrumental learning that has been documented at the behavioral level suggests that the underlying neural circuitry of instrumental behavior is equally complex. This is unlike the situation in Pavlovian conditioning. As we saw in Chapters 4 and 5, there are both simple and more complex forms of Pavlovian conditioning. Simple forms of Pavlovian excitatory conditioning are mediated by just an S-S association. More complex forms involve higher-order relations, B(A–US). In contrast, corresponding simple and complex forms of instrumental conditioning do not exist.

Instrumental learning involves both binary S-S* and higher-order **S(R-S*) associations**. This suggests that the neural mechanisms of instrumental conditioning are likely to be built of components that include the mechanisms of S-S learning as well as the mechanisms of higher-order Pavlovian relations.

IMPLICATIONS FOR CONSTRAINTS ON INSTRUMENTAL CONDITIONING

Understanding the associative structure of instrumental conditioning also provides insights into some enduring puzzles of instrumental learning. Thorndike, for example, tested subjects in a variety of different puzzle boxes (Thorndike, 1911). The young cats had to do different things in different boxes. In some boxes, the cats had to either yawn or scratch themselves to be let out. Learning proceeded slowly in these boxes. Even after extensive training, the cats did not make vigorous and genuine yawning responses. Rather, they came to perform rapid, abortive yawns. Thorndike obtained similar results with the scratch response. The cats made rapid, half-hearted attempts to scratch themselves. These two examples illustrate the general finding that self-care and grooming responses are difficult to condition with food reinforcement.

Another category of instrumental behavior that is difficult to condition with food reinforcement is the release of a coin or token. Two of Skinner's graduate students, Keller and Marion Breland, became fascinated with the possibilities of animal training and set up a business that supplied trained animals for amusement parks, department store windows, and zoos. As a part of their business, they trained numerous species of animals to do various entertaining things (Breland & Breland, 1961).

In one display, the Brelands tried to have a pig pick up a coin and drop it into a piggy bank to obtain food. Although the pig did what it was supposed to a few times, as training progressed, it became reluctant to release the coin and rooted it along the ground instead. This rooting behavior came to predominate, and the project had to be abandoned.

Several factors are probably responsible for the difficulties that have been encountered in conditioning grooming and coin-release behavior (Shettleworth, 1975). One of the most important factors seems to be the development of S-S* associations in instrumental conditioning (Timberlake, Wahl, & King, 1982). In the coin-release task, the coin becomes associated with the reinforcer and serves as stimulus S in the S-S* association. In instrumental reinforcement of grooming, stimulus S is provided by the contextual cues of the conditioning situation.

Because S-S* associations are much like Pavlovian associations between a CS and a US, Pavlovian conditioned responses related to the reinforcer come to be elicited by S. With food reinforcement, these responses are related to the anticipation of food. Food-anticipatory responses are incompatible with self-care and grooming. They are also incompatible with releasing, and thereby withdrawing from, a coin that has come to signal the availability of food.

Analyses of the associative structure of instrumental conditioning indicate that Pavlovian associations develop during the course of instrumental conditioning. These Pavlovian associations can yield CRs that are incompatible with the required instrumental response and prevent increases in certain instrumental responses such as grooming and coin-release responses.

Suggested Readings

COLWILL, R. M. (1994). Associative representations of instrumental contingencies. In D. L. Medin (Ed.), *The psychology of learning and motivation* (pp. 1–72). San Diego, CA: Academic Press.

RESCORLA, R. A., & SOLOMON, R. L. (1967). Two-process learning theory: Relationships between Pavlovian conditioning and instrumental learning. *Psychological Review, 74,* 151–182.

TIMBERLAKE, W., & LUCAS, G. A. (1989). Behavior systems and learning: From misbehavior to general principles. In S. B. Klein & R. R. Mowrer (Eds.), *Contemporary learning theories: Instrumental conditioning and the impact of biological constraints on learning* (pp. 237–275). Hillsdale, NJ: Erlbaum.

Technical Terms

Conditioned reinforcer
Constraints on learning
Discrete-trial method
Free-operant method
Instrumental behavior
Law of Effect
Marking stimulus
Operant behavior
Puzzle box
R-S* association

Rate of responding
Reinforcer
S(R-S*) association
S-R association
S-S* association
Secondary reinforcer
Shaping
Skinner box
Straight-alley runway
Two-factor theory

CHAPTER SEVEN

Schedules of Reinforcement and Response Choice

DID YOU KNOW THAT:

- Schedules of reinforcement determine rates and patterns of responding.
- Ratio schedules produce higher rates of responding than interval schedules.
- A pause after reinforcement occurs on both fixed ratio and fixed interval schedules.
- Training of a response chain does not have to begin with the last component of the chain.
- Reinforcement can be simultaneously available for two or more response alternatives.
- The Matching Law describes choice behavior.
- Rates and patterns of responding are determined by the feedback function created by a particular schedule of reinforcement.

I described examples of instrumental conditioning in Chapter 6 with the implication that the reinforcer is delivered each time the subject performs the instrumental response. Situations in nature in which there is a direct causal link between the response and the reinforcer come close to this ideal. Nearly every time you turn on the faucet, you get running water; nearly every time you pick up the telephone, you hear a dial tone; and most of the time when you buy an attractive piece of pastry, you end up with something good to eat. However, even in these cases, the relation between responding and the reinforcer is not perfect. The water main to your house may be broken, the telephone may malfunction, and the pastry may be stale. In many instrumental conditioning situations, not every occurrence of the instrumental response is successful in producing the reinforcer.

Whether a particular occurrence of the instrumental response results in the reinforcer can depend on a variety of factors. Sometimes, the response has to be repeated a number of times before the reinforcer is delivered. In other situations, the response is only reinforced after a certain amount of time has passed. In yet other cases, both repetition and the passage of time are critical. The rule that specifies which occurrence of the instrumental response is reinforced is called a **schedule of reinforcement.**

Schedules of reinforcement have been of great interest because they determine many aspects of instrumental behavior. The rate and pattern of instrumental responding in free-operant situations are determined by the schedule of reinforcement. Seemingly trivial changes in a reinforcement schedule can produce profound changes in the rate and pattern of responding. I will describe some of these effects in the present chapter. Schedules of reinforcement also determine the persistence of instrumental behavior when reinforcement is no longer available. I will describe persistence effects in Chapter 9.

The Cumulative Record

The rate and pattern of responding produced by various schedules of reinforcement are typically investigated with the use of free-operant procedures. Microcomputers are programmed to record occurrences of the operant response (lever-pressing in rats, for example) and also determine which response is reinforced. Training sessions last about an hour each day, and subjects receive repeated sessions. After extensive experience with a particular schedule of reinforcement, the rate and pattern of responding stabilize. The results are conveniently represented in terms of a **cumulative record.**

A cumulative record is a special kind of graph in which the horizontal axis represents the passage of time, and the vertical axis represents the total or cumulative number of responses that have occurred up to a particular point in time (see Figure 7.1). If the subject does not respond during a period of time, its total or cumulative number of responses stays the same; the

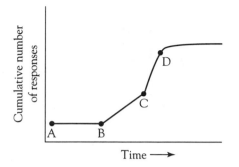

F I G U R E 7.1   An example of a cumulative record used to represent patterns of responding across time in free-operant studies of schedules of reinforcement.
The section from point A to point B represents no responding. The section from point B to point C represents a low rate of responding. The section from point C to point D represents a high response rate. After point D, the rate of responding gradually declines to zero.

---

resultant curve on the cumulative record is a flat horizontal line, as between points A and B in Figure 7.1. Each response is added to the previous total. Thus, each time the subject responds, the cumulative record shows an increment. Because responses cannot be taken away, the curve never goes down.

The slope of the cumulative record represents the subject's rate of responding. Slope is calculated by dividing the vertical displacement between two points on a graph by the horizontal displacement between those two points. Vertical displacement on a cumulative record represents a certain number of responses, and horizontal displacement represents time. Thus, the slope represents responses per time or rate of responding. Low rates of responding are represented by a shallow slope on the cumulative record (for example, from point B to point C in Figure 7.1). Higher response rates result in a steeper slope (for example, from point C to point D in Figure 7.1).

Simple Schedules of Reinforcement

In a simple schedule of reinforcement, only one factor determines whether a particular occurrence of the instrumental response is reinforced. That single factor may be the number of responses that have been performed since the last reinforcer or how much time has passed since the last reinforcer. If the delivery of the reinforcer depends only on the number of responses that have occurred, the procedure is called a **ratio schedule.** If reinforcement of a particular response depends on how much time has passed since the last reinforcer, the procedure is called an **interval schedule.**

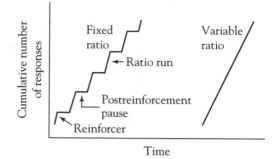

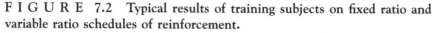

F I G U R E 7.2   Typical results of training subjects on fixed ratio and variable ratio schedules of reinforcement.
The data were obtained with pigeons pecking a response key on an FR 120 and a VR 360 schedule of food reinforcement. The hatch marks indicate when the reinforcer was delivered. (Based on Ferster and Skinner, 1957.)

RATIO SCHEDULES

Fixed ratio schedule of reinforcement.   There are basically two types of ratio schedules, fixed and variable. In a **fixed ratio schedule**, the subject has to perform a fixed number of responses for each delivery of the reinforcer. For example, each work sheet in a math class may have four problems on it, and students may receive a star for each work sheet they complete. This would be a fixed ratio 4 schedule of reinforcement, abbreviated FR 4.

The number of responses required for reinforcement on a fixed ratio schedule may be small or large. In some classes, each work sheet may have four problems on it; in other classes each sheet may have fifteen problems. Regardless of the number, if each sheet in a class has the same number of problems, a fixed ratio schedule of reinforcement is in effect.

Figure 7.2 illustrates the stable pattern of responding that results from two ratio schedules of reinforcement. The hatch marks in the records represent the delivery of the reinforcer. The typical result of reinforcing behavior on a fixed ratio schedule is shown on the left side of the figure. Two features of this pattern are noteworthy. First, notice that after each hatch mark or delivery of the reinforcer, the response rate is zero. The subject stops responding. This pause in behavior is called the **postreinforcement pause**. After the postreinforcement pause, a steady and high rate of responding occurs until the next delivery of the reinforcer. This is called the **ratio run**.

As illustrated in Figure 7.2, fixed ratio schedules produce a stop-run pattern of responding. Either the subject does not respond at all (in the postreinforcement pause) or it responds at a very steady and high rate (in the ratio run). The duration of the postreinforcement pause is related to the ratio requirement. As the ratio requirement of an FR schedule is increased (from FR 10, to FR 20, to FR 40, for example), the duration of the post-reinforcement pause increases (Felton & Lyon, 1966).

Variable ratio schedule of reinforcement. A **variable ratio** schedule is similar to a fixed ratio schedule in that the only factor that determines which repetition of the instrumental response is reinforced is also the number of responses that have been performed. The difference between fixed and variable ratio schedules is that in a variable ratio schedule, the number of responses required varies from one reinforcer delivery to the next.

In putting, for example, reinforcement is provided by getting the golf ball into the cup. You may get the ball into the cup on the first try, or you may have to hit the ball several times before you succeed. Whether or not the ball gets into the cup depends only on your hitting the ball with the putter. How long you take to get the job done is irrelevant. Therefore, this is a ratio schedule. But the number of putting responses varies from one putting green to another. Therefore, this is a variable ratio schedule.

A variable ratio schedule is abbreviated as VR. If on average, you need to hit the ball three times to get it into the cup, you would be on a VR 3 schedule of reinforcement.

The typical result of training subjects on a variable ratio schedule is illustrated in the right panel of Figure 7.2. Unlike fixed ratio schedules, variable ratio schedules result in a steady and high rate of responding with no predictable pauses.

INTERVAL SCHEDULES

In contrast to ratio schedules that are based on the number of responses the subject performs, interval schedules are based on the passage of time. As with ratio schedules, there are basically two types of interval schedules, fixed and variable.

Fixed interval schedule of reinforcement. In a **fixed interval (FI) schedule**, a fixed amount of time has to pass before a response can be reinforced. Fixed interval schedules occur in situations where it takes a certain amount of time for the reinforcer to be prepared. Consider making a gelatin dessert (Jello, for example). After the ingredients are mixed, the Jello has to be cooled in the refrigerator for a certain amount of time (let's say an hour) to harden and become good to eat. In this example, the reinforced response is taking the Jello out of the refrigerator to eat. If you take the Jello out too early, it will be too soft, and your response will not be reinforced. Attempts to eat the Jello before the hour is up will not be reinforced. Another important feature of this example is that once the reinforcer is ready, it remains available until the subject responds to obtain it. Once the

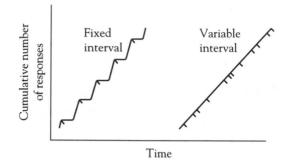

F I G U R E 7.3   Typical results of training subjects on fixed interval and variable interval schedules of reinforcement.
The data were obtained with pigeons pecking a response key on FI 4-min and VI 2-min schedules of food reinforcement. The hatch marks indicate when the reinforcer was delivered. (Based on Ferster and Skinner, 1957.)

Jello is done, you don't eat it right away. It will be there for you even if you don't try eating it until the next day.

In an FI schedule of reinforcement, a fixed amount of time has to pass before the reinforcer becomes available. However, the reinforcer is not provided automatically at the end of the set interval. To obtain the reinforcer, the subject has to perform the specified instrumental response. Early responses have no consequence. They do not make the reinforcer available earlier, and they do not result in a penalty. Finally, the reinforcer can be obtained any time after it becomes available. In a simple interval schedule, the subject does not have to respond within a limited period to obtain the reinforcer.

Fixed interval schedules are abbreviated FI, with a number afterward indicating the duration of the fixed intervals during which responding is not reinforced. Figure 7.3 shows data obtained from a pigeon pecking a response key on a free-operant, FI 4-min schedule of food reinforcement. On this schedule, delivery of the reinforcer at the end of one fixed interval starts the next fixed interval cycle. Four minutes after the start of the cycle, the reinforcer becomes available and can be obtained by making a key peck.

Responding on an FI schedule of reinforcement is similar to the pattern of responding that occurs on fixed ratio schedules. The subject does not respond at the beginning of the fixed interval. Because it occurs just after delivery of the previous reinforcer, this lack of responding at the beginning of the fixed interval cycle is the postreinforcement pause. Responding increases as the end of the interval gets closer, with the subject responding at a high rate just as the fixed interval ends. The entire response pattern is called an *FI scallop* because it resembles the ridges on the shell of a scallop.

Variable interval schedule of reinforcement. Variable interval (VI) schedules of reinforcement are similar to FI schedules except that the amount of time it takes to set up the reinforcer varies. Making a cup of coffee on a campfire illustrates a VI schedule. How long it takes for the coffee to brew varies from one occasion to the next, depending on how much heat the fire is generating. As in FI schedules, the instrumental response is reinforced only after a certain amount of time has passed since the start of the schedule cycle. Early responses have no consequence, and once the reinforcer has been set up, it remains available until the subject responds.

Variable interval schedules are abbreviated VI, with a number afterward indicating the average duration of the intervals during which responding is not reinforced. Figure 7.3 shows data obtained from a pigeon pecking a response key on a free-operant, VI 2-min schedule of food reinforcement. On this schedule, the reinforcer became available on average 2 minutes after the start of each schedule cycle.

Responding on a VI schedule is similar to responding on a VR schedule of reinforcement. A steady rate of behavior occurs, with no predictable pauses or changes in rate.

In simple interval schedules, once the reinforcer has become available it remains there until the subject responds and obtains the reinforcer. The cycle then starts over again. Picking up your letters from a mailbox, for example, is done on a VI schedule. Checking the mail before it is delivered doesn't speed up delivery of the mail, but once the letters have been placed in your mailbox, you don't have to pick them up right away. They will remain there even if you don't get them until the next day.

In some special cases, once the reinforcer has been set up, it remains available for just a limited period. For example, it takes a certain amount of time to bake a pan of cookies, but once the required time has passed, if you don't take the cookies out of the oven, they will get overdone. This is an interval schedule with a *limited hold*. The reinforcer is "held" for only a limited period after it becomes available, and the response has to occur during the hold period for the response to be reinforced.

Chained Schedules of Reinforcement

In simple schedules of reinforcement, only one operant response is involved. The subject is allowed to repeat that response in the same situation, and the schedule determines which occurrence of the response is reinforced. In contrast, a **chained schedule** involves a sequence of responses or response components, and each response component has its own associated stimulus.

The primary reinforcer is not presented until the subject has completed all of the components of the chain and has done so in the correct order.

HETEROGENEOUS CHAINS

The most familiar type of chained schedule involves a sequence of different responses, each of which is performed in the presence of a different stimulus. Consider, for example, putting on a pullover sweater. The goal is to have the sweater on your body. To get to that point, first you have to put each of your arms into the arms of the sweater. Then you have to lift the sweater above your head and pull it over your head and neck. Finally, you have to pull the bottom of the sweater down around your body.

Notice that putting on the sweater involves making a series of different responses. In addition, each response occurs in the presence of a different stimulus. You start with the sweater in front of you. That is the stimulus for putting your arms into the sweater. Having the sweater on your arms is the stimulus for pulling the sweater over your head. Having the sweater around your neck is the stimulus for pulling the bottom of it down around your body. The reinforcer is the enjoyment of wearing the sweater, and that is available only at the end of the chain of responses. No satisfaction or reinforcement is experienced if the response sequence is interrupted part way through— while the sweater is covering your head, for example.

Many activities can be analyzed as response chains: opening a can, doing your homework, or mowing the lawn. In all of these cases, the response chain is made up of a sequence of different activities, and each activity occurs in the presence of a different stimulus. If the response chain is made up of a sequence of different responses, it is called a *heterogeneous chain*.

HOMOGENEOUS CHAINS

Another type of chained schedule involves a *homogeneous chain* (see Figure 7.4). In a homogeneous chain, the various response components all involve the same response, but each component occurs in the presence of a different stimulus and involves a different schedule requirement. For example, a researcher could reinforce a pigeon for pecking a response key on an FR 15 - FI 3-min chained schedule. This schedule involves two response components, an FR 15 and an FI 3-min component, each with its associated stimulus, S_1 and S_2. During the S_1, the subject has to peck 15 times to satisfy the FR 15 requirement. At this point, the subject would not be reinforced, but S_2 would be presented and the FI 3-min requirement would come into effect. The primary reinforcer would be delivered for the first response after S_2 had been on for 3 minutes.

With a homogeneous chain, each component of the schedule produces a pattern of responding that is characteristic of the simple schedule in effect in that component. On an FR 15 - FI 3-min chained schedule, the

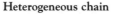

Heterogeneous chain

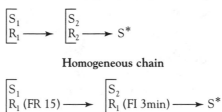

Homogeneous chain

FIGURE 7.4 Difference between heterogeneous and homogeneous chains.

In a heterogeneous chain, the subject has to perform a sequence of different responses (R_1 followed by R_2) to obtain the reinforcer S*. In a homogeneous chain, the subject has to perform the same response (R_1) on one reinforcement schedule (FR 15) followed by another (FI 3-min) to obtain the reinforcer S*. In both cases, each response component has its own associated stimulus.

subject would pause and then respond at a steady and high rate in the FR 15 component. It would then pause and show a scalloped pattern of pecking in the FI 3-min component.

TRAINING RESPONSE CHAINS

Techniques for the establishment of response chains are of great interest for teachers, especially if their students require extensive instruction. The conventional wisdom was that response chains are learned most readily with a *backward chaining* procedure (Ferster & Perrot, 1968). In backward chaining, the last response or response component of the chain is taught first because it is closest to the delivery of the reinforcer. Earlier response components are added after the subject has mastered the end of the chain.

In the case of putting on a sweater, for example, the last response is pulling the sweater over the body. To teach this response to a little girl, the teacher would place the sweater around the child's head and shoulders and encourage her to pull the sweater down. Once the child has mastered the last response, the response preceding the last one would be added. In this case, the sweater would be held above the child, and she would be encouraged to pull it over her head and then over her body. Gradually, the earlier steps would be added until the child could perform all of the responses in the sequence.

Backward chaining is an effective approach to training response sequences. However, response chains can also be effectively taught by starting from the beginning and initially reinforcing the first response in the chain. Once the first response is learned, the second one can be added, and then the third and fourth. Such a forward chaining procedure can be as effective as backward chaining (see Sulzer-Azaroff & Mayer, 1991).

Concurrent Schedules

In each of the schedules of reinforcement considered so far, the subject can either perform the specified instrumental response or not do so. These procedures are usually not considered to involve a choice, but in fact all instrumental conditioning situations involve a choice. With simple and chained schedules, the choice is to perform the response specified by the reinforcement schedule or do something else.

Investigators have become convinced that a complete understanding of instrumental behavior requires understanding why organisms choose to engage in one response rather than another. Unfortunately, simple and chained schedules of reinforcement are not adequate for analyzing the determinants of response choice. In simple and chained schedules, the alternative to the instrumental response—the "something else" the subject might do—is poorly specified and not measured. Concurrent schedules were designed to provide a clear "something else" for the subjects to do and provide a method for studying more directly why organisms elect to engage in one response rather than another.

As you might suspect, whether you do one thing or another depends on the benefits you derive from each type of activity. In the terminology of conditioning, how often you engage in activity A as compared to activity B will depend on the schedule of reinforcement in effect for response A compared to the schedule of reinforcement in effect for response B. On a playground, Joe could play with Peter, who likes to play vigorous physical games, or Joe could play with Matt, who prefers to play quietly in the sandbox. If Joe is not getting much enjoyment from playing with Peter, he can go play with Matt. This kind of situation is modeled in the laboratory with the use of a **concurrent schedule** of reinforcement.

A concurrent schedule provides two response alternatives, A and B (see Figure 7.5). Responding on alternative A is reinforced on one schedule of reinforcement (VI 5-min, for example), and responding on B is reinforced on a different schedule (VR 15, for example). Both response alternatives (and their corresponding reinforcement schedules) are available at the same time, and the subject can switch from one activity to the other at any time. Because the two choices are available simultaneously, the procedure is called a concurrent schedule.

Numerous factors determine how subjects distribute their behavior between two response alternatives. These include the nature of each type of response, the effort and time involved in switching from one response to the other, the attractiveness of the reinforcer provided for each response, and the schedule of reinforcement in effect for each response. Experi-

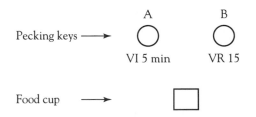

F I G U R E 7.5   Diagram of a concurrent schedule of reinforcement.
Pecking the response key on the left is reinforced on a VI 5-min schedule of reinforcement. Pecking the response key on the right is reinforced on a VR 15 schedule of reinforcement.

ments have to be designed carefully so that the effects of each of these factors can be observed without changes in other features of the choice situation.

Investigators of operant conditioning have been most interested how choice is determined by the schedule of reinforcement in effect for each response alternative. In an effort to focus on this variable, they have designed procedures that minimize the contribution of other factors. Studies of concurrent schedules are often carried out with pigeon subjects. One wall of the experimental chamber has two response keys positioned at about the height of the bird's head. A feeder through which the birds can obtain grain is centered below the two keys. This arrangement has the advantage that the two responses require the same effort. Although pecks on the right and left keys are reinforced on different schedules, the reinforcer in each case is the same type of food. Another advantage is that the pigeon can easily switch from one response to the other because the left and right keys are located near each other.

If the effort required for both the left and the right key-pecks is similar, if the same reinforcer is used for both responses, and if switching from one response to the other is fairly easy, the schedule of reinforcement in effect for each response determines how the subjects distribute their responses between the two alternatives. The results of numerous experiments involving concurrent schedules have been consistent with what is known as the **matching law** (Herrnstein, 1970). According to the matching law, *the relative rate of responding on a response alternative is equal to the relative rate of reinforcement obtained with that response alternative.*

In a concurrent choice situation, organisms tend to match relative rates of responding to relative rates of reinforcement. Departures from matching occur if the response alternatives are unequal in their effort requirement, if different reinforcers are used for each response alternative, and if switching from one response to the other is made more difficult (Davison & McCarthy, 1988; Williams, 1988).

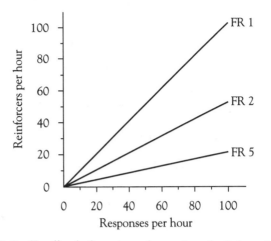

F I G U R E 7.6 Feedback functions for ratio schedules of reinforcement.
Notice that each feedback function is a straight line. Because of that, every increase in the response rate results in a corresponding increase in the rate of reinforcement.

Mechanisms of Schedule Performance

So far, I have described procedural factors involved in different schedules
of reinforcement and patterns of responding produced by the schedules. Another important issue concerns the underlying mechanisms of
schedule effects. A key concept involved in the analysis of the mechanisms of schedule effects is the feedback function that characterizes the
schedule.

Reinforcement of an instrumental response can be viewed as feedback
for that response. Schedules of reinforcement determine how this feedback
is arranged. One way to describe the arrangement is to show how the rate
of reinforcement the organism earns is related to the rate of its responding.
This is called the **feedback function.**

FEEDBACK FUNCTIONS FOR RATIO SCHEDULES

Feedback functions for ratio schedules are perhaps the easiest to understand.
In a ratio schedule, how soon (and how often) the subject gets reinforced is
determined only by how rapidly it makes the required number of responses.
The faster the subject responds, the faster it obtains reinforcement.

Figure 7.6 shows examples of feedback functions for several ratio
schedules. On an FR 1, or continuous reinforcement schedule, the subject
is reinforced for each occurrence of the instrumental response. Therefore, the

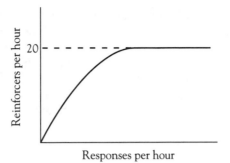

F I G U R E 7.7 **Feedback function for a variable interval, 3-min schedule of reinforcement.**
The subject is assumed to distribute its responding randomly in time. Notice that no matter how rapidly the subject responds, its maximum reinforcement rate is 20 per hour.

rate of reinforcement is equal to the rate of responding. This results in a feedback function with a slope of 1.0.

If more than one response is required for reinforcement, the rate of reinforcement will be less than the rate of responding, and the slope of the feedback function will be less than 1.0. For example, on an FR 5 schedule of reinforcement, the subject receives one reinforcer for every fifth response. Under these circumstances, the rate of reinforcement is one-fifth the rate of responding, and the slope of the feedback function is 0.2.

Regardless of their slope, feedback functions for ratio schedules are always straight lines. Because of that, an increase in the rate of responding always yields an increase in the rate of reinforcement. This is true for both FR and VR schedules.

FEEDBACK FUNCTIONS FOR INTERVAL SCHEDULES

Interval schedules have feedback functions that differ markedly from those of ratio schedules. Figure 7.7 shows the feedback function for a VI 3-min schedule of reinforcement. On such a schedule, the reinforcer becomes available on average 3 minutes after the last time it was delivered. Therefore, no matter how often or how rapidly the subject responds, the maximum number of reinforcers it can obtain is limited to 20 per hour.

Although responding on an interval schedule is not reinforced until sufficient time has passed to make the reinforcer available, if the subject hardly ever responds, it will hardly ever be reinforced. As the subject increases its response rate above zero, it will also increase its chances of getting whatever reinforcers become available. Therefore, up to a point, increases in the rate of responding are accompanied by increases in the rate of reinforcement. However, once the subject responds fast enough to get all of the 20 reinforcers that can become available each hour, any further increase in response rate will have no further benefit. Thus, the feedback function for an interval schedule becomes flat (has a slope of zero) once the maximum possible reinforcement rate has been achieved.

FEEDBACK FUNCTIONS AND SCHEDULE PERFORMANCE

The differences in the feedback functions of ratio and interval schedules allow us to understand differences in the motivating effects of these two types of schedules. Since the feedback function for an interval schedule reaches a maximum with a particular rate of reinforcement, there is no incentive for any increases in response rate beyond that point. In contrast, no such maximum is reached with ratio schedules. Therefore, ratio schedules tend to motivate much higher rates of responding than do interval schedules (Reynolds, 1975; McDowell & Wixted, 1988; Peele, Casey, & Silberberg, 1984).

Although the concept of the feedback function is important in explanations of schedule performance, feedback functions can be difficult to characterize. This is true, for example, for interval-based schedules. In interval schedules, reinforcement depends not only on the rate of responding but also on how responding is distributed in time. In my characterization of the feedback function for a VI 3-min schedule (Figure 7.7), I made the simplifying assumption that the subject distributed its responses randomly in time. With other assumptions, the initial increasing portion of the feedback function would have been different. In spite of such complications, however, many investigators believe that the nature of schedule performance is ultimately determined by how schedules of reinforcement provide feedback for instrumental behavior.

Suggested Readings

FERSTER, C. B., & SKINNER, B. F. (1957). *Schedules of reinforcement.* New York: Appleton-Century-Crofts.

RACHLIN, H. C. (1978). A molar theory of reinforcement schedules. *Journal of the Experimental Analysis of Behavior, 30,* 345–360.

SHIMP, C. P. (1969). Optimum behavior in free-operant experiments. *Psychological Review, 76,* 97–112.

WILLIAMS, B. A. (1988). Reinforcement, choice, and response strength. In R. C. Atkinson, R. J. Herrnstein, G. Lindzey, & R. D. Luce (Eds.), *Stevens' handbook of experimental psychology* (Vol. 2, pp. 167–244). New York: Wiley.

Technical Terms

Chained schedule

Concurrent schedule

Cumulative record

Feedback function

Fixed interval

Fixed ratio

Interval schedule

Matching law

Postreinforcement pause

Ratio run

Ratio schedule

Schedule of reinforcement

Variable interval

Variable ratio

CHAPTER EIGHT

Theories of Reinforcement

DID YOU KNOW THAT:

- Reinforcers need not reduce a biological drive or need.

- Responses, not just stimuli, can serve as reinforcers.

- According to contemporary perspectives, reinforcement does not "strengthen" the instrumental response.

- Instrumental conditioning procedures not only increase the rate of the instrumental response; they also decrease the rate of the reinforcer response.

- Instrumental conditioning procedures restrict how a subject distributes its behavior among its response alternatives.

- Reinforcement effects are a by-product of the new response choices a subject makes when its activities are constrained by an instrumental conditioning procedure.

In Chapter 7, I discussed various types of instrumental conditioning procedures and their behavioral outcomes. There is no doubt that reinforcement procedures can produce dramatic changes in behavior. The issue I shall turn to next is how reinforcement procedures produce their effects. That question is addressed by *theories of reinforcement.*

All good theories have to be consistent with the findings they are intended to explain. In addition, good theories may stimulate new research that serves to evaluate and increase the precision of the theory. Good theories also provide new insights and new ways of thinking about familiar phenomena.

The story of the development of theories of reinforcement is a marvelous example of creativity in science. The story is peppered with examples of small refinements in thinking that brought a particular theory in line with new data. The story also includes dramatic new departures and new ways of thinking about reinforcement. And, there are interesting examples in which incremental changes in thinking culminated in major new perspectives on the problem.

Any successful theory of reinforcement has to answer two types of questions about instrumental conditioning. The first type of question concerns the identity of reinforcers: *What makes something effective as a reinforcer,* or how can we predict whether something will be an effective reinforcer? The second type of question concerns the mechanism of reinforcement effects: *How does a reinforcer produce its effects,* or how does a reinforcer produce an increase in the probability of the reinforced response?

Thorndike and the Law of Effect

The first systematic theory of reinforcement was provided by Thorndike soon after his discovery of instrumental conditioning (Bower & Hilgard, 1981). According to Thorndike, a positive reinforcer is a stimulus that produces a "satisfying state of affairs." However, Thorndike did not go on to consider why something was satisfying, so his answer to our first question—What makes something effective as a reinforcer?—was not very illuminating.

An observer can determine whether a stimulus, such as a pat on the head for a dog, is a satisfier by seeing whether the subject increases a response that results in getting patted on the head. However, such evidence does not reveal why a pat on the head is a reinforcer. By calling reinforcers satisfiers, Thorndike provided a label for reinforcers, but he did not provide an explanation for what makes something effective as a reinforcer.

Thorndike was a bit more forthcoming on the second question—How does a reinforcer produce an increase in the probability of the reinforced response? His answer was provided in what he called the *Law of Effect.* As I noted in Chapter 6, according to the Law of Effect, a reinforcer establishes an association or bond between the instrumental response R and the

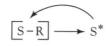

FIGURE 8.1 Diagram of Thorndike's Law of Effect.
The reinforcer S* acts retroactively to strengthen the S-R association.

stimulus S in the presence of which the response is performed. The reinforcer produces an S-R association (see Figure 8.1).

The Law of Effect explains how reinforcement increases the future probability of the instrumental response. Because of the S-R association that is established by reinforcement, stimulus S comes to produce the instrumental response R in much the same way that any elicited response is produced by its eliciting stimulus. The basic mechanism of the Law of Effect was considered a reasonable explanation of increased instrumental responding and was accepted by major behavioral theorists during the next 50 years. However, in hindsight, acceptance of the Law of Effect is rather remarkable.

Although the Law of Effect predicts increased instrumental responding in the training environment, it does so by a bit of magic rather than by a well-established process. Thorndike did not tell us how a reinforcer that is provided after an instrumental response has occurred can act retroactively to strengthen an association between the response and the stimulus in the presence of which the response was made. That part of the Law of Effect had to be taken on faith. Furthermore, despite the widespread acceptance of the Law of Effect in the next 50 years, no one has filled in the gap left by Thorndike. No one has provided an explanation for how a reinforcer can act backward in time to strengthens an S-R association.

In summary, Thorndike provided no more than a name in answer to the question, What makes something effective as a reinforcer? His answer to the question, How does a reinforcer produce an increase in the probability of the reinforced response? was successful in that it accurately predicted the behavioral effect of reinforcement. But the answer was superficial because it simply stated that an S-R association was formed without saying how this came about.

Hull and Drive Reduction Theory

The next major theorist we will consider is Clark Hull. (For a contemporary review of Hullian theory, see Amsel & Rashotte, 1984.) Hull accepted the S-R mechanism of the Law of Effect and concentrated instead on the question that Thorndike had pretty much ignored, What makes something effective as a reinforcer? To answer this question, Hull made use of the

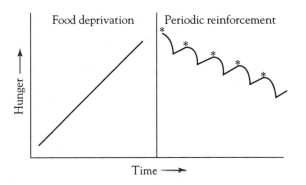

F I G U R E 8.2 Illustration of the mechanisms of drive reduction rein-forcement using hunger as an example.
Deliveries of the food reinforcer are indicated by the asterisks.

concept of **homeostasis** that had been developed to explain the operation of physiological systems.

According to a homeostatic model, organisms defend a stable state with respect to certain biologically critical factors. Consider, for example, food intake (see Figure 8.2). For survival, organisms have to maintain a stable or optimal supply of nutrients. Food deprivation creates a challenge to the nutritional state of the organism. It creates a need for food. The psychological consequence of this need is the motivational or drive state of hunger, which can be reduced by the ingestion of food. According to Hull, food is an effective reinforcer because it reduces the hunger drive. More generally, Hull proposed that what makes a stimulus reinforcing is its effectiveness in reducing a **drive state**. Hence, his theory is called the **drive reduction theory of reinforcement.**

PRIMARY REINFORCERS

Many common laboratory examples of instrumental reinforcement are consistent with Hull's drive reduction theory. Mild food deprivation is routinely used to make food an effective instrumental reinforcer for rats and pigeons in laboratory situations. Similarly, mild water deprivation makes water an effective reinforcer. Rats will respond to obtain heat when they are in a cold environment and respond to obtain cold air in a hot environment. Deprivation procedures and other circumstances that challenge a biological homeostatic system create drive states, and stimuli that reduce those drive states are effective reinforcers for instrumental behavior.

Hull's drive reduction theory provides a successful account of reinforcers such as food and water. Stimuli that are effective in reducing a biological need without prior training are called **primary reinforcers.** However, if Hull's theory could only characterize reinforcers that reduce primary biological drives, it would be rather limited. Many stimuli that do not satisfy a biological drive or need can reinforce instrumental behavior. You may find the smell of Italian food reinforcing, but the smell of food does not reduce hunger.

SECONDARY REINFORCERS AND ACQUIRED DRIVES

Hull's theory has been successfully extended to stimuli like the smell of food by adding the principle of Pavlovian conditioning. As one repeatedly eats spoonfuls of a particular food, the smell of that food becomes associated with the reduction of hunger through Pavlovian conditioning. That makes the food's aroma a conditioned or secondary reinforcer. Thus, Hull's theory was extended to stimuli that do not reduce a drive state directly but gain their reinforcing properties through association with a primary reinforcer.

Another way Hull's theory has been extended beyond events that involve primary biological drives is through the concept of a **conditioned drive state**. Stimuli that become associated with a primary drive state are assumed to elicit a **conditioned** or **acquired drive.** Reduction of a conditioned or acquired drive is assumed to be reinforcing in the same manner as the reduction of a primary or biological drive state.

The concept of conditioned or acquired drive has been used most extensively in the analysis of aversively motivated behavior. You can lose your balance and fall on a moving escalator. If the fall is severe enough, you will become afraid of escalators. Such conditioned fear is an example of a conditioned or acquired drive. According to Hull's drive reduction theory, a reduction in the intensity of the acquired drive will be re-inforcing. Therefore, any response that enables you to escape from the conditioned fear of escalators will be reinforced. Walking away from the escalator and using an elevator will be reinforced by reduction of the conditioned fear elicited by the escalator. (I will have more to say about fear conditioning in Chapter 11.)

SENSORY REINFORCEMENT

Although Hull's theory was successfully extended to situations that do not involve primary biological drives, the theory has not been successful in explaining all instances of reinforcement. For example, investigators have found that rats kept in the dark will press a response lever to turn on a light, and rats kept in an illuminated chamber will press a response lever to produce periods of darkness. Chimpanzees have been found to perform instrumental responses that are reinforced by nothing more than the opportunity to watch an electric toy train move around a track. These are all examples of **sensory reinforcement.** In many situations, sensory stimuli with no apparent relation to a biological need or drive state can serve as effective reinforcers (see Berlyne, 1969). Examples of sensory reinforcers for people are music, beautiful paintings, and other works of art.

The growing weight of evidence for sensory reinforcement, along with the success of alternative conceptualizations of reinforcement, led to abandonment of Hull's drive reduction theory. As we will see, the new theories were highly creative and involved radical new ways of thinking about the issues of instrumental reinforcement.

Reinforcers as Responses

The modern era in reinforcement theory was ushered in by the work of David Premack, who considered reinforcement from an entirely different perspective than Hull. Like Hull, Premack considered situations like a rat pressing a response lever for food. However, instead of thinking about the reinforcer as a pellet of food, he thought about the reinforcer as the act of eating food. For Premack, the question was not what made food a reinforcing stimulus but what made eating a reinforcing response. Premack stated the issues of reinforcement in terms of responses, not in terms of stimuli (Premack, 1965).

THE PREMACK PRINCIPLE

What makes eating different from pressing a response lever in a standard Skinner box? Many answers are possible. The rat has to learn to press the lever, but it does not have to learn to eat. Eating can occur not just in the Skinner box but anywhere the rat finds food. Eating involves a special set of muscles and activates digestive processes. Another difference is that a food-deprived rat in a Skinner box is much more likely to eat than it is to press the lever if it is given free access to both activities. Premack focused on this last fact and elevated it to a general principle.

According to Premack, the critical precondition for reinforcement is not a drive state. Rather, it is the existence of two responses that differ in their likelihood of occurrence when the subject is given free access to both activities. Given two such responses, Premack proposed that *the opportunity to perform the higher-probability response will serve as a reinforcer for the lower-probability response*. This general claim is known as the **Premack principle.** A more descriptive name for it is the differential probability principle.

According to the differential probability principle, the specific nature of the instrumental and reinforcer responses does not matter. Neither of them has to involve eating or drinking, and the organism need not be hungry or thirsty. The only requirement is that one response be more likely than the other. Given such a differential response probability, the more likely response can serve as a reinforcer for the less likely response.

THE PREMACK REVOLUTION

The Premack principle took the scientific community by storm. It was a radical departure from previous ways of thinking about reinforcers. For the first time, scientists started thinking seriously about reinforcers as responses rather than as special kinds of stimuli, and for the first time, the distinction between conditioned and unconditioned reinforcers became irrelevant.

For Hull, all reinforcers were ultimately related to unconditioned biological needs or drives. Secondary or conditioned reinforcers were effective only through association with primary reinforcers. In contrast, Premack was unconcerned with how one response might have come to be more likely than another. For him, the only thing that mattered was that the reinforcer response be more likely than the instrumental response.

The Premack principle was important because it liberated us from the grip of stimulus views of reinforcement and views of reinforcement rooted in biological needs and drives. In addition, the Premack principle provided a convenient tool for the application of instrumental conditioning procedures in a variety of educational settings, including homes, classrooms, psychiatric hospitals, mental retardation centers, and correctional institutions.

APPLICATIONS OF THE PREMACK PRINCIPLE

In all educational settings, students are encouraged to learn and perform new responses. The goal is to get the students to do things they did not do before and things they would not do without special encouragement. In other words, the goal is to increase the likelihood of low-probability responses. Instrumental conditioning procedures are ideally suited to accomplish this task, but the teacher first has to find an effective reinforcer. Withholding a student's lunch so that food may be used as a reinforcer is not socially acceptable and would create a great deal of resentment. Candy and other food treats are effective reinforcers for young children without food deprivation but are not good for them nutritionally.

The Premack principle provides a way out of this conundrum (Homme, deBaca, Devine, Steinhorst, & Rickert, 1963). According to Premack, a reinforcer is any activity the subject is more likely to engage in than the instrumental response. Some students may like to watch television a lot; others may enjoy some time on the playground; still others may enjoy helping the teacher. Whatever the high-probability response may be, the Premack principle suggests that a teacher can take advantage of it by training a student to engage in a less likely behavior. All that is necessary is to provide access to the high-probability response only if the subject first performs lower-probability behavior (Charlop, Kurtz, & Casey, 1990).

Consider, for example, a mentally retarded boy who enjoys playing on swings and is a messy eater; thus he ends up with food all over his clothes after each meal. The goal is to teach this student to eat more carefully. The Premack principle suggests that an effective instrumental conditioning procedure could be set up in which eating neatly is reinforced by the opportunity to play on a swing after the meal.

Premack's principle facilitated the application of instrumental conditioning to a variety of educational settings. It enables teachers to use a variety of activities rather than food items as reinforcers, and it encourages taking advantage of each student's unique set of preferred activities. In this way, training procedures can be tailor-made to fit a student's unique likes and dislikes.

THEORETICAL PROBLEMS

The Premack principle continues to be used in many educational settings. However, it has been superseded by other concepts in theoretical analyses of reinforcement. The differential response probability principle has two major shortcomings. One problem is the measurement or calculation of response probabilities. We all have an intuitive sense of what we mean when we say that one response is more likely than another, but assigning a precise numerical value to the probability of a response can be difficult. Furthermore, the likelihood of a given response may change unexpectedly. A youngster may enjoy playing baseball one day but not another.

There is no satisfactory solution to the theoretical problems posed by the fact that response probabilities fluctuate and are difficult to measure. However, there are ways to get around such problems in practical applications of the Premack principle. For example, a system can be set up in which students are given points for performing the target instrumental response correctly. The students could then be permitted to exchange their points for various response opportunities (watching television, reading a comic book, going out to the playground, getting some crayons and paper, and so forth), depending on what they wanted to do at the moment. Such systems are called *token economies* and have been instituted in a wide range of behavioral settings (Kazdin, 1985). If a wide enough range of reinforcer activities is provided, there is no need to obtain precise measurements of the probability of each reinforcer response or worry about fluctuations in reinforcer preferences.

The second major theoretical problem of the Premack principle is that it is just a formula or rule for finding reinforcers. It does not reveal how reinforcers work. It answers the question, What makes something effective as a reinforcer? but it does not answer the question, How does a reinforcer produce an increase in the probability of the reinforced response?

The Response Deprivation Hypothesis

The next major development in theories of reinforcement was the **response deprivation hypothesis** proposed by Timberlake and Allison (1974). The response deprivation hypothesis was designed to solve some of the theoretical problems that were left unresolved by the Premack principle.

Timberlake and Allison followed in Premack's footsteps in thinking about reinforcers as responses rather than as stimuli, and their starting point was also to think about the difference between an instrumental response and a reinforcer response. However, their consideration of this question led them in a different direction than Premack. Timberlake and Allison suggested that the critical difference between the instrumental response and the reinforcer response is that in an instrumental conditioning situation, the subject is free to perform the instrumental response but is restricted in performing the reinforcer response.

In a typical Skinner box, for example, the rat can press the response lever any time, but it is not free to eat pellets of food any time. Eating can occur only after the rat has pressed the lever, and even then the rat can only eat a little bit because small portions of food are provided. Timberlake and Allison suggested that these restrictions on the reinforcer response are what make eating an effective reinforcer. In a sense, instrumental conditioning situations deprive the subject from free access to the reinforcer response—hence, the name response deprivation hypothesis.

RESPONSE DEPRIVATION AND THE LAW OF EFFECT

The response deprivation hypothesis captures an important idea. The idea is obvious if you consider what would happen if there were no restriction on eating for a rat in a Skinner box. Imagine a situation in which the rat receives a week's supply of food each time it presses the response lever. According to Thorndike's Law of Effect, a week's worth of food should be a highly satisfying state of affairs; therefore, it should result in a strong S-R bond and should produce a large increase in lever-pressing. But that hardly seems sensible from the rat's point of view. A more sensible prediction is that if the rat received a week's supply of food for each lever-press, it would press the response lever about once a week, when its food supply was nearly depleted.

According to the response deprivation hypothesis, what makes food an effective reinforcer is not that food satisfies hunger or that eating is a high-probability response. Rather, the critical factor is that an instrumental conditioning procedure places a restriction on eating. It is this response deprivation that makes eating reinforcing. If the response deprivation is removed (by providing a week's supply of food), instrumental responding will not increase; the instrumental response will not be reinforced.

RESPONSE DEPRIVATION AND RESPONSE PROBABILITY

Notice that the response deprivation hypothesis avoids the computational problem that plagued the Premack principle. The response deprivation hypothesis does not require computing response probabilities. To apply the idea, simply determine the rate of a response during a baseline period in the absence of any restrictions and then limit access to the reinforcer response below the baseline level.

An interesting prediction of the response deprivation hypothesis is that even a low-probability response can be made into a reinforcing event. According to the hypothesis, the opportunity to perform a low-probability response can be used to reinforce a higher-probability behavior if access to the low-probability response is restricted below its already low baseline rate. Such a prediction is contrary to the Premack principle but has been confirmed by experimental evidence (Allison & Timberlake, 1974; Eisenberger, Karpman, & Trattner, 1967).

RESPONSE DEPRIVATION AND THE LOCUS OF REINFORCEMENT EFFECTS

In addition to avoiding the problems involved in computing response probabilities, the response deprivation hypothesis shifts the locus of the explanation of reinforcement. In earlier theories, reinforcement was explained in terms of factors that are outside the instrumental conditioning procedure itself. With drive reduction theory, the external factor involves procedures that establish a drive state. With the Premack principle, the external factor involves the baseline probabilities of the reinforcer and instrumental responses. In contrast, with the response deprivation hypothesis, the locus of reinforcement rests with how the instrumental conditioning procedure constrains the organism's activities. This is a new idea. Never before had someone suggested that reinforcement effects are determined by the response restrictions that are inherently involved in all instrumental conditioning procedures.

The response deprivation hypothesis moved our understanding of reinforcement forward in that it avoided some of the problems of the Premack principle. However, as was true of the Premack principle, the response deprivation hypothesis only provided an answer to the question, What makes something effective as a reinforcer? The second major question, How does a reinforcer produce an increase in the probability of the reinforced response? was not addressed by the hypothesis.

The Behavioral Regulation Approach

In many ways, the **behavioral regulation** approach is similar to the response deprivation hypothesis in that it rejects the assumption that reinforcers are special kinds of stimuli or special kinds of responses. In addition, the behavioral regulation approach accepts the idea that reinforcement effects are determined by how an instrumental conditioning procedure restricts an organism's activities. In fact, the behavioral regulation approach builds on this idea and strives to answer the second question about reinforcement,

How does a reinforcer produce an increase in the probability of the reinforced response? (Allison, 1989; Timberlake, 1980, 1984).

The behavioral regulation approach borrowed the concept of homeostasis from physiology and drive reduction theory and extended it to response choice. Behavioral homeostasis is analogous to physiological homeostasis in that both involve defending an optimal or preferred level of a system. Physiological homeostatic mechanisms exist to maintain physiological parameters (blood concentrations of oxygen and glucose, for example) close to what is ideal. The homeostatic balance is "defended" in the sense that deviations from the target blood concentrations of oxygen or glucose trigger compensatory physiological mechanisms that return the systems to their respective homeostatic levels.

THE BEHAVIORAL BLISS POINT

In behavioral regulation, what is defended is the organism's preferred distribution of activities—its **behavioral bliss point.** The behavioral bliss point refers to how an organism elects to distribute its activities among available response options in the absence of procedural restrictions. It refers to the subject's preferred response choices before an instrumental conditioning procedure is imposed.

Consider, for example, a teenager named Kim. Left to her own devices, during the course of a 24-hour day, Kim might elect to spend 3 hours a day talking to friends on the telephone, 1.5 hours eating, 4 hours driving around, 10 hours sleeping, 2 hours watching television, 3 hours listening to music, and a half hour doing school work. This distribution of activities would constitute the behavioral bliss point for Kim. Notice that at the bliss point, Kim devotes only a half hour a day to doing school work.

IMPOSING AN INSTRUMENTAL CONTINGENCY

Kim's parents may want to introduce an instrumental conditioning procedure to increase the amount of time Kim devotes to school work. They could do this by restricting her access to music. For example, they could require that Kim spend a minute doing school work for every minute she gets to listen to music.

Before the instrumental contingency, listening to music and doing homework were independent activities for Kim. How much time she spent on one activity had little to do with how much time she spent on the other. This characterized the bliss point. The behavioral bliss point for listening to music and studying is illustrated in the upper left quadrant of Figure 8.3.

Requiring Kim to spend a minute on homework for every minute of music listening ties the two activities together in a special way. Now, time spent on homework has to equal time spent on music. This relationship is illustrated by the 45° line in Figure 8.3. This is also called the **schedule line.**

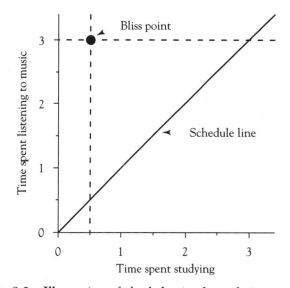

F I G U R E   8.3   Illustration of the behavioral regulation approach to instrumental conditioning.
The Bliss Point represents how much time the subject spends studying and listening to music in the absence of an instrumental conditioning procedure or schedule constraint. The Schedule Line represents how much time the subject can devote to each activity when she is required to spend 1 minute studying for each minute spent listening to music.

With the instrumental conditioning procedure in effect, studying is no longer independent of listening to music. The two activities are tied together and restricted to the schedule line.

The contingency between studying and listening to music illustrated by the schedule line in Figure 8.3 restricts Kim's behavior so that she can no longer distribute her responses as she did at the behavioral bliss point. The schedule line does not go through the behavioral bliss point. Because of that, the instrumental contingency is a challenge to the behavioral bliss point in the same sense that a drive state is a challenge to physiological homeostasis.

The behavioral regulation approach is similar to physiological homeostatic models in that deviations from a preferred level are assumed to trigger mechanisms of adjustment that move the system back toward the preferred level. In behavioral regulation, these mechanisms of adjustment involve moving the subject's response choices or her distribution of activities back toward the behavioral bliss point.

Once the instrumental conditioning procedure has been put into effect for Kim (one minute of music listening for one minute of school work), she can never get all the way back to her preferred response allocation. Every possible route for returning to the behavioral bliss point involves some cost or disadvantage. If Kim elects to listen to music for as long as she would like (ideally 3 hours a day), she would have to do much more school work than she likes. On the other hand, if she spent as little time doing school work as she prefers (a half hour a day), she would have to settle for much less music than she likes.

Instrumental conditioning procedures constrain response options. They disrupt the free flow of behavior and interfere with how an organism selects among its available response alternatives. Furthermore, most cases are like Kim's in that the instrumental conditioning procedure does not allow the subject to return to the behavioral bliss point. The best the organism can achieve is to approach the bliss point under the constraints of the instrumental conditioning procedure.

RESPONDING TO SCHEDULE CONSTRAINTS

How an organism goes about moving back toward its behavioral bliss point after an instrumental contingency has been imposed depends on the costs and benefits of various strategies. If doing school work is much more unpleasant for Kim than the potential loss of music listening time, then she will not increase her school work much but will give up time spent listening to music. In contrast, if the potential loss of music time is much more aversive for Kim than increased effort devoted to school work, she will adjust to the constraint imposed by the instrumental conditioning procedure by substantially increasing her time doing school work.

A particularly important factor determining how an individual responds to schedule constraints is *the availability of substitutes* for the reinforcer activity (Burkhard, Rachlin, & Schrader, 1978; Green & Rachlin, 1991). Instrumental conditioning procedures are powerful if no substitutes are available for the reinforcer activity. However, if the subject has something it can substitute for the reinforcer, restricting access to the reinforcer will not increase instrumental responding.

In my example, the reinforcer activity is listening to music. If Kim loves music and cannot derive the same satisfaction from any other type of activity (if Kim has no substitutes for music), music will be a very powerful reinforcer. In this case, Kim will adjust to the instrumental procedure with a large increase in school work. Quite a different outcome would occur if Kim did not like music any more than watching television. If watching television were a good substitute for listening to music, the instrumental contingency would have little effect on how much school work Kim did. In this case, she would respond to the schedule constraint by substituting watching television for listening to music, without any increase in time spent on school work.

CONTRIBUTIONS OF BEHAVIORAL REGULATION

The behavioral regulation approach has advanced our understanding of instrumental behavior because it has encouraged us to think about instrumental conditioning and reinforcement within the context of the organism's entire behavioral repertoire. Behavioral regulation focuses attention on the fact that an instrumental conditioning procedure disrupts the free flow of behavior; it disrupts how the organism allocates its behavior among available response options. Behavioral regulation also focuses attention on the fact that constraints on response choices can have effects not only on the instrumental and the reinforcer responses but also on related or substitutable responses that are not directly a part of the instrumental procedure.

The behavioral regulation approach encourages us to think about the behavior of a subject as an organized system. It focuses attention on how the system is organized and how that organization determines the effects of schedule constraints. These ideas are a far cry from the more limited stimulus-response perspective that dominated early conceptions of reinforcement theory.

Suggested Readings

ALLISON, J. (1983). *Behavioral economics*. New York: Praeger.

PREMACK, D. (1965). Reinforcement theory. In D. Levine (Ed.), *Nebraska symposium on motivation* (Vol. 13, pp. 123–180). Lincoln: University of Nebraska Press.

STADDON, J.E.R. (1979). Operant behavior as adaptation to constraint. *Journal of Experimental Psychology: General, 108,* 48–67.

TIMBERLAKE, W., & ALLISON, J. (1974). Response deprivation: An empirical approach to instrumental reinforcement. *Psychological Review, 81,* 146–164.

Technical Terms

Acquired drive

Behavioral bliss point

Behavioral regulation

Conditioned drive state

Drive reduction theory of reinforcement

Drive state

Homeostasis

Premack principle

Primary reinforcer

Response deprivation hypothesis

Schedule line

Sensory reinforcement

CHAPTER NINE

Extinction

D I D   Y O U   K N O W   T H A T :

- Extinction is not the opposite of acquisition; it does not involve "unlearning."
- Extinction of Pavlovian conditioned behavior is very similar to habituation.
- Extinction of instrumental behavior depends on the schedule of reinforcement in effect during acquisition.
- Reinforcing a response every time it occurs facilitates loss of responding in extinction.
- Intermittent reinforcement produces persistence by teaching subjects to keep going in the face of failure.

In Chapters 3–8, I showed how the acquisition of conditioned behavior depends on relations between stimuli and reinforcers (Pavlovian conditioning) and relations between responses and reinforcers (instrumental conditioning). The presentation of a reinforcer contingent on a prior stimulus or contingent on a prior response can produce profound changes in behavior. An obvious question I have avoided so far is, What happens if the reinforcer is no longer provided? Once a response has been acquired as a result of either a Pavlovian or an instrumental conditioning procedure, does it persist if the reinforcer is no longer presented? Or do training procedures have to remain in effect to maintain conditioned responding?

A procedure in which the unconditioned stimulus or reinforcer is no longer delivered is called an **extinction procedure.** In Pavlovian conditioning, extinction involves repeatedly presenting the conditioned stimulus (CS) without the unconditioned stimulus (US). In instrumental conditioning, extinction involves allowing the subject to perform the instrumental response but without the subsequent presentation of the reinforcer. As might be suspected, both Pavlovian and instrumental extinction procedures ultimately result in a decline in the previously conditioned response. Such a decline in conditioned behavior is called an **extinction effect.**

Extinction effects are of interest from two points of view. One perspective focuses on how rapidly conditioned behavior declines when the US (reinforcer) is no longer presented. The primary evidence of interest in this perspective is the **rate of extinction** of the conditioned behavior. The other perspective focuses on how long conditioned behavior continues to occur after an extinction procedure has been introduced. Here, the primary evidence of interest is the **persistence** of the conditioned behavior in the absence of reinforcement.

Rate of extinction and persistence are different ways of looking at the same thing. However, response persistence has historically been of greater interest in studies of extinction following instrumental conditioning, whereas rate of extinction has been of greater interest in studies of Pavlovian conditioning.

In some cases, persistence of conditioned behavior is highly desirable. In other cases, persistence may be problematic. Consider, for example, a girl who has learned to brush her teeth properly because she was praised for doing so by her parents. For such instrumental conditioning to be useful, the child should continue to brush properly even if her parents no longer supervise and praise her behavior. In contrast, consider a boy who has become frightened of dogs because of an encounter with a large dog that knocked him down in playful exuberance. In this case, persistence of the conditioned behavior is undesirable because it prevents the child from enjoying the company of friendly dogs.

The persistence of conditioned behavior in the absence of reinforcement is also of interest from a theoretical perspective. Early investigators of learning considered the persistence of conditioned behavior to be a measure of how well the response was originally learned. This notion was captured in the concept of **response reserve.** According to the concept of response reserve, conditioning procedures build up response reserve, or associative strength. When the reinforcer is no longer presented, the response reserve is lost or dissipated. Highly effective conditioning procedures were assumed to establish more response reserve or produce stronger associative strength than ineffective procedures. Therefore, highly effective conditioning procedures were expected to produce greater persistence of conditioned behavior during extinction.

As we will see, the concept of response reserve has been thoroughly refuted by studies of extinction. Subjects do not continue responding in extinction because of the strength of their prior learning. Rather, subjects are persistent because of the kinds of things they previously learned. Certain kinds of learning lead to much more responding in extinction than other types of learning.

Extinction of Pavlovian Conditioned Behavior

Procedures for extinction following Pavlovian conditioning are very similar to the procedures for habituation that I described in Chapter 3. In both cases, a stimulus is repeatedly presented by itself, and behavior elicited by that stimulus is observed to decline. The critical difference is that in habituation procedures the subject has no particular prior experience with the eliciting stimulus. In contrast, in extinction the eliciting stimulus previously served as the CS in a Pavlovian conditioning procedure. Despite this difference, many Pavlovian extinction phenomena are similar to effects we previously encountered in studies of habituation.

EXTINCTION AND HABITUATION

One important similarity between habituation and Pavlovian extinction is that in both cases, responding recovers after a long period without stimulation (Brooks & Bouton, 1993; Robbins, 1990). As we saw in Chapter 3, recovery of a habituated response following a period of rest is called spontaneous recovery. The recovery of extinguished responding that occurs after a period of rest is also called spontaneous recovery.

Another similarity between habituation and Pavlovian extinction is that in both phenomena the presentation of a novel stimulus can cause a temporary recovery of the response. Habituated responding can recover temporarily due to the presentation of an arousing or sensitizing stimulus. As I said in Chapter 3, this phenomenon is called dishabituation. The presentation of a novel stimulus can also result in the temporary recovery of a conditioned response following extinction (Pavlov, 1927). In this case, the phenomenon is called **external inhibition** or **disinhibition.**

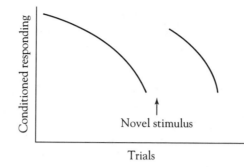

FIGURE 9.1   Illustration of disinhibition in extinction.
Following extinction of a conditioned response, presentation of a novel stimulus with the CS produces temporary recovery of conditioned responding. (Hypothetical data.)

To observe disinhibition, subjects are first repeatedly presented a previously conditioned stimulus by itself until they stop responding to the CS. The CS is then presented with a novel stimulus, and the conditioned behavior is observed to recover (see Figure 9.1).

Notice that the responding that occurs in the disinhibition effect cannot be attributed to the novel stimulus. Novel stimuli do not elicit conditioned responses. Rather, the novel stimulus appears to release the extinguished response from some sort of inhibitory influence.

EXTINCTION AS UNLEARNING

The phenomena of spontaneous recovery and disinhibition have important implications for theories of extinction. Superficially, extinction looks like the opposite of acquisition. During Pavlovian acquisition, conditioned responding progressively increases. In contrast, during extinction, conditioned responding progressively declines. This symmetry suggests that the processes of extinction are simply the opposite of the processes of acquisition. Acquisition involves the establishment of associative linkages between the CS and the US. The assumption that extinction is the opposite of acquisition suggests that extinction involves the loss, or unlearning, of the CS-US association.

The phenomena of spontaneous recovery and disinhibition are important because they show that extinction is not the opposite of acquisition. If responding declines during extinction because the CS-US association is lost or unlearned, then a period of rest should not produce recovery of the behavior. The phenomenon of spontaneous recovery suggests that extinction does not result in the loss or unlearning of the CS-US association.

The idea that extinction involves unlearning also cannot explain the phenomenon of disinhibition. If extinction involved the unlearning of a CS-US association, presentation of a novel stimulus could not reinstitute the conditioned response.

EXTINCTION AS A FORM OF INHIBITION

The phenomena of spontaneous recovery and disinhibition suggest that extinction involves some form of inhibition of the conditioned response. The inhibition appears to be lost with a period of rest, resulting in spontaneous recovery of the extinguished response. Presentation of a novel stimulus also appears to disrupt the inhibition created by extinction, producing the phenomenon of disinhibition.

Yet another phenomenon that supports the idea that extinction involves some form of inhibition rather than unlearning is the **renewal effect** (for example, Bouton, 1993). The renewal effect was discovered during the course of research on transfer of training. The basic question in such studies is how the learning that occurs in one situation transfers to other circumstances or contexts. For example, if you learn something in a noisy dormitory lounge, will that learning transfer to a quiet classroom in which you have to take a test? An equally important question concerns the transfer of extinction. If extinction is conducted in one situation so that the CS no longer elicits conditioned responding there, will the CS also be ineffective in other situations?

The transfer of extinction is often of considerable clinical and practical significance. For example, if a little boy's conditioned fear of dogs is extinguished in the office of a therapist, we would want those effects of extinction to transfer to situations outside the office. We would want the child to be willing to approach dogs that he encounters at a friend's house or in a park.

Much of the research on the renewal effect has been conducted with laboratory rats. The animals are conditioned in an experimental chamber with a particular level of illumination and a particular odor. (Let us call this conditioning chamber *context A.*) They are then moved to another chamber with less lighting and a different odor and receive an extinction procedure there. (Let us call the second chamber *context B.*) The reason for moving the subjects to context B for extinction training is to see if the effects of extinction will transfer back to context A (see Figure 9.2).

If extinction involves the unlearning of a conditioned response, then returning the subjects to context A after extinction in context B should not produce a recovery of the conditioned behavior. Contrary to that prediction, the effects of extinction training in context B do not transfer back to the original training context A. Rather, when subjects are returned to context A, conditioned responding recovers. Conditioned responding is "renewed" when subjects are returned to the experimental chambers in which they were originally trained—hence, the name, renewal effect.

Spontaneous recovery, disinhibition, and the renewal effect illustrate

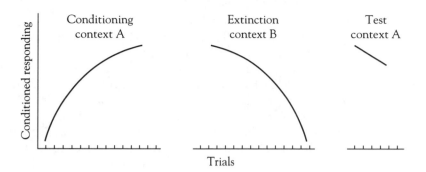

F I G U R E 9.2   Illustration of the renewal effect.
Subjects originally acquire the conditioned response in context A. They then receive extinction training in context B, which results in a decline of the conditioned response. In the third phase, they are returned to context A for testing. The conditioned response is "renewed" when the subjects are returned to context A. (Hypothetical data.)

that extinction does not result in the unlearning of conditioned behavior. Rather, extinction appears to involve some form of inhibition that results in the suppression of conditioned responding. Furthermore, the suppression of responding is not permanent but can be reversed by various manipulations.

CLINICAL IMPLICATIONS

Spontaneous recovery, disinhibition, and the renewal effect have important implications for using extinction in therapeutic situations. The therapeutic goal of using an extinction procedure is to reduce an undesired conditioned response. Extinction may be used, for example, to reduce an undesired conditioned drug craving or an undesired conditioned fear. Spontaneous recovery, disinhibition, and the renewal effect can all contribute to relapse after the therapeutic application of an extinction procedure.

The renewal effect in particular suggests that differences between the context in which a conditioned response is acquired and the context in which it is extinguished can determine the likelihood of relapse (Bouton & Swartzentruber, 1991). If therapeutic extinction is conducted in a context very different from the context in which the undesired response was originally acquired, returning the subject to the original learning situation may result in serious relapse of the problematic behavior.

EXTINCTIVE INHIBITION VS. CONDITIONED INHIBITION

We previously encountered the concept of inhibition when I described Pavlovian conditioned inhibition in Chapter 5. Although extinction also involves an inhibitory process of some sort, evidence suggests that extinctive inhibition is very different from Pavlovian conditioned inhibition.

Traditionally, two behavioral tests have been used to identify conditioned inhibition, the retardation-of-acquisition test and the compound stimulus test (Hearst, Besley, & Farthing, 1970; Rescorla, 1969). The retardation-of-acquisition test requires that a conditioned inhibitory stimulus be slower to acquire conditioned excitatory properties than a "neutral" stimulus (see Chapter 5). The compound stimulus test requires that a conditioned inhibitory stimulus reduce responding elicited by a conditioned excitatory stimulus when the two stimuli are presented at the same time (in compound).

A CS that has been extinguished fails to pass either the retardation-of-acquistion test or the compound test of inhibition (for example, Reberg, 1972). Therefore, extinction does not appear to involve the same kind of inhibition as Pavlovian conditioned inhibition. The most reasonable judgment at the present time is that extinctive inhibition is more akin to habituation processes than to conditioned inhibition.

Extinction of Instrumentally Conditioned Behavior

The procedure for the extinction of instrumentally conditioned behavior is remarkably simple. The subject is permitted to perform the instrumental response, but the reinforcer is not delivered. Organisms that have experienced instrumental conditioning continue responding for some time after the reinforcer is no longer available. However, the absence of reinforcement eventually results in a decline in behavior.

Extinction of instrumentally conditioned behavior exhibits some of the same properties as extinction of Pavlovian conditioned responding. As in Pavlovian extinction, giving organisms a period of rest after an extinction session can result in spontaneous recovery of an extinguished instrumental response. The phenomenon of disinhibition also occurs in the extinction of instrumental behavior. Presentation of a novel stimulus can result in a temporary recovery of the extinguished instrumental response. Another similarity between Pavlovian and instrumental extinction is the renewal effect. If subjects experience the extinction in a situation that is distinctively different from the training context, the instrumental behavior will recover when the subject is returned to the training context.

Although extinction of instrumental behavior has some of the same characteristics as extinction of Pavlovian conditioned behavior, research in these two paradigms has developed largely independently of each other. In studies of the extinction of instrumental behavior, investigators have focused on how various training or reinforcement procedures influence the persistence of responding when extinction is introduced.

The most important training variable that influences instrumental

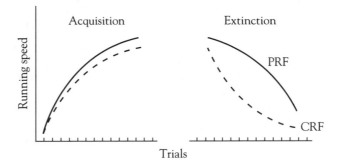

F I G U R E 9.3   Illustration of the partial reinforcement extinction effect, or PREE.
During the acquisition phase, the instrumental response is conditioned on a partial reinforcement (PRF) schedule for one group of subjects and on a continuous reinforcement (CRF) schedule for the second group. During extinction, when responding is not reinforced for either group, Group PRF shows more persistence than Group CRF.

---

responding during extinction is the schedule of reinforcement. Hundreds of experiments have been conducted to investigate the effects of schedules of reinforcement on the persistence of instrumental behavior. Most of these studies have dealt with the partial reinforcement extinction effect.

THE PARTIAL REINFORCEMENT EXTINCTION EFFECT

As I noted in Chapter 7, schedules of reinforcement can take many different forms. There are ratio schedules, interval schedules, and concurrent schedules that combine two (or more) simpler schedules. Those various schedule arrangements have been investigated in great detail in studies employing free-operant methodology. In contrast, much of the research on how schedules of reinforcement determine extinction of instrumental behavior has been conducted in straight-alley runways. These studies have shown that the most important factor determining the persistence of responding in extinction is whether the instrumental response was initially trained with continuous reinforcement (CRF) or partial reinforcement (PRF). With continuous reinforcement, the subject is reinforced each time it reaches the goal box; with partial reinforcement, the reinforcer is provided only some of the times that the subject reaches the goal box. In general, responding in extinction is much more persistent following partial reinforcement than following continuous reinforcement (see Figure 9.3). This is known as the **partial reinforcement extinction effect** or PREE.

The partial reinforcement extinction effect was first observed by Humphreys (1939), and for some time it was known as Humphreys's paradox.

Before the demonstration of the PREE, responding in extinction was considered to reflect the associative strength of the conditioned response, or how well the conditioned response had been learned. In addition, the associative strength of an instrumental response was assumed to be determined by how often that response had been reinforced. The assumption was that the more often a response is reinforced, the better it would become learned, and the more persistent it would be in extinction.

The instrumental response is reinforced more often in continuous reinforcement than in intermittent reinforcement. Therefore, continuous reinforcement was expected to yield more persistent responding in extinction than partial reinforcement. The PREE is contrary to this prediction. According to the PREE, more persistence occurs after partial reinforcement than after continuous reinforcement. Therefore, the PREE was considered a paradoxical finding.

Since Humphreys's initial demonstration, the PREE has been documented in a wide variety of instrumental conditioning situations and species (for example, Bitterman, 1975). The phenomenon may still be considered paradoxical, but it is not an anomaly. Rather, it is a common characteristic of instrumental behavior. Gamblers, aspiring actors and musicians, and research scientists are all on intermittent schedules of reinforcement, and all display considerable persistence in their behavior.

EXPLANATIONS OF THE PREE

The discrimination hypothesis. The first and perhaps the simplest account of the PREE was the **discrimination hypothesis.** The introduction of an extinction procedure after a period of training in which the instrumental response was reinforced represents a change in the contingencies of reinforcement—a change in the rules of the game, if you will. Proponents of the discrimination hypothesis pointed out that introducing extinction after continuous reinforcement involves a bigger change for the subject than introducing extinction after partial reinforcement.

During continuous reinforcement, every occurrence of the instrumental response results in delivery of the reinforcer. This is dramatically different from extinction, when the reinforcer is never delivered. In contrast, the change from partial reinforcement to extinction is not as remarkable. Responses are occasionally not reinforced during a PRF schedule, and responses are also not reinforced during extinction. Thus, a partial reinforcement procedure is in some ways similar to extinction. The discrimination hypothesis assumes that responding is more persistent after PRF than CRF because extinction is more difficult to detect following PRF training.

Although the discrimination hypothesis is intuitively reasonable, it is too simplistic as an explanation of the persistence of instrumental behavior. The hypothesis was definitively disproved by the results of an elegant experiment, independently conceived by Theios (1962) and Jenkins

	Acquisition phase 1	Acquisition phase 2	Extinction
Group C	CRF	CRF	no S*
Group P	PRF	CRF	no S*

F I G U R E 9.4 **Design of experiments demonstrating the PREE in spite of interpolated continuous reinforcement before extinction.**
Group C receives CRF training in the first phase of acquisition, during which Group P receives partial reinforcement. During the second phase of acquisition, responding for both groups is reinforced on a CRF schedule. Then, both groups receive extinction.

(1962). The design of the Theios and Jenkins experiments is shown in Figure 9.4.

The extinction performance of two groups of subjects was compared. As is true for all studies of the PREE, Group C received continuous reinforcement (CRF) training initially, and Group P received partial reinforcement (PRF) training. In a second phase of acquisition, both groups received CRF training, and then both groups received extinction. The phase of acquisition, in which both groups received CRF training, was intended to make the change from reinforcement to extinction equivalent for both groups. With the interpolated CRF training, introduction of the extinction procedure should have been just as noticeable for Group P as it was for Group C.

According to the discrimination hypothesis, an interpolated phase of CRF training should eliminate the PREE. Contrary to this prediction, however, both Theios and Jenkins observed greater persistence in Group P than in Group C. The PREE was not eliminated by giving Group P CRF training just before extinction.

The results of the Theios and Jenkins experiments are important because they show that persistence following PRF training does not result from possible perceptual difficulties in detecting the onset of extinction. Evidently, the PREE does not result from the nature of the transition from acquisition to extinction. Rather, the PREE appears to result from something subjects in Group P learn long before extinction starts—something they learn during PRF training at the beginning of the experiment.

The results of the Theios and Jenkins experiments suggest that persistence created by PRF training is not erased by subsequent continuous reinforcement. A man who has become a persistent gambler because of partial reinforcement will not change his habits after an unbroken string of wins (continuous reinforcement).

The next two theories we will consider—the sequential hypothesis and

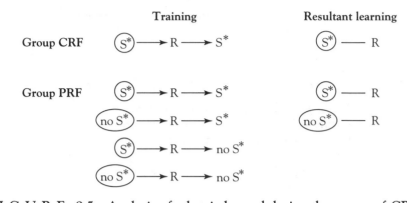

F I G U R E 9.5   **Analysis of what is learned during the course of CRF and PRF training according to the sequential theory of the PREE.**
$\textcircled{S*}$ = memory of reinforcement; $\textcircled{noS*}$ = memory of nonreinforcement; R = instrumental response; S* = reinforcement; and noS* = nonreinforcement.

frustration theory—offer different explanations for what subjects learn during PRF training that makes them persistent in extinction. Both of these theories were developed in the context of research in which laboratory rats were required to run from the start box to the goal box of a straight-alley runway for food reinforcement. The theories can be extended to other instrumental conditioning situations as well. However, for the sake of simplicity, I will describe the theories as they apply to discrete trial runway experiments.

Sequential theory. **Sequential theory** was developed by John Capaldi and is based on the idea that memories can be an important source of the stimuli in the presence of which an instrumental response occurs. Capaldi assumed that when subjects are placed in a runway at the start of a trial, they are able to remember whether or not they were reinforced for running on the preceding trial (Capaldi, 1967, 1971). Therefore, on each trial, the instrumental running response occurs in the presence of the memory of the outcome of the preceding trial. How this basic idea may contribute to the PREE is illustrated in Figure 9.5.

On a CRF schedule, each trial is reinforced. Therefore, the memory of the outcome of the preceding trial is always the memory of reinforcement. Because of this, continuously reinforced subjects learn to run in response to the memory of reward. If the memory of reward is represented by $\textcircled{S*}$, this type of learning is represented as $\textcircled{S*}$-R.

What happens with partially reinforced subjects is a bit more complicated. To simplify the analysis, let us consider only what happens on the reinforced trials of a partial reinforcement schedule, because it is only the reinforced trials that are relevant to conditioning persistence. A reinforced trial can occur following either reinforcement or nonreinforcement on the preceding trial. Thus, on a PRF schedule, the instrumental response may be reinforced in the presence of the memory of prior reinforcement (S^*) or in the presence of the memory of prior nonreinforcement (noS^*). As a result, subjects learn to respond when they remember prior reinforcement (S^*-R), just as with CRF training. In addition, with PRF training, subjects also learn to respond when they remember prior nonreinforcement (noS^*-R).

The noS^*-R association is the critical factor that produces persistence in extinction after PRF training. Extinction involves a series of nonreinforced trials. After the first extinction trial when the subject is placed back in the runway, it will remember the nonreward (noS^*) of the preceding trial. PRF subjects have learned to respond to the memory of nonreward because of the noS^*-R association, and that will encourage them to respond in extinction. In contrast, CRF subjects have not learned to respond to the memory of nonreward. Therefore, they will be much less pesistent in extinction.

According to sequential theory, subjects with a history of partial reinforcement will persist in responding during extinction because they learn to respond when they remember not having been reinforced on the preceding trial; CRF training does not result in such learning. Therefore, CRF training does not build persistent behavior. The difference in how the instrumental response becomes conditioned to the memories of reward and nonreward is assumed to be responsible for the PREE.

Frustration theory. **Frustration theory** as an explanation of the PREE was developed by Abram Amsel (1958, 1967, 1992). Unlike sequential theory, frustration theory takes into consideration the emotional effects of nonreward. The absence of reinforcement can be very upsetting. Consider, for example, losing money in a broken soft drink machine. We expect to get a soft drink when we put money in a soft drink machine and are therefore highly disappointed if the machine malfunctions. As this example illustrates, nonreinforcement is especially upsetting when we anticipate being reinforced.

According to frustration theory, the emotional consequences of nonreinforcement depend on the subject's history. If you have never been reinforced in a particular situation, you will not expect reward there, and the absence of reinforcement will not be upsetting or frustrating. In contrast, if you are consistently reinforced (you get a soft drink each time you put money in a vending machine), the absence of reinforcement will be highly frustrating. According to frustration theory, **frustration** occurs when a subject expects to be rewarded but reinforcement does not occur. Frustration is elicited by the unexpected absence of reinforcement.

Frustration is an unpleasant experience, and the usual (unconditioned) response to frustration is to withdraw from the situation. In a straight-alley runway, frustration is elicited in the goal box when the subject encounters no food after a series of reinforced trials or after continuous reinforcement. The response to this frustration is to withdraw or stop running to the goal box. Such unconditioned withdrawal behavior to frustration is used in frustration theory to explain why extinction produces a rapid decline in responding after continuous reinforcement. What about partial reinforcement?

Sequential theory explained persistence after partial reinforcement as the result of learning to respond in the face of the memory of not having been reinforced on the preceding trial (see Figure 9.5). Frustration theory explains persistence as the result of learning to respond in the face of anticipated frustration. How might such learning occur?

On the reinforced trials of a PRF procedure, subjects learn to expect getting food. Once they have learned to expect being reinforced, the absence of food elicits frustration. As PRF training progresses, subjects continue receiving reinforced and nonreinforced trials. After a number of encounters with frustration during the course of PRF training, the subjects also come to expect being frustrated. Thus, after a while, partial reinforcement produces both the anticipation of reward and the anticipation of frustration.

The initial or unconditioned response to the anticipation of frustration is withdrawal from the goal box. However, withdrawal is not productive because if PRF subjects stopped going to the goal box altogether, they would miss the food that is available there some of the time. Because food is sometimes available on a PRF schedule, subjects can get reinforced for responding when they anticipate being frustrated. As a result of such reinforcement, PRF subjects eventually learn to make the instrumental response in the face of anticipated frustration. Such learning is the basic mechanism of persistence in frustration theory.

Subjects given continuous reinforcement do not have the opportunity to learn to make the instrumental response when they anticipate being frustrated. They never encounter frustration during acquisition and therefore are never reinforced for running in the presence of anticipated frustration. When CRF subjects first encounter frustration in extinction, frustration elicits unconditioned withdrawal responses and the subjects quickly stop making the instrumental response. In contrast, because PRF subjects previously learned to make the instrumental response in the face of anticipated frustration, they continue to respond when they encounter repeated nonreinforced trials in extinction.

Comparison of frustration theory and sequential theory. Numerous experiments have been conducted to test frustration theory and sequential theory, and many of the predictions of each theory have been confirmed. Thus, one theory is not more accurate than the other; rather, the two theories help us understand different aspects of the PREE.

Sequential theory focuses on the effects of trial sequences and transitions from nonreinforced to reinforced trials in a PRF schedule. These transitions are needed for PRF subjects to learn to respond when they remember not having been reinforced on the preceding trial. The specific sequence of rewarded and nonrewarded trials is not as important for frustration theory. Rather, frustration theory focuses on the emotional effects of nonreward and on learning about expectancies of reward and expectancies of frustration.

Frustration theory and sequential theory are similar in that both theories assume that the instrumental response becomes conditioned to internal cues. In sequential theory, the internal cues are assumed to be provided by the memory of reward or nonreward on the prior trial. In frustration theory, the internal cues are assumed to be provided by the expectancy of frustration. This difference turns out to be highly significant.

The persistence mechanism of frustration theory takes a number of trials to develop during the course of PRF training. As I noted earlier, for nonreward to elicit frustration, the subjects first have to learn to anticipate being rewarded. After that, learning to anticipate frustration takes additional trials. Therefore, subjects cannot learn to respond to the anticipation of frustration until a substantial amount of PRF training has taken place. Because of that, frustration theory can only explain the persistence that occurs after substantial numbers of PRF trials. In contrast, the memory mechanisms of sequential theory are operative from the start of PRF training. Therefore, sequential theory is better equipped to explain PRF extinction effects that occur after only a few training trials.

Suggested Readings

AMSEL, A. (1992). *Frustration theory: An analysis of dispositional learning and memory.* Cambridge, UK: Cambridge University Press.

BOUTON, M. E. (1993). Context, time, and memory retrieval in the interference paradigms of Pavlovian learning. *Psychological Bulletin, 114,* 80–99.

CAPALDI, E. J. (1971). Memory and learning: A sequential viewpoint. In W. K. Honig & P.H.R. James (Eds.), *Animal memory* (pp. 115–154). Orlando, FL: Academic Press.

ROBBINS, S. J. (1990). Mechanisms underlying spontaneous recovery in autoshaping. *Journal of Experimental Psychology: Animal Behavior Processes, 16,* 235–249.

Technical Terms

Discrimination hypothesis   External inhibition
Disinhibition   Extinction effect

Extinction procedure
Frustration
Frustration theory
Partial reinforcement extinction
    effect

Persistence
Rate of extinction
Renewal effect
Response reserve
Sequential theory

CHAPTER TEN

Stimulus Control of Behavior

DID YOU KNOW THAT:

- Differential responding is used to identify control of behavior by a particular stimulus.
- Even simple stimuli have many features or dimensions.
- Control of behavior by one training stimulus often generalizes to other, similar stimuli.
- Stimulus generalization and stimulus discrimination are complementary concepts.
- Generalization of behavior from one stimulus to another depends on the subject's training history with the stimuli.
- Intradimensional discrimination training produces more precise stimulus control than interdimensional discrimination training.

Throughout the book, I have been discussing how various aspects of behavior are controlled by environmental events. Elicited behavior and responding that result from Pavlovian conditioning are obvious examples of behavior that occurs in response to specific stimuli. As we saw in Chapter 6, instrumental behavior can also be regarded as responding that occurs because of the presence of antecedent stimuli. These antecedent stimuli may activate the instrumental response directly or may activate a representation of the response-reinforcer relation.

Clearly, much of learned behavior occurs because of the presence of particular environmental events. Up to this point, however, our discussion of learning has left two critical issues about the stimulus control of behavior unanswered. The first issue concerns the measurement of stimulus control. How can we determine to what extent a specific stimulus or feature of the environment is responsible for a particular response? Are some types of stimuli more important than others in controlling a particular response? If so, how can we measure such differences in the degree of stimulus control?

Once we know how to measure stimulus control, we can tackle the second issue, which concerns the determinants of stimulus control. What determines which stimulus will gain control over a particular response, and what determines the degree to which that stimulus comes to control the behavior? Why does a response come to be controlled more by one feature of the environment than another?

Questions about stimulus control arise in part because of the complexity of environmental events. Even something as simple as a dial tone on the telephone is a complex stimulus with multiple features. The tone can be characterized in terms of its loudness, pitch, how suddenly it begins and ends, tonal complexity, and location in space. How do we determine which of these stimulus features is critical, and what makes those features critical?

Measurement of Stimulus Control

Analyzing the stimulus control of behavior in a new situation or in a new species is not unlike trying to figure out what is happening if you are a visitor from a different culture or a different planet. Assume that you are a creature from Mars seeing cars, streets, and traffic lights on earth for the first time. Periodically, the cars drive past the traffic light. At other times, they stop and wait. You want to figure out what makes the drivers stop some of the time and continue driving at other times. How might you approach this problem? What kind of an experiment could you perform to determine what is controlling the behavior of the drivers?

The first step would be to formulate a hypothesis or guess about what is going on. The possibilities are limited only by your imagination. Perhaps drivers stop because a sensor in the road near an intersection signals an on-board computer to stop the car. Alternatively, drivers may be sending signals to each other, with a particular gesture indicating "stop" and another indicating "go." Another possibility is that the drivers come to a stop when they need a short break and continue when they have rested a bit. Or, there may be an elaborate schedule, known to all drivers, according to which they have to stop at certain times of day and are allowed to continue at other times. Yet another possibility is that stops and starts are controlled by the traffic lights.

IDENTIFYING RELEVANT STIMULI

How could you determine which stimulus causes cars to stop at an intersection? The various possibilities may be tested in different ways. For example, you may test whether drivers are signaling each other by comparing what happens when there is just one car on the road to what happens when several cars are using the road at the same time. To determine whether the traffic lights have anything to do with it, you could see whether the cars are less likely to stop when the traffic lights are covered up. To determine whether sensors in the road are relevant, you could try to find the sensors and see what happens when they are deactivated.

Notice that each of the above tests involves observing the behavior of interest in the presence and absence of the stimulus that we guessed might be responsible for the behavior. To test whether the drivers were signaling each other to stop, we compared stopping when such signals could not have been transmitted (when there was only one car on the road) to stopping when such signals could have occurred (when there were several cars on the road at the same time). In testing the possibility that the traffic lights were responsible for the stops and starts, we observed what happened when the lights were covered up. These examples illustrate a basic manipulation involved in the measurement of stimulus control:

> The stimulus control of behavior is measured by comparing the behavior
> of interest in the presence and absence of the test stimulus.

If the presence and absence of the test stimulus do not produce differences in responding, we may conclude that the stimulus does not control the behavior in question. Cars are just as likely to stop at a traffic light whether or not there are other cars on the road. Therefore, we may conclude that stops and starts are not cued by signals between drivers. In contrast, cars are much more likely to stop when the traffic lights are visible than when they are covered up. This provides evidence that the traffic lights control the behavior of interest and illustrates the basic criterion for the stimulus control of behavior:

> A response is said to be under the control of a particular stimulus if the
> response is altered by changes in that stimulus.

A change in responding related to changes in a stimulus is called **differential responding.** Which possible stimulus is responsible for the target behavior is identified by differential responding related to changes in that

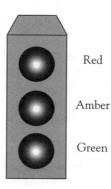

Red

Amber

Green

F I G U R E **10.1**   **Stimulus features of traffic lights.**
The lights differ in both color and position.

stimulus. If responding is altered by changes in a stimulus, that stimulus is involved in the control of the behavior. If responding is not altered by changes in a stimulus, that stimulus is not relevant to the control of the behavior.

IDENTIFYING RELEVANT STIMULUS FEATURES

Identifying the fact that stops and starts on a road are somehow controlled by traffic lights is progress. However, many details need to be filled in before we know exactly how drivers respond to traffic lights. For example, traffic lights are often arranged in a vertical array, with the top light being red and the bottom one green (see Figure 10.1). Which feature is important? Does it matter which color is lit, or is the relative position of the illuminated light critical? Do drivers stop when they see a red light and go when they see a green light? Or do they stop when the top light is on and go when the bottom one is illuminated? These considerations concern the particular feature of a traffic light (color or position) that is important in controlling the behavior in question.

How can we determine which feature of a traffic light is most important? The strategy for identifying relevant stimulus features is similar to the strategy for identifying relevant stimuli. To determine whether a particular stimulus feature is important, we have to vary that stimulus feature without altering any other feature and see whether the behavior of interest changes accordingly. For example, to determine whether color is important in traffic lights, we have to test a red and a green light presented in the same position (always on top perhaps) and see if drivers stop when the light is red and go when the light is green. To determine whether the position of the light is important, we have to test lights of the same color in different positions. For example, we might present a red light in either the top or the bottom position and see if drivers stop when the light is on top and go when the light is on the bottom.

When we vary one feature of a stimulus while keeping all other features constant, we are testing the importance of a particular **stimulus dimension** for the behavior in question. When we present red and green lights always in the top position of a set of traffic lights, we are testing the importance of the color dimension of traffic lights. When we present the same color light in different positions (top vs. bottom), we are testing the importance of the position dimension.

Different stimulus dimensions may be important for different drivers. Drivers who are color-blind and cannot distinguish red from green have no choice. They have to focus on the position of the illuminated traffic light. They have to stop when the top light is on and go when they see the bottom light illuminated. Other drivers may respond primarily to the color dimension of traffic lights. Still others may respond to both the color and stimulus position.

MEASUREMENT OF THE DEGREE OF STIMULUS CONTROL

A particular response is usually not controlled exclusively by a single stimulus feature. Rather, behavior is influenced to different degrees by different stimulus features. Differential responding in tests of the presence and absence of a stimulus identifies that stimulus as involved in the control of the behavior. However, testing the presence versus absence of a stimulus does not tell us how precisely the behavior is tuned to a particular stimulus feature.

We may find, for example, that a driver stops whenever a red traffic light is on, regardless of the position of the light. This indicates that the driver's behavior is controlled by the red light. However, it does not tell us how precisely the behavior is tuned to a particular shade of red. Red traffic lights are not uniform. Some are more reddish than others. To analyze the stimulus control of a driver's behavior more precisely, we would have to test a variety of colors, including several different shades of red.

The wavelength of red light is at the short end of the visual spectrum. Longer wavelengths of light appear less red and more orange. As the wavelength of light becomes even longer, the light appears more and more yellow. A detailed test of stimulus control by different colors requires systematically testing subjects with lights of different wavelengths.

Stimulus generalization gradients. Several different outcomes may occur if a variety of test colors are presented, ranging from deep red to deep yellow. These are illustrated in Figure 10.2. If the driver were paying very close attention to color, she would stop only if the light had a perfect red color. Lights that had a tinge of orange would not cause her to stop. This possibility is illustrated by the curve A of Figure 10.2

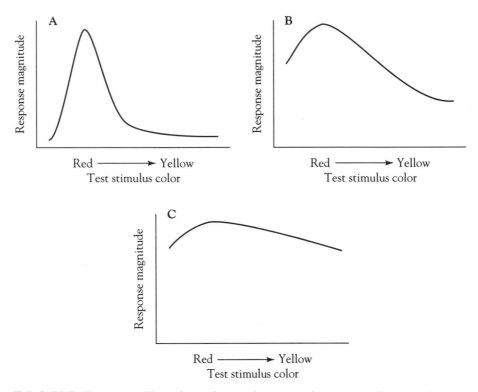

F I G U R E 10.2 Hypothetical stimulus generalization gradients indicating different degrees of control of responding by the color of a stimulus. Curve A illustrates strongest stimulus control by color; curve C illustrates weakest stimulus control by color.

At the other extreme, the driver may stop when she sees any color that has a vague resemblance to red. This possibility is illustrated by the curve C of Figure 10.2. As the driver encounters lights that are less and less reddish, her responding declines, but in curve C, responding is less precisely under the control of the color of the lights than behavior represented by curve A.

An intermediate outcome is also possible, as illustrated by curve B of Figure 10.2. In this case, the driver's behavior shows considerable sensitivity to differences in color, but responding is not as closely limited to a particular shade of red as in curve A.

The curves presented in Figure 10.2 illustrate that a gradation of responding can occur as the color of the light is systematically altered. Each of the curves in Figure 10.2 is a **stimulus generalization gradient.** We previously encountered the concept of a stimulus generalization gradient when we discussed the stimulus generalization of habituation (see Figure 3.2). A stimulus generalization gradient shows how behavior changes as a

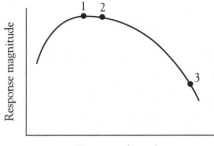

F I G U R E 10.3 A hypothetical generalization gradient for responding to different colored stimuli.
Points 1 and 2 illustrate the phenomenon of stimulus generalization. Points 1 and 3 illustrate the phenomenon of stimulus discrimination.

function of systematic variations of a particular feature of a stimulus. In Figure 10.2, the feature in question is color. In Figure 3.2, the feature in question was stimulus position.

Generalization gradients can be obtained for any stimulus feature, including stimulus position, size, brightness, shape, height, and so forth. As Figure 10.2 illustrates, stimulus generalization gradients can be very steep (curve A) or rather shallow (curve C). The steepness or slope of the generalization gradient indicates how closely the behavior being measured is controlled by the stimulus feature in question. A steep generalization gradient indicates strong control by the stimulus feature or dimension. A shallow or flat generalization gradient indicates weak stimulus control.

Stimulus generalization and stimulus discrimination. Stimulus generalization gradients involve two important phenomena—stimulus generalization and stimulus discrimination. **Stimulus generalization** is said to occur if responding elicited by one stimulus is also observed when a different stimulus is presented. In this case, the behavior is said to generalize from the first stimulus to the second. Points 1 and 2 in Figure 10.3 illustrate the phenomenon of stimulus generalization.

Stimulus discrimination is said to occur if changes in a stimulus result in different levels of responding. Stimulus discrimination is identified by differential responding. Points 1 and 3 in Figure 10.3 illustrate the phenomenon of stimulus discrimination.

In a generalization gradient, stimulus generalization and stimulus discrimination are complementary phenomena. More of one is necessarily accompanied by less of the other. A great deal of generalization among stimuli indicates lack of stimulus discrimination, and a great deal of discrimination among stimuli indicates the lack of stimulus generalization.

Theories of generalization.   Why do subjects respond similarly to different stimuli? Why do they generalize from one stimulus to another? Early investigators (Pavlov, 1927, for example) suggested that responses conditioned to one stimulus will generalize to other stimuli because the effects of training spread to stimuli that are similar to the originally trained cue. When a little boy first learns the word for a cow, he is likely to use the word "cow" not only when he sees a cow but also when he sees a bull, or perhaps even a horse. According to the spread-of-effect interpretation, such generalization occurs because bulls and horses are similar to cows and the learned response to cows spreads to other, similar animals.

The spread-of-effect interpretation was challenged by Lashley and Wade (1946), who proposed that subjects respond similarly to different stimuli because they have not learned to distinguish between them. According to this interpretation, the little boy will use the word "cow" when he sees cows, bulls, and horses because he has not learned yet to distinguish among those different animals.

The Lashley-Wade hypothesis suggests that stimulus generalization can be limited by appropriate training. I will describe evidence confirming this prediction when I describe learning factors as determinants of stimulus control. However, before I get to that, let us consider the effects of stimulus and organismic factors in stimulus control.

Determinants of Stimulus Control: Stimulus and Organismic Factors

Having identified how to measure the stimulus control of behavior, and having identified the complementary phenomena of stimulus generalization and stimulus discrimination, we are ready to tackle the second major question, namely, What factors determine which features of a stimulus will gain control over a particular response? In addressing this question, we will first consider factors related to the type of stimulus and organism involved.

SENSORY CAPACITY

Perhaps the most obvious factor determining whether a particular stimulus feature will influence behavior is the sensory capacity of the organism. An organism cannot respond to a stimulus if it lacks the sense organs needed to detect the stimulus. People are unable to respond to radio waves, ultraviolet light, and sounds above about 20,000 cycles per second because they lack the sense organ to detect such stimuli. Dogs, in contrast, are able to hear sounds of much higher frequency than human beings and are therefore capable of responding to ultrasounds that are inaudible to people.

Sensory capacity sets a limit on the kinds of stimuli that can come to control an organism's behavior. However, sensory capacity is just a precondition for stimulus control. It does not ensure that behavior will be influenced by a particular stimulus feature. People with a normal sense of smell can distinguish the aroma of different fine wines. However, without special training, most people find it difficult to make fine discriminations among wines. Without a sense of smell, you could never learn to distinguish the aroma of different wines, but a normal sense of smell is not enough. Sensory capacity is just the starting point for bringing behavior under the control of a particular stimulus feature.

SENSORY ORIENTATION

Another prerequisite for stimulus control is the sensory orientation of the subject. For a stimulus to gain control over some aspect of a subject's behavior, the stimulus has to be accessible to the relevant sense organ. If you have a cold and have to breathe through your mouth, olfactory stimuli are not likely to reach the nasal epithelium, and you will be unable to make fine distinctions among different odors.

Some stimuli such as sounds and overall levels of illumination spread throughout an environment. Therefore, such stimuli are likely to be encountered whether or not the subject is oriented toward the source of the stimulus. You can see a lamp light up a room, for example, even if you are not facing the light. For this reason, tones and overhead lights are popular stimuli in learning experiments conducted in laboratories. In contrast, localized visual cues may present a problem because such a stimulus is encountered only if the subject is looking toward it. For example, if you are watching for instructional signs on the right side of a road, you may miss a sign placed on the left side.

STIMULUS INTENSITY OR SALIENCE

Other things being equal, behavior is more likely to come under the control of more intense or salient stimuli than weak stimuli (for example, Kamin, 1965). In fact, the presence of an intense stimulus can interfere with the control of behavior by a less intense cue. This phenomenon was first identified by Pavlov (1927) and is referred to as **overshadowing.**

In one demonstration of overshadowing (Kamin, 1969), two groups of rats were compared in their acquisition of conditioned fear to a fairly soft, 50 db noise using the conditioned suppression procedure. For the overshadowing group, the noise CS was presented simultaneously with a light on each conditioning trial. For the control group, the noise was presented without the light. After eight conditioning trials, the fear response of both groups was measured to the noise CS presented alone.

The results of the noise-alone test trials are summarized in Figure 10.4. A modest but reasonable level of conditioned fear was observed in the control group. In contrast, much less conditioned fear to the noise occurred

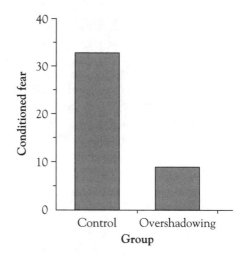

F I G U R E 10.4 Levels of conditioned fear elicited by a 50 db noise CS after pairings with foot shock in which the CS was presented simultaneously with a light CS (overshadowing) or without the light (control). (Based on Kamin, 1969.)

in the overshadowing group. This outcome indicates that the presence of the light during the conditioning trials interfered with, or overshadowed, conditioning of the noise CS.

MOTIVATIONAL FACTORS

The extent to which behavior comes under the control of a particular stimulus is also determined by the motivational state of the organism. Motivational factors in the stimulus control of behavior have not been investigated extensively. However, the available evidence indicates that attention can be shifted away from one type of stimulus to another by a change in motivation. LoLordo and his associates have found that pigeons conditioned with food as the reinforcer come to respond to visual cues more than auditory cues. In contrast, pigeons conditioned to avoid pain are more likely to respond to auditory cues than to visual cues (Foree & LoLordo, 1973; Shapiro, Jacobs, & LoLordo, 1980).

The motivational state of the organism (or the unconditioned stimuli the subject receives) appears to activate a stimulus filter and biases the attention of the organism in favor of certain types of cues. When pigeons are hungry and are motivated to find food, they appear to be especially sensitive to visual cues. In contrast, when pigeons are fearful and are motivated to avoid danger, they are especially sensitive to auditory cues. For other species, these motivational influences may take different forms. A species that hunts at night, for example, may be especially attentive to auditory cues when hungry.

Determinants of Stimulus Control: Learning Factors

Given the required sensory capacity and sensory orientation, perhaps the most important factor that determines the extent to which behavior will be controlled by a particular stimulus is the significance or validity of that stimulus. As Pavlov pointed out, biologically significant stimuli (such as food for a hungry animal) can control behavior unconditionally or without prior training. In addition, stimuli that are not significant at the outset can become so through association with stimuli or events that are already significant.

PAVLOVIAN AND INSTRUMENTAL CONDITIONING

An initially ineffective stimulus can come to control behavior through a direct or an indirect association with a US. As I said in Chapter 4, simple Pavlovian conditioning procedures make an initially ineffective stimulus significant by establishing an association between that stimulus and the US.

Stimulus significance can also be established through instrumental conditioning. In this case, the US, or reinforcer (S*), is presented contingent on a response (R) in the presence of an initially neutral stimulus (S). The S-R-S* instrumental procedure may increase the significance of stimulus S by establishing an association between S and the reinforcer S* or by having stimulus S signal when the R-S* contingency is in effect (see Chapter 6). In the second case, stimulus S comes to set the occasion for the R-S* relation.

Simple Pavlovian and instrumental conditioning procedures increase control of behavior by an initially ineffective stimulus (the CS in Pavlovian conditioning and stimulus S in instrumental conditioning). However, such procedures do not determine which feature(s) of the CS or stimulus S come to exert the greatest influence on the conditioned response. Consider, for example, a case in which the CS or stimulus S is an audiovisual cue, with both auditory and visual features. Whether the visual or the auditory component of the stimulus will gain predominant control over the conditioned response will depend on the stimulus and organismic factors discussed previously. If the organism has a keen sense of sight but poor hearing, the visual component of the stimulus will be predominant. If the subject is motivated by fear, the auditory component may be more important. If the visual component is more intense or salient than the auditory feature, then the visual component will gain more control over the behavior.

Simple Pavlovian and instrumental conditioning procedures bring behavior under the control of initially ineffective stimuli, but sensory capacity, sensory orientation, stimulus intensity, and motivation still determine which features of a complex event predominate in the control of the conditioned response.

How is it then that people and other animals are able to respond differentially to stimuli that are very similar in their sensory effects? Consider, for example, a car that has been recently filled with gas and one that is about to run out of gas. There is little difference between these two types of cars in terms of the modality and intensity of the stimuli a driver encounters. The only difference is in the fuel gauge indicator, and that difference is likely to be very small. Nevertheless, drivers respond very differently to cars that have plenty of gas and those that are about to run out of gas. People also respond very differently to reading the word "fire" as compared to the word "hire," even though the visual stimuli involved with these two words are nearly identical. How do such highly similar stimuli come to control differential responding? The answer rests with more complex conditioning procedures that provide differential reinforcement in the presence of different stimuli.

STIMULUS DISCRIMINATION TRAINING

Procedures that provide differential reinforcement in the presence of different stimuli are called *stimulus discrimination procedures*. **Stimulus discrimination training** can be conducted in either Pavlovian or instrumental conditioning. Simple cases of Pavlovian and instrumental conditioning involve only one CS or stimulus condition. In contrast, stimulus discrimination training requires two conditioned stimuli or stimulus conditions. One of these is called the S^+ and the other is called the S^-. Any two stimuli that are initially ineffective in generating the conditioned or instrumental response may serve as S^+ and S^-. For example, S^+ and S^- may be the letters "f" and "h," a tone and a buzzer, or a light and a noise.

In a Pavlovian discrimination procedure, each presentation of S^+ is paired with the US. In contrast, the US is omitted on trials when S^- occurs. Thus, S^+ and S^- are associated with different outcomes or differential reinforcement. S^+ and S^- may be two orange cats, for example, one rather friendly and the other aloof. The friendly cat (S^+) is paired with tactile pleasure because it allows people to pet her. The aloof cat (S^-) does not let people pet her and is therefore not paired with the positive, tactile US.

Typical results of a discrimination procedure are illustrated in Figure 10.5. During the initial stages of training, the conditioned response comes to be elicited by the S^+, and this responding generalizes to S^-. The outcome is that the subject responds to some extent to both the S^+ and the S^- early in training. With continued discrimination training, responding to S^+ continues to increase, whereas responding to S^- gradually declines. The final result is that the subject responds much more to S^+ than to S^-. At this point, the subject is making a distinction between the two stimuli. The two stimuli are said to be discriminated.

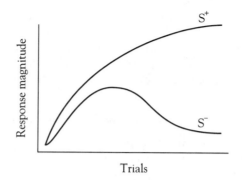

F I G U R E 10.5. Typical results of a Pavlovian discrimination training procedure in which S⁺ is paired with a US and S⁻ is presented equally often alone.
The conditioned responding that develops initially to S⁺ generalizes to S⁻. However, with continued training, a strong discrimination develops between S⁺ and S⁻.

Let's consider again our example of two cats, one friendly and the other aloof. As you start to associate one of the cats with tactile pleasure, any affection that you develop for her may generalize to the other cat. However, as you have further pleasant encounters with one cat but not the other, you will come to react to the two cats differently. Your response to the friendly cat will increase, and your response to the aloof cat will decline.

Discrimination training is conducted in an analogous fashion in instrumental conditioning. In this case, the instrumental response is reinforced on trials when S⁺ is presented (S⁺ → R → S*). In contrast, the response is not reinforced when S⁻ is presented (S⁻ → R → noS*). Thus, S⁺ and S⁻ are again associated with differential reinforcement. As with Pavlovian discrimination procedures, during initial stages of training, responding to S⁺ may generalize to S⁻. However, as discrimination training progresses, the subject comes to respond vigorously to S⁺ and little, if at all, to S⁻, as in Figure 10.5.

In all stimulus discrimination procedures, different stimuli are associated with different outcomes. In the above examples, differential reinforcement was provided by the delivery versus omission of the US, or reinforcer. The presence versus absence of reinforcement represents a common but special case in discrimination training procedures. Any form of differential reinforcement can be used in discrimination training, not just the presence versus absence of reinforcement.

Infants, for example, quickly learn to discriminate mom from dad. This does not occur because mom is a source of reinforcement whereas dad is not. Both mom and dad provide pleasure for the infant, but they are likely to provide different types of pleasure. One parent may provide more tactile comfort and nutritional reinforcement, whereas the other may provide sensory stimulation by tickling the infant or swinging it from side to side. Each type of reinforcer is associated with a different parent, and that leads the infant to discriminate between the parents.

MULTIPLE SCHEDULES OF REINFORCEMENT

Differential reinforcement may be also programmed in terms of different schedules of reinforcement in the presence of different stimuli. For example, a VI schedule may be in effect in the presence of stimulus A, and an FI schedule may be in effect in the presence of stimulus B. Such a procedure is called a **multiple schedule of reinforcement.** As a result of training on a multiple VI-FI schedule of reinforcement, subjects will come to respond to stimulus A in a manner typical of VI performance and will respond to stimulus B in a manner typical of FI performance.

Listening to different instructors in different classes, for example, is reinforced on a multiple schedule. The reinforcer is the new information provided in each class. Some professors say many important things during their classes, thereby reinforcing listening behavior on a dense VI schedule. Other professors predictably make just four or five important points during a lecture and spend about 10 minutes elaborating each point. This reinforces listening behavior on an FI schedule. Each schedule of reinforcement is in effect in the presence of the distinct stimuli of each professor and class. Therefore, across both classes, listening behavior is reinforced on a multiple schedule, and this results in differential listening behavior. Students will listen at a steady rate without predictable pauses in classes where listening is reinforced on a VI schedule and will show postreinforcement lapses in attention in classes where listening is reinforced on an FI schedule.

DIFFERENTIAL REINFORCEMENT AND STIMULUS CONTROL

Differential reinforcement in the presence of different stimuli typically produces differential responding to those stimuli. Therefore, discrimination training typically increases the stimulus control of behavior. Furthermore, these effects may extend far beyond the particular stimuli that served in the discrimination procedure.

The far-reaching effects of discrimination training on stimulus control were first identified by Jenkins and Harrison (1960). They compared the stimulus control of pecking behavior in two groups of pigeons. Group D was first conditioned to discriminate between the presence and absence of a tone. These pigeons were reinforced for pecking a response key in the presence of a tone with a frequency of 1000 Hz (S^+) and were not reinforced when the tone was absent (S^-). Group C, the control group, received similar reinforcement for pecking the response key, but for them the tone was

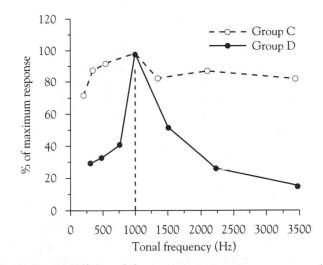

F I G U R E 10.6 Effects of discrimination training on control of the pecking behavior of pigeons by the frequency of different tones.
Prior to the generalization test, Group D received discrimination training in which the S⁺ was a 1000 Hz tone and the S⁻ was the absence of the tone. In contrast, Group C received just reinforcement for keypecking in the presence of the 1000 Hz tone. (After Jenkins & Harrison, 1960.)

---

present at all times during the training sessions. Thus, Group C did not receive discrimination training or differential reinforcement associated with the tone.

Following this contrasting training history, the response of both groups to tones of various frequencies was measured in a test of stimulus generalization. The results of the generalization test are summarized in Figure 10.6. The control group that did not receive discrimination training responded vigorously to the tone that had been present during training (the 1000 Hz tone). They also responded vigorously to most of the other tones, which they encountered for the first time during the generalization test. Thus, in the absence of discrimination training, a fairly flat generalization gradient was obtained.

The results were dramatically different with the pigeons in Group D, which were first trained to discriminate between the presence and absence of the 1000 Hz tone. These subjects showed a steep generalization gradient. They responded a great deal to the 1000 Hz tone (the S⁺), but their responding quickly dropped off when tones of other frequencies were presented. This is a remarkable outcome because the other tones had not been presented during prior discrimination training. None of the other tones had served as the S⁻ in the discrimination procedure. Even though Group

D had not encountered nonreinforcement in the presence of tones during training, tones other than S^+ did not support pecking behavior.

As the results presented in Figure 10.6 illustrate, generalization gradients obtained from subjects that have received discrimination training are much steeper than gradients obtained from subjects that have not. Furthermore, the effects of discrimination training extend beyond the specific stimuli that are used as S^+ and S^- in the discrimination procedure. In the Jenkins and Harrison experiment, discrimination training increased attention to tones of a variety of different frequencies.

INTERDIMENSIONAL VERSUS INTRADIMENSIONAL DISCRIMINATIONS

So far, I have stressed the importance of differential reinforcement in discrimination training procedures. However, the effects of discrimination training on stimulus control are determined not only by differential reinforcement but also by the types of stimuli that serve as S^+ and S^-. An important factor that determines the nature of discrimination learning is the number of ways in which S^+ and S^- differ. If S^+ and S^- differ in several respects, the discrimination is said to be an **interdimensional discrimination.** If S^+ and S^- differ in only one respect, the discrimination is said to be an **intradimensional discrimination.**

Interdimensional discriminations. Perhaps the most common forms of interdimensional discrimination training are simple Pavlovian or discrete-trial instrumental conditioning procedures, although we don't usually think of these as involving discrimination training. A simple Pavlovian procedure involves just one CS and one US. Presentations of the CS end in delivery of the US. In contrast, the US is not delivered when the CS is absent. Thus, the discrimination is between times when the CS is present and times when the CS is absent (the intertrial interval). All of the features of the CS (its modality, intensity, and location) serve to distinguish times when the CS is present from times when the CS is absent. Therefore, this is an example of an interdimensional discrimination.

In simple discrete-trial instrumental conditioning, the subject is reinforced for responding in the presence of particular stimuli (when the subject is placed in the start box of a runway, for example) and is not reinforced in the absence of those cues (when it is removed from the runway). Thus, simple discrete-trial instrumental conditioning similarly involves a discrimination between trial stimuli and stimuli that are present during the intertrial interval. Because numerous stimulus features distinguish the trial stimuli from the intertrial interval, this is also an interdimensional discrimination.

Interdimensional discriminations can also be set up between discrete stimuli serving as S^+ and S^-. The discrimination between a red and a green traffic light, for example, is an interdimensional discrimination because red and green traffic lights differ in both color and position. The discrimination learned by an infant between mom and dad is also an interdimensional discrimination. Mom and dad differ in many respects, including visual features, ways of holding the infant, sounds of their voices, time of day they interact with the infant, and so on.

Intradimensional discriminations. Interdimensional discriminations are effective in establishing stimulus control. However, they do not establish a high degree of control over behavior by any particular stimulus feature. For example, since many things distinguish mom from dad, the infant may not respond a great deal to any one distinguishing feature. The most effective procedure for increasing the stimulus control of behavior is through intradimensional discrimination training (Jenkins & Harrison, 1960, 1962), in which the stimuli associated with differential reinforcement differ in only one respect.

Many forms of expert performance involve intradimensional discriminations. Reading, for example, requires discriminating between letters that differ in only one respect. The letters "E" and "F" differ only in the horizontal bottom stem, which is present in "E" but not in "F." The physical difference is very small, but the differential consequences in terms of meaning can be substantial. The letters "B" and "P," and "M" and "N" are other pairs that are similar physically but differ greatly in significance. Learning to read involves learning to respond differentially to such similar letters. Reading requires learning many intradimensional discriminations.

One of the interesting things about learning fine intradimensional discriminations is that the subject is not likely to be aware of the physical difference between the stimuli at the outset of training. Initially, the letters "E" and "F" may appear to be the same to a child. The child may recognize "E" and "F" as being different from "O" but may not be able to tell the difference between "E" and "F." The child may come to recognize the visual difference between the two letters only after being taught to say one thing when shown "E" and something else when shown "F." Differential reinforcement serves to focus attention on physical differences that are otherwise ignored.

Similar effects occur in the acquisition of other forms of expertise. Children learning to sing may not be able to tell at first when they are singing on key or off key. However, this skill develops through differential reinforcement from a teacher. Likewise, ballet students learn to pay close attention to proprioceptive cues indicating the precise position of their arms and legs, and pool players learn to make precise judgments about angles and trajectories. Intradimensional discrimination training brings behavior under precise control of small variations in a stimulus and thereby serves to increase sensitivity to those small stimulus variations. Thus, sensitivity to variations in environmental stimuli depends not only on sensory capacity but also on a person's history of discrimination training.

Suggested Readings

BALSAM, P. D. (1988). Selection, representation, and equivalence of controlling stimuli. In R. C. Atkinson, R. J. Herrnstein, G. Lindzey, & R. D. Luce (Eds.), *Stevens' handbook of experimental psychology* (Vol. 2, pp. 111–166). New York: Wiley.

MACKINTOSH, N. J. (1977). Stimulus control: Attentional factors. In W. K. Honig & J.E.R. Staddon (Eds.), *Handbook of operant behavior* (pp. 481–513). Englewood Cliffs, NJ: Prentice-Hall.

RILLING, M. (1977). Stimulus control and inhibitory processes. In W. K. Honig and J.E.R. Staddon (Eds.), *Handbook of operant behavior* (pp. 432–480). Englewood Cliffs, NJ: Prentice-Hall.

Technical Terms

Differential responding	S^-
Interdimensional discrimination	Stimulus dimension
Intradimensional discrimination	Stimulus discrimination
Multiple schedule of reinforcement	Stimulus discrimination training
Overshadowing	Stimulus generalization
S^+	Stimulus generalization gradient

CHAPTER ELEVEN

Avoidance Learning

DID YOU KNOW THAT:

- Avoidance is a form of instrumental conditioning in which the instrumental response prevents the delivery of an aversive stimulus.
- No major theory of avoidance learning assumes that avoidance behavior is reinforced by the absence of the avoided aversive stimulus.
- Although avoidance is a form of instrumental behavior, theories of avoidance learning rely heavily on concepts from Pavlovian conditioning.
- In many situations, avoidance learning is assumed to involve learning about internal temporal cues and proprioceptive or feedback cues.
- Avoidance behavior is strongly determined by the preexisting defensive behavior of the subject.

We do a lot of things that prevent bad things from happening. Putting out your hand when approaching a door prevents the discomfort of walking into a closed door; grabbing a handrail prevents the discomfort of slipping on a flight of stairs; slowing down while driving prevents a collision with the car in front of you; putting on a coat prevents you from catching a chill. All of these are avoidance responses. Avoidance conditioning is a form of instrumental conditioning in which the instrumental response prevents the occurrence of an unpleasant event or **aversive stimulus.**

As do other instrumental conditioning procedures, avoidance procedures involve a contingency between an instrumental response and a motivating or reinforcing stimulus. In the instances of instrumental conditioning that I described in Chapters 6–8, the reinforcing stimulus was an appetitive or pleasant event (delivery of food to a hungry organism, for example), and there was a positive contingency between the instrumental response and the reinforcer. If the subject performed the instrumental response, the reinforcing stimulus was presented.

Avoidance conditioning differs from instances of positive reinforcement in two ways. The motivating stimulus is an unpleasant or aversive event, and the contingency between the instrumental response and the motivating stimulus is negative. With a negative contingency, if the subject performs the instrumental response, the aversive event is not delivered. Thus by responding, the subject prevents the delivery of the aversive reinforcer.

Since I have already discussed instrumental conditioning procedures, and since people are highly familiar with avoidance learning from personal experience, you might suppose that analysis of avoidance conditioning would be fairly straightforward, if not self-evident. Unfortunately, that is not the case. In fact, avoidance learning has been one of the most difficult forms of learning to analyze and explain.

Dominant Questions in the Analysis of Avoidance Learning

Theoretical considerations of avoidance learning have been dominated by two questions. The first question is, *How can the absence of something reinforce instrumental behavior?*

Avoidance procedures are clear enough: the subject performs an instrumental response that prevents the delivery of an aversive stimulus. However, it is not clear what in such a procedure reinforces the instrumental response. A successful avoidance response prevents the delivery of an aversive stimulus. Therefore, a successful avoidance response is followed by nothing. But, how can "nothing" reinforce behavior? As Mowrer and Lamoreaux (1942) pointed out more than 50 years ago, the fact that successful avoidance responses result in "nothing" presents a major theoretical challenge for analyses of avoidance learning.

Various hypotheses and theories have been offered to explain how "nothing" can reinforce avoidance responding. The hypotheses and theories differ in many ways. However, all of the major explanations reject the common sense idea that avoidance responses occur because they prevent the delivery of the aversive event. As we will see, a number of ingenious proposals have been offered in an effort to explain avoidance learning without relying on the theoretically vacuous idea that "nothing" serves as a reinforcer.

The second major question in the analysis of avoidance behavior is, *How are Pavlovian conditioning processes involved in avoidance learning?* As we have seen, Pavlovian conditioning processes have also been discussed in analyses of positively reinforced instrumental behavior. However, Pavlovian conditioning concepts have not dominated thinking about positively reinforced instrumental behavior as they have dominated analyses of avoidance learning. Historically, avoidance learning was regarded as a special case of Pavlovian conditioning. In fact, to this day some accounts of avoidance learning regard avoidance behavior as entirely the product of Pavlovian conditioning mechanisms.

Origins of the Study of Avoidance Learning

Avoidance learning was first investigated by the Russian scientist Bechterev (1913), who set out to study Pavlovian conditioning in human subjects. For obvious reasons, he did not want to study conditioning in people the way Pavlov and his students studied conditioning in dogs. Bechterev looked for some way to study Pavlovian conditioning without implanting salivary fistulae to measure conditioned and unconditioned responding. The procedure he devised was fairly simple.

Bechterev asked human subjects to place a finger on a metal plate resting on a table. Mild current could be passed through the metal plate, and this caused the subject to lift the finger. Thus, the unconditioned response was finger withdrawal. To turn the situation into one involving classical conditioning, Bechterev presented a brief warning stimulus immediately before the shock on each trial. As you might suspect, the subjects quickly learned to lift their fingers when the CS was presented, and this was considered the conditioned response.

Although Bechterev considered his finger-withdrawal technique to be a convenient way to study Pavlovian conditioning, more careful consideration of his procedure revealed that in fact it was an instrumental rather than a Pavlovian conditioning procedure. Recall that the metal plate rested on the surface of a table; it was not attached to the subject's finger. Therefore, by lifting the finger in response to the CS, the subject could entirely avoid getting shocked. This differs from standard Pavlovian conditioning procedures in which the occurrence of the conditioned response does not alter the delivery of the US. Bechterev had inadvertently given the subject control

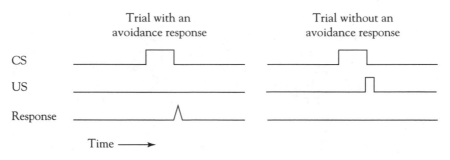

F I G U R E 11.1 **Diagram of discriminated, or signaled, avoidance procedure.**
If the subject responds during the warning signal or CS, the CS is turned off and the aversive US is not delivered. In contrast, if the subject fails to respond during the warning signal or CS, the CS continues to be presented for its full duration and ends in the presentation of the aversive US.

over presentation of the US. This made the finger-withdrawal technique an instrumental rather than a Pavlovian conditioning procedure.

Contemporary Avoidance Conditioning Procedures

Two types of avoidance conditioning procedures are commonly used in contemporary research—the discriminated avoidance procedure and the nondiscriminated, or free-operant avoidance procedure.

DISCRIMINATED AVOIDANCE

Without knowing it, Bechterev invented what has come to be known as the **discriminated avoidance** procedure. Discriminated avoidance is a discrete trial procedure. The response-reinforcer contingency is not always in effect. Rather, responding prevents delivery of the reinforcer only during discrete periods or trials when a CS is presented. As illustrated in Figure 11.1, what happens during these trials depends on the subject's behavior. If the subject responds, the CS is turned off and the aversive US is not delivered. In contrast, if the subject fails to respond during the conditioned stimulus, the CS continues to be presented for its full duration and ends in the presentation of the aversive US. Thus, a discriminated avoidance procedure involves two types of trials—response trials and no-response trials—and the aversive US only occurs on no-response trials. Because the aversive stimulus occurs at the end of the CS if the subject does not respond, the CS is also called the **warning stimulus** or **warning signal.**

The discriminated avoidance procedure has been adapted in various

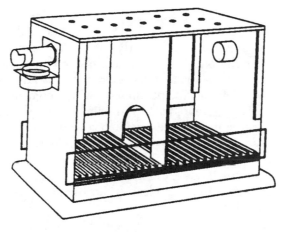

F I G U R E 11.2 Shuttle box used in studies of avoidance learning.
The subject has to cross from one compartment to the other to avoid mild
shock through the grid floor. (Domjan & Burkhard, 1993.)

ways for use with nonhuman subjects as well. In fact, most of the research
on the theoretical mechanisms of avoidance learning has been done with
laboratory animals, primarily laboratory rats. Typically, the aversive US has
been mild electric shock because stimulus intensity and duration can be
controlled more easily with shock than with other aversive stimuli. In
addition, shock is unlike any other aversive stimulus subjects are likely to
have encountered before.

In some experiments, the subjects have to press a response lever during
the CS to avoid receiving the shock. In other experiments, they have
to run from one side to the other of a **shuttle box.** Figure 11.2 illustrates
a typical shuttle box. It consists of two compartments set side-by-side.
The subject is allowed to move from one compartment to the other
through an open doorway. Mild shock is administered through a grid floor.
Each trial starts with presentation of a CS, a light or a tone, on one
side of the apparatus. If the subject moves to the other side before the
end of the CS, the shock does not occur. If the shuttle avoidance response
is not made, the mild shock is turned on and remains on until the subject
escapes to the other side.

The shuttle box can be used to implement either a one-way or a two-way
avoidance procedure. In a **one-way avoidance** procedure, the subject is
always placed in the same compartment at the start of each trial (the left side,
for example). Because each trial starts on the same side (left), the avoidance
response always is in the same direction (left to right).

Notice that in a one-way avoidance procedure, the side the subject starts
on is always potentially dangerous because if the subject doesn't run to the

other side it gets shocked. In contrast, the other side is always safe. The subject never gets shocked on the other side. Thus, a one-way avoidance procedure has a consistently safe side and a consistently dangerous side. This makes the one-way avoidance task rather easy to learn.

In a **two-way avoidance** procedure, trials can start either on the left side or the right side, depending on which compartment the subject happens to occupy. The avoidance response is always going to the other side. If the subject starts on the left, it has to go to the right to avoid shock. If the subjects starts on the right, it has to go to the left side to avoid shock. Because trials can start on either side, both sides of the shuttle box are potentially dangerous. The lack of a consistently safe side makes the two-way avoidance task more difficult to learn than the one-way procedure (Theios, Lynch, & Lowe, 1966).

NONDISCRIMINATED OR FREE-OPERANT AVOIDANCE

In discriminated avoidance procedures, responding is effective in preventing the aversive stimulus only if the response occurs during the trial period when the CS is presented. Responses made during the intertrial interval have no effect. In fact, in many studies the subjects are removed from the apparatus during the intertrial interval. In contrast to such traditional discrete trial procedures, in 1953 Sidman devised a **nondiscriminated** or **free-operant avoidance** procedure (Sidman, 1953).

Sidman's free-operant procedure was developed in the Skinnerian or operant tradition. In this tradition, trials are not restricted to periods when a discrete stimulus (CS) is present, and the subject is free to repeat the instrumental response at any time. On an FR schedule in a Skinner box, for example, the subject can respond at any time and earn credit toward completion of the ratio requirement. Sidman extended these features of operant methodology to the study of avoidance behavior.

In the free-operant avoidance procedure, an explicit CS is not used, and there are no discrete trials. The subject has the opportunity to repeat the avoidance response at any time, and responding always provides some measure of benefit. A brief shock is scheduled to occur periodically throughout the training session. For example, a half-second shock may be scheduled every 15 seconds if the subject does not respond. This specifies the shock-shock or **S-S interval.** By making an avoidance response, the subject can establish a duration of safety, during which no shocks are given. The safe period may be 30 seconds. This is the response-shock or **R-S interval** (see Figure 11.3).

An important aspect of free-operant avoidance procedures is that the R-S interval is reset and starts over again each time the subject responds. Thus, if the R-S interval is 30 seconds, each response resets the R-S interval and starts the 30-second period of safety all over again. Because of this

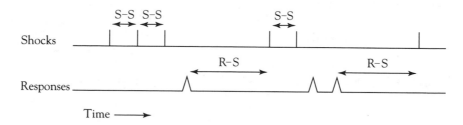

FIGURE 11.3   Diagram of a nondiscriminated, or free-operant, avoidance procedure.

As long as the subject fails to respond, a brief shock is scheduled to occur periodically, as set by S-S interval. Each occurrence of the avoidance response creates a period without shock, as set by the R-S interval. (Domjan & Burkhard, 1993.)

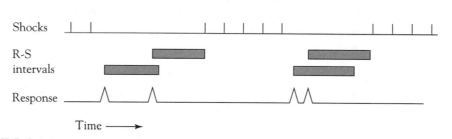

FIGURE 11.4   Effects of repeating the avoidance response early or late in an R-S interval in a free-operant avoidance procedure.

The R-S intervals are indicated by the shaded horizontal bars. On the left, the response was repeated late in an R-S interval; on the right, the response was repeated early in an R-S interval. Notice that the total time without shocks is longer if the response is repeated late in an R-S interval.

feature, each occurrence of the avoidance response provides some benefit. However, the degree of benefit depends on exactly when the response occurs.

If the subject responds when the R-S interval is already in effect, the R-S interval will start over again and time left on the R-S clock will be lost. The net benefit of responding will depend on whether the response occurs early or late in the R-S interval (see Figure 11.4). If the subject responds late in the R-S interval, it will lose little time remaining on the R-S clock, and the net benefit of responding will be substantial. In contrast, if the subject responds early in the R-S interval, it will lose a lot of time remaining on the R-S clock, and the net benefit of responding will be much smaller. In either case, however, if the subject always responds before the end of the R-S interval, it will reset the R-S interval over and over again and thereby successfully avoid all shocks.

Theoretical Approaches to Avoidance Learning

Because the study of avoidance learning emerged from studies of Pavlovian conditioning, Pavlovian concepts have always been very important in the analysis of avoidance learning. In fact, avoidance learning was considered initially to be entirely due to Pavlovian conditioning. As I noted earlier, Bechterev considered his finger-withdrawal task to be a Pavlovian conditioning procedure. In keeping with that interpretation, he considered the avoidance response to be a classically conditioned response to the CS, much like salivation conditioned to a visual cue paired with food. According to such an interpretation, the fact that the avoidance response prevents the delivery of the aversive US is entirely irrelevant to the acquisition of avoidance behavior.

TEST OF THE ROLE OF THE INSTRUMENTAL CONTINGENCY

The idea that the instrumental contingency is entirely irrelevant to avoidance learning is counterintuitive and has been found to be wrong. A powerful test of the idea was conducted by Brogden, Lipman, and Culler (1938), who studied the avoidance conditioning of guinea pigs in a running wheel apparatus. Each trial started with a tone CS or warning signal. One group of subjects received a strictly Pavlovian conditioning procedure. For them, the warning signal always ended in a brief shock through the grid floor of the running wheel. A second group of subjects (the instrumental group) received a conventional discriminated avoidance procedure. If they rotated the wheel during the warning signal, the CS was turned off and the shock scheduled on that trial was omitted.

Notice that from the perspective of Pavlovian conditioning, the instrumental group received a rather poor conditioning procedure. For the instrumental group, pairings of the warning signal with shock occurred only on trials when the subjects did not respond. In contrast, for the Pavlovian group the warning signal ended in shock on every trial. Therefore, if Pavlovian conditioning were entirely responsible for avoidance learning, the Pavlovian group should show higher rates of responding than the instrumental group.

The results turned out just the opposite. Instead of responding at a higher rate, the Pavlovian group responded significantly less often than the instrumental group. Within eight sessions, subjects given the instrumental procedure were responding on 100% of the trials. In contrast, subjects in the Pavlovian group responded on just 20–30% of the trials even after extensive training (see Figure 11.5).

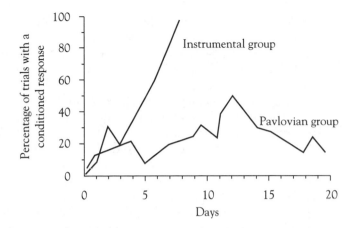

F I G U R E 11.5   Results of the experiment by Brogden, Lipman, and Culler (1938).
The Pavlovian group received a pure Pavlovian conditioning procedure. The Instrumental group received a discriminated avoidance procedure. (Brogden, Lipman, & Culler, 1938).

The results of the study by Brogden, Lipman, & Culler (1938) indicated clearly that the instrumental contingency makes a significant contribution to avoidance learning, but the two dominant questions about avoidance learning remained unresolved. The experiment left no doubt that response consequences are important, but the reinforcer for avoidance responding remained unidentified. Successful avoidance responses were followed by nothing, and the experiment provided no hints about how "nothing" could serve as an effective reinforcer. The experiment also did not clarify what the role of Pavlovian conditioning might be in avoidance learning. Was Pavlovian conditioning entirely irrelevant to avoidance learning? If Pavlovian conditioning was not irrelevant, how was it involved?

TWO-FACTOR THEORY OF AVOIDANCE

The questions left unresolved by the Brogden, Lipman, & Culler (1938) experiment were answered by a two-factor theory of avoidance behavior proposed about ten years later (Mowrer, 1947; see also Miller, 1951). According to this theory, avoidance learning involves both Pavlovian and instrumental conditioning processes (hence the name "two-factor" theory). However, Mowrer did not describe either of these processes in ways that are intuitively obvious.

Let us consider first the Pavlovian conditioning process in two-factor theory. Instead of thinking about the Pavlovian process as resulting directly in the conditioning of avoidance behavior (the way Bechterev thought about it), Mowrer proposed that the Pavlovian process results in the conditioning of a hypothetical emotional state called "fear." On trials when the subject fails to make the avoidance response, the CS or warning stimulus is paired with the aversive US, and this is assumed to result in the conditioning of fear to the warning stimulus.

Conditioned fear presumably is an unpleasant or aversive state. Therefore, the reduction or elimination of fear is assumed to be reinforcing. Fear reduction brings into play the second process in two-factor theory. On trials when the subjects make the avoidance response, the response turns off the warning stimulus and prevents the delivery of the US. Turning off the warning stimulus is assumed to result in the reduction of conditioned fear, and this fear reduction is assumed to provide instrumental reinforcement for the avoidance response. Thus, the second factor in the two-factor theory of avoidance is instrumental conditioning of the avoidance response through fear reduction.

Notice that according to two-factor theory, avoidance behavior is not reinforced by "nothing" occurring after the avoidance response. Rather, avoidance behavior is reinforced by fear reduction. Fear reduction is a form of **negative reinforcement** (removal of an aversive stimulus contingent on behavior). In two-factor theory, the instrumental response is considered to be an escape response—a response that escapes fear. Instead of focusing on the fact that avoidance behavior prevents delivery of the aversive US, two-factor theory treats avoidance behavior as a special type of escape behavior.

Interactions between the Pavlovian and instrumental factors. Two-factor theory provides answers to many questions about avoidance learning. The answers were innovative when they were first proposed and have shaped the course of research on avoidance conditioning ever since. According to the theory, both Pavlovian and instrumental processes contribute to avoidance learning. Furthermore, the two processes are interdependent in various ways.

Before fear reduction can provide instrumental reinforcement for the avoidance response, fear first has to become conditioned to the warning stimulus. Thus, the Pavlovian conditioning of fear is a prerequisite for the instrumental component of two-factor theory. The instrumental process depends on the integrity of the Pavlovian process.

The Pavlovian process is in turn influenced by the instrumental contingency, but in this case the influence is disruptive. Each time the subject makes an avoidance response, the aversive US is omitted and the warning stimulus ends up being presented without the US. According to the principles of Pavlovian conditioning, presentation of the warning stimulus without the US should result in extinction of the fear that had been conditioned to the warning stimulus. Thus, frequent avoidance responding should result in Pavlovian extinction of conditioned fear.

Extinction of fear in turn undermines the effectiveness of fear reduction as a source of instrumental reinforcement. If the instrumental avoidance response is no longer followed by fear reduction, the response will undergo extinction. As the avoidance response becomes extinguished, the warning stimulus will again end in presentation of the aversive US. This in turn should reactivate the conditioning of fear to the warning signal. Once fear has become reconditioned to the warning stimulus, fear reduction can again serve as an effective reinforcer for instrumental responding. Thus, according to two-process theory, avoidance behavior is determined by a continually changing or dynamic interaction of Pavlovian and instrumental processes.

Challenges to two-factor theory. Many predictions of two-factor theory have been substantiated. Despite these successes, however, the theory has been challenged by certain striking results. One set of findings that has been challenging (but not impossible) for two-factor theory is free-operant avoidance behavior. As I noted earlier, in a free-operant avoidance procedure, shocks occur periodically without an explicit warning stimulus, and each occurrence of the avoidance response initiates a period of safety (the R-S interval). Since the mechanisms of two-factor theory seem to require a warning stimulus, it is not obvious how two-factor theory might explain free-operant avoidance behavior.

Another challenging phenomenon for two-factor theory is the common observation that once well learned, avoidance responding often persists at high levels for long periods of time, even though shocks are no longer delivered. As I noted earlier, a long string of avoidance responses should result in Pavlovian extinction of fear, which in turn should result in extinction of the instrumental avoidance response. This does not seem to happen (Solomon, Kamin, & Wynne, 1953).

A third major finding that has been challenging for two-process theory is that after subjects become proficient in avoiding the aversive US, they do not seem to be very fearful. In fact, levels of conditioned fear often decline with increased proficiency in avoidance responding (Mineka & Gino, 1980). Common experience also suggests that not much fear exists once an avoidance response becomes well learned. Steering a car so that it does not drift off the road is basically avoidance behavior; a competent driver avoids having the car get too close to the side of the road or to another lane of traffic. Yet, proficient drivers show no fear under normal traffic conditions.

CONDITIONED TEMPORAL CUES

Findings that are difficult to explain in terms of the two-factor theory of avoidance have encouraged modifications of, and additions to, the theory. Efforts to integrate new findings with two-factor theory have often involved postulating internal stimuli and ascribing important functions to those internal cues. For example, one approach to explaining nondiscriminated or free-operant avoidance behavior in terms of two-factor theory involves assuming that internal cues related to the passage of time (**temporal cues**) acquire conditioned aversive properties (Anger, 1963).

Recall that in a nondiscriminated avoidance procedure, explicit warning stimuli are not provided before each shock the subject receives. However, shocks occur at predictable times. Free-operant avoidance procedures are constructed from two types of intervals (S-S intervals and R-S intervals), both of which are of fixed duration. Therefore, a subject can use the passage of time to predict when the next shock will occur. With both S-S and R-S intervals, shock occurs when the intervals have been completed.

Free-operant avoidance learning can be explained in terms of two-factor theory by assuming the existence of internal temporal cues. Temporal cues characteristic of the end of the S-S and R-S intervals are presumably different from temporal cues characteristic of the beginning of these intervals. At first, subjects probably do not distinguish between the beginning and the end of the S-S and R-S intervals. However, these points in time have different consequences; they are differentially reinforced. Temporal cues that characterize the beginning of the S-S and R-S intervals are never paired with shock. If shock occurs, it always occurs at the end of these intervals. Because of this differential reinforcement, subjects can learn to distinguish the early-time stimuli from the temporal cues they experience near the end of S-S and R-S intervals, just as you can tell whether you just started waiting for a bus or have been waiting for a long time.

Temporal cues characteristic of the end of an S-S or R-S interval are paired with shock and can acquire conditioned aversive properties. An avoidance response starts a new R-S interval and thereby reduces the conditioned aversiveness of temporal cues characteristic of the end of the S-S and R-S intervals (see Figure 11.6). In this way, an avoidance response can result in reduction of conditioned fear and satisfy the tenets of two-factor theory.

SAFETY SIGNALS IN AVOIDANCE LEARNING

The next explanation of avoidance learning that we will consider—the **safety signal** hypothesis—also originated from a consideration of internal cues that subjects may experience during the course of avoidance conditioning. However, instead of focusing on cues that might predict danger, the safety signal hypothesis focuses on signals for the absence of shock or signals for safety (Dinsmoor, 1977).

In an avoidance procedure, periods of safety are best predicted by the occurrence of the avoidance response. After all, avoidance behavior is defined as responding that cancels the delivery of an aversive simulus. We know from biology that the movements of muscles and joints that are involved in making responses can give rise to internal **proprioceptive cues.** Such cues are also called response feedback cues or just **feedback cues.** The feedback cues that are produced by an avoidance response are followed by

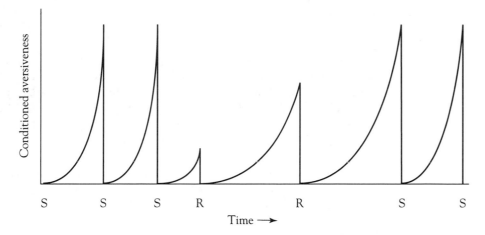

FIGURE 11.6 The presumed conditioned aversiveness of temporal cues during R-S and S-S intervals in a free-operant avoidance procedure. "R" represents occurrence of the avoidance response; "S" represents occurrence of a brief shock. Notice the low levels of conditioned aversiveness at the beginning of each S-S and R-S interval and high levels of aversiveness at the end of these intervals. The occurrence of a response always reduces the aversiveness of temporal cues because each response starts a new R-S interval.

a predictable period without the aversive US or a predictable period of safety. As we saw in Chapter 5, stimuli that reliably predict the absence of a US can acquire Pavlovian conditioned inhibitory properties. Therefore, feedback cues generated by avoidance responses may also acquire Pavlovian conditioned inhibitory properties.

The safety signal explanation of avoidance learning is based on the above ideas. According to the safety signal hypothesis, feedback cues from the avoidance response acquire Pavlovian conditioned inhibitory properties and thereby become signals for safety. In a situation involving potential danger, safety signals are assumed to be reinforcing. According to the safety signal hypothesis, avoidance behavior is positively reinforced by conditioned inhibitory safety signals.

Although the safety signal hypothesis is similar to the temporal cue hypothesis in relying on stimuli internal to the organism, it has been more accessible to experimental verification. The safety signal hypothesis has been evaluated by introducing an external stimulus (a brief tone, for example) at the time the interoceptive feedback cue is presumed to occur. That is, a brief tone is presented when the subject performs the avoidance response. If the safety signal hypothesis is correct, such an exteroceptive cue should acquire conditioned inhibitory properties. In addition, these conditioned inhibitory properties should make the feedback stimuli effective as a positive reinforcer for instrumental behavior. Both of these predictions have been confirmed (for example, Morris, 1974, 1975; Weisman & Litner, 1972).

Another, less obvious, prediction is that avoidance learning should be facilitated by increasing the salience of safety signal feedback cues. Consistent with that prediction, the introduction of an external response feedback stimulus (which is presumably more salient than internal proprioceptive cues) substantially facilitates avoidance conditioning (for example, D'Amato, Fazzaro, & Etkin, 1968).

The safety signal hypothesis is not incompatible with two-factor theory and need not be viewed as an alternative to that theory. Rather, positive reinforcement through a conditioned inhibitory safety signal is a third factor that can contribute to avoidance learning.

AVOIDANCE LEARNING AND UNCONDITIONED DEFENSIVE BEHAVIOR

As I noted in Chapter 2, learning procedures are superimposed on an organism's preexisting behavioral tendencies, and learned responses are the product of the interaction between conditioning procedures and that preexisting behavioral structure. Two-factor theory and safety signal mechanisms are based on a simple view of the organism's preexisting behavior structure. For these learning mechanisms to operate, all we have to presume is that organisms find some stimuli aversive. Given an aversive stimulus, fear can become conditioned to stimuli that predict the aversive event, safety can become conditioned to stimuli that predict the absence of the aversive event, and fear reduction and safety can serve as reinforcers for any instrumental behavior.

Starting about 25 years ago, it became evident that the preexisting behavioral tendencies organisms bring into an avoidance conditioning situation are a lot more complex than is presumed by two-factor theory and the safety signal hypothesis. Organisms come into an avoidance conditioning situation not only with certain stimuli they find aversive but also with a rich behavioral repertoire for dealing with aversive situations. The existence of this unconditioned behavioral repertoire was first emphasized by Bolles (1970).

Bolles suggested that organisms could not survive with just the ability to detect aversive stimuli and the ability to learn about them through the Pavlovian and instrumental conditioning mechanisms presumed by traditional theories. The mechanisms of two-factor theory and safety signal learning require extensive training to generate avoidance responses. An animal first has to learn about signals for danger and signals for safety. It then has to learn what instrumental responses are required to turn off the danger signals and produce the safety signals.

Bolles pointed out that in their natural habitat, animals may not have the time to learn about danger and safety signals. An animal being pursued by a predator has to effectively avoid the danger the first time or it may not be alive to face that predator for a second or third conditioning trial. Because dangerous situations require effective coping mechanisms without much opportunity for learning, Bolles suggested that organisms respond to aversive situations with a hierarchy of unconditioned defensive responses. Bolles called these **species-specific defense responses** (SSDRs).

The SSDR theory of avoidance. Because SSDRs are unconditioned responses to aversive stimuli, they are assumed to predominate during the initial stages of avoidance training. SSDRs include freezing, fleeing, and fighting. Bolles suggested that which particular SSDR occurs depends on the nature of the aversive stimulus and the response opportunities provided by the environment. If a familiar and effective means of escape is available, the subject is most likely to try to flee when it encounters the aversive stimulus. Without a familiar escape route, freezing will be the predominant defensive response, and in a social situation fighting will predominate.

In addition to describing what subjects are likely to do initially in an aversive situation, the SSDR theory also specifies how an avoidance conditioning procedure can shape the future actions of the organism. In contrast to the negative and positive reinforcement mechanisms of two-factor theory and the safety signal hypothesis, the response shaping or response selection mechanism of SSDR theory is punishment.

If the SSDR the subject performs during the first few trials of an avoidance conditioning procedure is not effective in preventing the aversive US, the aversive stimulus will occur and the SSDR will end up being punished. Suppression by punishment of the first SSDR the subject makes will result in a switch to the next most likely SSDR in that situation. If that response also turns out to be ineffective in preventing delivery of the aversive US, it will also be punished and suppressed. That in turn will result in the subject switching to the third SSDR in its response hierarchy.

According to SSDR theory, as each ineffective SSDR becomes suppressed by punishment, the subject will eventually end up performing the required avoidance response. The required avoidance response will not come to predominate in the situation because it is reinforced by shock avoidance, fear reduction, or safety signals. Rather, the required avoidance response will emerge because it is the only response that is not followed by the aversive US and is therefore the only response not suppressed by punishment.

SSDR theory advanced our knowledge of avoidance learning a great deal because it emphasized that avoidance learning is influenced by the preexisting defensive behavior of the organism. However, details of SSDR theory have not stood up well in light of subsequent empirical scrutiny. Punishment has not been found to be effective in suppressing SSDRs (for example, Bolles & Riley, 1973). In addition, SSDRs appear to be organized by the imminence of injury rather than by response opportunities provided by the environment.

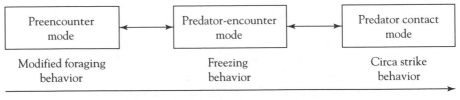

Increased levels of predatory imminence
(Perceived likelihood of injury)

FIGURE 11.7   The predatory imminence continuum.
Different modes of defensive behavior are activated at different levels of predatory imminence. The preencounter mode represents the defensive behavior of
an animal before it encounters a predator. The predator-encounter mode represents defensive behavior after the animal has encountered a predator, and the
predator contact mode represents its behavior after the predator has made
physical contact.

The predatory imminence continuum. Animals seem to do one thing
when they perceive a low likelihood of injury and other things when they
perceive the likelihood of injury to be higher. The different defensive
responses that are elicited by different degrees of perceived danger constitute
what is called the **predatory imminence** continuum (Fanselow & Lester,
1988).

The predatory imminence continuum has been investigated most
extensively in laboratory rats (Fanselow, 1989, 1994). Rats are subject to
predation by, among other things, snakes. Different modes of defensive
behavior are activated, depending on the rat's perceived likelihood of injury.
The preencounter mode is activated if, during the course of its foraging, a
rat wanders into an area where there is some chance of finding a snake, but
the snake has not been encountered yet. In the preencounter mode, the rat
may move to a safer area. If a safer area is not available, the rat will become
more cautious in its foraging. It will go out of its burrow less often and eat
larger meals (Fanselow, Lester, & Helmstetter, 1988).

If the preencounter defensive responses are not successful and the rat
encounters the snake, the predator-encounter mode will be activated. In the
predator-encounter mode, freezing is the predominant response. Finally, if
this defensive behavior is also unsuccessful and the rat is struck by the snake,
the predator contact mode will be activated. In the predator contact mode,
the rat will suddenly leap into the air, performing what is called a *circa strike
response* (see Figure 11.7).

Preexisting behavioral tendencies are likely to predominate during early
avoidance conditioning trials, before much learning has taken place. With
continued training, the Pavlovian and instrumental mechanisms presumed
by two-factor theory and the safety signal hypothesis will become activated.

However, the predatory imminence continuum is likely to be also reflected in the behavioral manifestations of the learning processes that are activated by an avoidance procedure.

As I noted in Chapter 4, conditioning involves incorporating new stimuli into a preexisting behavior system. In an avoidance conditioning situation, the aversive US involves the highest level of predatory imminence and activates the predator contact mode. The warning stimulus that occurs before the aversive US is highly predictive of the US and activates the predator-encounter mode. Finally, a conditioned safety signal involves the total absence of predatory imminence. We may expect responses such as freezing that are characteristic of the predator-encounter mode to develop to conditioned stimuli that become associated with an unconditioned aversive event. In contrast, safety signals should elicit recuperative and relaxation responses. These considerations illustrate that even when subjects learn about an aversive situation, their behavior is heavily influenced by the preexisting organization of their defensive behavior system.

Suggested Readings

BOLLES, R.C. (1972). The avoidance learning problem. In G.H. Bower (Ed.), *The psychology of learning and motivation* (Vol. 6). Orlando, FL: Academic Press.

FANSELOW, M.S., & LESTER, L.S. (1988). A functional behavioristic approach to aversively motivated behavior: Predatory imminence as a determinant of the topography of defensive behavior. In R.C. Bolles & M.D. Beecher (Eds.), *Evolution and learning* (pp. 185–212). Hillsdale, NJ: Erlbaum.

HERRNSTEIN, R.J. (1969). Method and theory in the study of avoidance. *Psychological Review, 87,* 49–69.

McALLISTER, D.E., & McALLISTER, W.R. (1991). Fear theory and aversively motivated behavior: Some controversial issues. In M.R. Denny (Ed.), *Fear, avoidance, and phobias* (pp. 135–163). Hillsdale, NJ: Erlbaum.

Technical Terms

Aversive stimulus
Discriminated avoidance
Feedback cue
Free-operant avoidance
Negative reinforcement
Nondiscriminated avoidance
One-way avoidance
Predatory imminence
Proprioceptive cues

R-S interval
S-S interval
Safety signal
Shuttle box
Species-specific defense response (SSDR)
Temporal cues
Two-way avoidance
Warning stimulus or warning signal

CHAPTER TWELVE

Punishment

DID YOU KNOW THAT:

- Punishment does not have to involve physical pain.
- When properly applied, punishment can produce permanent suppression of behavior in a single trial.
- Intermittency and delay reduce the effectiveness of punishment.
- Warnings and mild punishment for initial offenses habituate individuals to further punishment.
- Severe punishment for initial offenses sensitizes individuals to further punishment.
- The effectiveness of punishment is greatly increased by positive reinforcement of alternative behavior.
- Punishment facilitates responding if it signals positive reinforcement or if the punished response is a form of escape behavior.

In a punishment procedure, an aversive stimulus is delivered contingent on performance of an instrumental response. Thus, like avoidance, **punishment** involves a relation between an instrumental response and aversive stimulation. However, in punishment, responding produces the aversive stimulus rather than prevents it. Punishment involves a positive rather than a negative contingency between an instrumental response and an aversive stimulus.

Punishment is the most controversial aspect of conditioning and learning. It readily conjures up visions of cruelty and abuse, and it is the only conditioning procedure whose application is regulated by law. However, punishment need not involve unusual forms of physical cruelty or pain. A variety of aversive events have been used effectively in punishment procedures, including verbal reprimands, monetary fines, placement in a time-out corner or a time-out room, loss of earned privileges or positive reinforcers, demerits, various restitution procedures, and even water mist and a squirt of lemon juice in the mouth. Electric shock is rarely used with human subjects but is common in animal research because the intensity and duration of shock can be controlled more easily than the intensity of other forms of aversive stimulation.

The stage for the punishment debate was set by Thorndike in the early part of the twentieth century. Thorndike (1932) claimed that punishment is an ineffective procedure for producing significant and lasting changes in behavior and therefore should not be used. Based on his own studies, Skinner (1953) adopted a similar point of view. He argued that we should make every effort to eliminate the use of punishment in society because punishment is cruel and ineffective. Whether punishment is cruel or not cannot be decided by empirical evidence alone. However, the other aspect of the argument—that punishment is ineffective—can be tested experimentally, and such tests have indicated that punishment can in fact be effective in suppressing behavior if the punishment is properly applied.

Effective and Ineffective Punishment

Casual observation suggests that Thorndike's and Skinner's claims that punishment is ineffective may be correct. Violations of traffic laws are punished by fines and other unpleasant consequences. Nevertheless, we often see people driving through red lights and driving faster than the posted speed limit. Students scolded by a teacher for not having their homework completed will not necessarily finish their next assignment on time, and a drug dealer apprehended for selling cocaine or heroin is likely to return to selling drugs after being released from jail.

In contrast to the above examples, sometimes punishment is remarkably effective. A child who accidentally gets shocked while playing with an electric outlet is unlikely to poke a finger into the outlet ever again. A person who falls and gets hurt rushing down a slippery staircase will slow down next time those stairs have to be negotiated. Someone who tips over a canoe by leaning too far to one side the first time out will be much more careful about staying in the middle of the canoe after that.

Why is punishment highly effective in suppressing behavior in some cases and ineffective in other instances? Let us first consider the cases in which punishment fails.

When Punishment Fails

Why do drivers often exceed the speed limit even though speeding can result in a fine? Punishment in the enforcement of traffic laws is similar to punishment in much of the criminal justice system and in many social situations. In all of these cases, punishment is administered by an individual rather than being an automatic environmental consequence of the punished response. A police officer has to detect whether a driver is going too fast, and an officer of the court has to judge the severity of the offense and decide what penalty to apply. Requiring people to detect the punished response and administer the aversive stimulus can make punishment ineffective for a variety of reasons.

One consequence of requiring a police officer to detect speeders is that drivers are not caught every time they exceed the speed limit. In fact, the chances of getting caught are fairly low. A driver may exceed the speed limit 50 times or more undetected for each time his or her speed is recorded by a patrol officer. Thus, *punishment is highly intermittent.*

On the rare occasion that a driver is detected exceeding the speed limit, chances are that this will not be detected right away but only after the person has been going too fast for some time. Therefore, *punishment is delayed* after the initiation of the behavior targeted for punishment. Further delays in punishment occur because, typically, fines do not have to be paid right away. Fines also can be appealed, and an appeal may take several months.

If the appeal is unsuccessful, punishment for the first offense is likely to be fairly mild. The driver will probably just have to pay a fine. More severe penalties are imposed only if the driver is repeatedly ticketed for speeding. Thus, *punishment is initially mild and is increased in severity only after repeated offenses.* This kind of gradual escalation of the severity of punishment is a fundamental aspect of societal uses of punishment. Someone who does something undesirable is first given a warning and a second chance. We get serious about punishment only after repeated offenses.

Another reason punishment is not effective in regulating the speed of traffic is that drivers can often tell when they are likely to be checked for speeding. In some cities, the location of traffic police is announced on the

TABLE 12.1   Characteristics of Punishment

For Driving Too Fast	For Poking Fingers into an Electric Outlet
Intermittent	Continuous
Delayed	Immediate
Low-intensity aversive stimulus at first	High-intensity aversive stimulus every time
Signaled by a discriminative stimulus	Not signaled

radio each morning. The presence of traffic police is also obvious from the distinctive markings of patrol cars. And, many drivers have installed radar detectors in their cars that signal the presence of a radar patrol. Patrol cars and radar detectors provide discriminative stimuli for punishment. Thus, *punishment is often signaled by a discriminative stimulus*.

WHEN PUNISHMENT SUCCEEDS

Compared to the ineffectiveness of punishment in discouraging speeding, why does punishment work well in discouraging children from poking their fingers into electric outlets? A child shocked while playing with an electric outlet is unlikely to ever do that again and may develop a strong fear of outlets. What are the critical differences in the punishment contingencies involved in driving too fast and playing with an electric outlet?

First, there is *no intermittency* to punishment for sticking your fingers into an electric outlet. Every time you do that, you will get shocked. If you touch an outlet so as to come in contact with the electrodes, you are sure to get shocked. The physical configuration of the outlet guarantees that punishment is delivered on an FR 1 schedule.

Second, *punishment is immediate*. As soon as you make contact with the electrodes, you will get shocked. There is no elaborate detection or decision process involved to delay delivery of the aversive stimulus.

Third, *punishment is intense for the first transgression*. The outlet does not give you a warning the first time you touch the electrodes. The first offense is treated the same way as the tenth one. Each time you make the response, you get an intense shock.

Finally, punishment is not limited to times when a police officer or observer is watching. Thus, *punishment is not signaled* by a discriminative stimulus. No matter who is present in the room, sticking your fingers in the outlet will get you shocked. Severe and immediate punishment is always in effect for each occurrence of the target response.

Research Evidence on Punishment

All of the factors that characterize punishment for touching the electrodes in an electric outlet have been found to be important in carefully conducted experiments on punishment. In addition, research has identified several additional factors that strongly determine the effectiveness of punishment. Ironically, much of the research was done under the leadership of one of Skinner's former students, Nathan Azrin (Azrin & Holz, 1966). Complementary studies were performed in a research program conducted by Church (1969). Azrin used pigeons for much of his research, whereas Church used laboratory rats. Contrary to the early claims of Thorndike and Skinner, these experiments demonstrated that punishment can be a highly effective technique for producing rapid and long-term changes in behavior.

RESPONSE-REINFORCER CONTINGENCY

Punishment is similar to positive reinforcement in that it involves a positive contingency between the instrumental response and the reinforcer. The reinforcer is delivered only if the subject previously performed the target instrumental response. The primary difference between punishment and positive reinforcement is that in punishment the reinforcer is an aversive stimulus.

As with other instrumental conditioning procedures, a fundamental variable in punishment procedures is the response-reinforcer contingency. This refers to the extent to which delivery of the aversive stimulus depends on the prior occurrence of the target response. If an aversive stimulus is administered independent of the target instrumental response, the procedure is a form of Pavlovian aversive conditioning rather than punishment. As we saw in Chapter 4, Pavlovian aversive conditioning results in the conditioning of fear, and this is often evident in freezing or the general suppression of ongoing behavior.

Some general suppression of ongoing behavior can result from punishment. However, punishment also produces behavioral suppression specific to the target response (Camp, Raymond, & Church, 1967; Goodall, 1984). The specificity of the behavioral suppression depends on the degree of response-reinforcer contingency. The stronger the response-reinforcer contingency, the more specific is the response suppression produced by punishment.

RESPONSE-REINFORCER CONTIGUITY

As we saw in Chapter 6, the response-reinforcer contingency is just one aspect of the relation between an instrumental response and a reinforcer. Another important feature of the response-reinforcer relation is the interval between the target response and delivery of the reinforcer. In a punishment procedure, this is the interval between the target response and the aversive stimulus.

Response-reinforcer contiguity is just as important with punishment as it is with positive reinforcement. Punishment is most effective if the aversive stimulus is presented without delay after the target response (Camp, Raymond, & Church, 1967). If the aversive stimulus is delayed after the target response, some suppression of behavior may occur. However, the response suppression will not be specific to the punished response.

INTENSITY OF THE AVERSIVE STIMULUS

As might be suspected, the response-suppressing effects of punishment are directly related to the intensity of the aversive stimulus. Low intensities of punishment produce only mild suppression of behavior. In contrast, dramatic suppressions of behavior can result from the use of intense aversive stimuli (Azrin, 1960). More importantly, the effects of the intensity of punishment depend largely on the subject's prior experience with punishment. In general, subjects tend to respond to a new punishment procedure in a manner similar to how they responded during earlier encounters with punishment.

The first exposure to punishment can lead to somewhat unexpected results. Consider, for example, subjects that are initially exposed to a low intensity of punishment. Weak aversive stimuli produce only mild, if any, suppression of responding. Subjects exposed to low-intensity punishment learn to continue to respond with little disruption in their behavior. Furthermore, their persistent responding in the face of mild punishment generalizes to higher intensities of aversive stimulation (Azrin, Holz, & Hake, 1963; Miller, 1960). As a result, the subjects also continue to respond if the intensity of punishment is subsequently increased. In a sense, exposure to mild aversive stimulation serves to immunize individuals against the effects of more intense punishment (see Figure 12.1).

Interestingly, a history of exposure to intense punishment can have just the opposite effect. Initial exposure to intense punishment can increase the impact of subsequent mild punishment (see Figure 12.2). High-intensity aversive stimulation produces dramatic suppression of the punished response, and this severe suppression of responding persists when the intensity of the aversive stimulus is subsequently reduced (Church, 1969). The outcome is that mild punishment produces much more severe suppression of behavior in subjects who previously received intense punishment than in subjects who were not punished previously. Exposure to intense punishment sensitizes individuals to subsequent mild aversive stimulation.

SIGNALED PUNISHMENT

As is the case with positive reinforcement and avoidance, punishment contingencies can be in effect at all times or only in the presence of

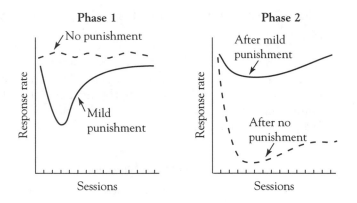

FIGURE 12.1   Immunizing effects of prior experience with mild punishment.
During Phase 1, one group of subjects is exposed to mild punishment while another group is permitted to respond without punishment. During Phase 2, both groups receive intense punishment. (Hypothetical data.)

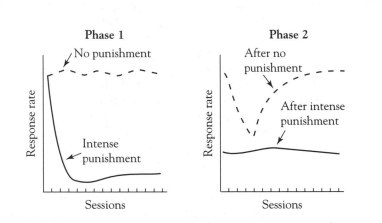

FIGURE 12.2   Sensitizing effects of prior experience with intense punishment.
During Phase 1, one group of subjects is exposed to intense punishment while another group is permitted to respond without punishment. During Phase 2, both groups receive mild punishment. (Hypothetical data.)

particular discriminative stimuli. If the punishment procedure is signaled by a discriminative stimulus, it is called **discriminative punishment.** A child, for example, may be reprimanded for running through the living room when her parents are home but not when her grandparents are in charge. In this case, punishment would be signaled by cues associated with the presence of the child's parents. The parents would be discriminative stimuli for punishment.

As you might suspect, a child reprimanded by her parents but not by her grandparents will learn to suppress running when her parents are home but will not show such restraint when the grandparents are in charge. Discriminative punishment procedures result in discriminative suppression of behavior (Dinsmoor, 1952). Responding becomes suppressed in the presence of the discriminative stimulus but continues unabated when the discriminative stimulus is absent.

Discriminative control of a punished response can be problematic. A parent may try to get a child to not use foul language by punishing the child for cursing. This may discourage the child from cursing in the presence of the parent but not from cursing around friends. The suppression of foul language will be under discriminative control, and the parent's goal will not be achieved.

In other cases, the discriminative control of punished behavior is not problematic. For example, if a little girl starts talking loudly in a religious service, she is likely to be reprimanded. If the punishment procedure is effective, the child will cease talking during the service, but this will not stop her from talking boisterously elsewhere. Having the response suppressed only under the discriminative stimulus control of the church service is not a problem.

PUNISHMENT AND THE MECHANISMS MAINTAINING THE PUNISHED RESPONSE

Punishment procedures are typically applied to responses that already occur for one reason or another. Often, punished responses are maintained by some form of positive reinforcement. Because of this, the effects of punishment depend both on the type of reinforcement and the schedule of reinforcement that supports the target response.

A child may talk during a church service to attract attention or to enjoy the camaraderie that comes from talking with a friend. If the child is reprimanded for talking, the aversiveness of the reprimand is pitted against the positive reinforcement of the attention and camaraderie. The outcome of the punishment procedure depends on how the subject solves this cost-benefit problem. In general, punishment will be less effective if the target response is reinforced often than if the target response is reinforced only once in a while (Church & Raymond, 1967).

The outcome of punishment also depends on the particular schedule of positive reinforcement that maintains the target response. With VI and FI schedules, punishment reduces the overall level of responding but does not change the temporal distribution of behavior (for example, Azrin & Holz, 1966). In contrast, if the instrumental response is maintained on an FR schedule of reinforcement, punishment tends to increase the postreinforcement pause (Azrin, 1959; Dardano & Sauerbrunn, 1964).

PUNISHMENT AND REINFORCEMENT OF ALTERNATIVE BEHAVIOR

As we saw in the preceding section, the outcome of punishment procedures can be analyzed in terms of the relative costs and benefits of performing the target response. This cost-benefit analysis involves not only the punished response but also other activities the subject may perform. A powerful technique for increasing the effects of punishment is to provide positive reinforcement for some other behavior (Perry & Parke, 1975). Effective parents are well aware of this principle. Punishing children on a long car ride for quarreling among themselves is relatively ineffective if the children are not given much else to do. Punishment of quarreling is much more effective if it is accompanied by an alternative reinforced activity such as listening to a story or playing with a new toy.

PARADOXICAL EFFECTS OF PUNISHMENT

The factors that I have described so far determine the extent to which punishment will suppress the target response. Punishment will not be very effective if the punished response is maintained by a highly motivating schedule of positive reinforcement, if there is no positive reinforcement for alternative behavior, and if the punishment procedure involves a weak response-reinforcer contingency, delayed aversive stimulation, and a mild aversive stimulus. Weak punishment parameters make punishment ineffective. In contrast, under other circumstances punishment can produce paradoxical effects and facilitate responding instead of suppressing behavior.

Punishment as a signal for positive reinforcement. One circumstance that leads to a paradoxical effect is when punishment serves as a signal for positive reinforcement (Holz & Azrin, 1961). Attention, for example, is a powerful source of reinforcement for children. A young boy may be ignored by his parents most of the time as long as he is not doing anything dangerous or disruptive. If he starts playing with matches, he is severely reprimanded and sent to his room. Will punishment suppress the target response in this case? Not likely. Notice that the child receives attention from his parents only after he does something bad and is being punished. Under these circumstances, punishment can become a signal for positive reinforcement, with the outcome that the child will seek out punishment as a way of obtaining attention.

Punishment of escape behavior. Another circumstance in which punishment may produce paradoxical effects is if the punished response is an escape response—if the punished response is maintained by negative

F I G U R E 12.3 Diagram of an escape or negative reinforcement procedure.
The escape response occurs during the aversive stimulus and results in termination of the aversive stimulus.

reinforcement. A negatively reinforced response serves to terminate an aversive stimulus.

Negative reinforcement is a bit unusual because before a subject can escape from an aversive stimulus, the aversive stimulus has to be presented or turned on. Therefore, a negatively reinforced escape response is performed in the presence of an aversive stimulus (see Figure 12.3). That makes the presence of the aversive stimulus a discriminative cue for the escape response.

Punishment of an escape response facilitates rather than suppresses that response (for example, Dean & Pittman, 1991). This paradoxical effect of punishment occurs because the aversive stimulus used to punish the response preserves the conditions that motivated the escape response in the first place. Hence, the escape response persists even though it is being punished.

Paradoxical effects of punishment are not common, and they should not encourage us to jump to the conclusion that punishment produces unpredictable results. Rather, if a paradoxical effect of punishment is observed, the situation should be examined carefully to determine whether punishment had come to serve as a signal for positive reinforcement. If that does not seem likely, perhaps the target response was previously reinforced as an escape response.

Can and Should We Create a Society Free of Punishment?

As I noted at the outset, both Thorndike and Skinner advocated that punishment not be used because they regarded punishment as ineffective in producing significant and lasting changes in behavior. Contrary to the views of Thorndike and Skinner, punishment can be highly effective in decreasing undesired behavior. Does this mean that we should go ahead and use punishment whenever we are interested in discouraging some activity? Or should we work to try to build a society entirely free of punishment? Answers to these questions depend in part on what one considers to be just and ethical human conduct. Ethical issues are outside the scope of this discussion. However, we can consider how empirical evidence about the effectiveness of punishment may constrain the kinds of decisions we make about societal uses of punishment.

First, can we create a punishment-free society? That is unlikely. Punishment is programmed by various aspects of the physical and biological environment. If you mishandle a cat, the cat is likely to scratch you. If you don't hold your glass steady as you pour from a pitcher, you are likely to spill the liquid and get your clothes wet. If you lift a pot out of the oven without a pot holder, you are likely to burn yourself. It would be very difficult, and perhaps impossible, to redesign our environment so as to eliminate all sources of punishment.

What kinds of punishment could we try to eliminate, and would doing that be sensible? The kind of punishment that people in our culture find most objectionable is physical pain inflicted by one person in an effort to suppress an undesired response on the part of someone else. We have laws against the use of corporal punishment in schools. We also have laws against child abuse and spousal abuse in the home. Such laws are often justified on moral and ethical grounds. Do such laws also make sense from the perspective of empirical principles of punishment? I think so.

Interpersonal interactions involving punishment require one individual to inflict pain on another. An important factor is the willingness of the person administering the punishment to hurt the recipient. A parent may claim to be punishing a child for having received a poor grade in school, and a husband may say that he is punishing his wife for getting home late. However, whether or not the punishment takes place is often related to the emotional state of the person who administers the punishment. People are likely to administer punishment if they are frustrated and angry, and under those circumstances, effective principles of punishment are rarely followed.

If punishment is administered out of frustration and anger, it is not likely to be closely related to an undesired response. A poor grade on a school assignment will not aggravate a parent every time. Therefore, the punishment is likely to be intermittent. Frustrative punishment is also likely to occur some time after the target response has taken place. A parent may become abusive when a child brings home a poor report card, even though the responses that contributed to the poor grades occurred over a period of weeks earlier.

Frustrative punishment is also often under discriminative stimulus control, and the discriminative stimulus is unrelated to the punished behavior. A parent may become upset by a poor report card when the parent's emotional resources are strained by events entirely unrelated to the child's behavior. The parent may be irritable because of stresses at work, ill health, or drug abuse. Under these circumstances, the likelihood of punishment will be signaled by the parent's irritability, and the child will learn that he or she can get a report card signed without being punished by waiting until the next day or the weekend when the parent is more relaxed.

Another shortcoming of frustrative punishment is that it is rarely accompanied by positive reinforcement of alternative behavior. When a parent punishes a child out of irritability and anger, the parent is not likely to have the presence of mind to accompany the punishment with a programmatic effort to provide positive reinforcement for more constructive activities.

Punishment as an act of aggression and frustration violates many of the parameters of effective punishment and therefore does not produce constructive changes in behavior. Because punishment out of frustration is poorly related to the targeted behavior, frustrative punishment is abusive and cannot be justified as a systematic behavior modification procedure. To avoid administering punishment out of frustration, a reasonable rule of thumb is not to administer punishment when you feel like it. If punishment is used at all, it should be a part of a systematic and well-planned program of behavior modification rather than a way to act out irritability.

Suggested Readings

AZRIN, N. H., & HOLZ, W. C. (1966). Punishment. In W. K. Honig (Ed.), *Operant behavior: Areas of research and application* (pp. 380–447). New York: Appleton-Century-Crofts.

CHURCH, R. M. (1969). Response suppression. In B. A. Campbell & R. M. Church (Eds.), *Punishment and aversive behavior* (pp.111–156). New York: Appleton-Century-Crofts.

REPP, A. C., & SINGH, N. N. (Eds.). (1990). *Perspectives on the use of nonaversive and aversive interventions for persons with developmental disabilities*. Sycamore, IL: Sycamore.

Technical Terms

Discriminative punishment
Punishment

CHAPTER THIRTEEN

Memory Mechanisms

DID YOU KNOW THAT:

- Learning and memory are integrally related.
- Tasks testing memory mechanisms have to be specially designed so they cannot be solved without the use of memory.
- Memory even for simple stimuli is not a passive, automatic process.
- Memory can improve with learning.
- Memory can be brought under stimulus control.
- Memory can be prospective and involve future rather than past events.
- Failures of memory can be caused by remembering too much or by not remembering enough.
- Seemingly trivial aspects of a learning situation can stimulate retrieval of the learning.

Learning and memory mechanisms are integrally related. Learning cannot occur without memory. Both are concerned with how experiences with stimuli and responses at one point in time influence the actions of an organism some time later.

Memory mechanisms have been investigated with human subjects since the time of the ancient Greeks, and such investigations continue as a prominent aspect of contemporary studies of human cognitive processes. In contrast, studies of memory mechanisms in animals have a much shorter history. Only in the last quarter century has much systematic work on memory been conducted with animal subjects (Honig & James, 1971; Kendrick, Rilling, & Denny, 1986; Medin, Roberts, & Davis, 1976; Spear & Miller, 1981). Research on memory mechanisms in animals is of particular interest because such experiments make extensive use of the basic conditioning procedures that have been described in earlier chapters of this book.

Animal research on memory mechanisms is important for several reasons. It promises to inform us about the evolution of cognitive processes (Sherry & Schachter, 1987), and it promises to help us understand basic mechanisms of conditioning and learning (for example, Miller, Kasprow, & Schachtman, 1986). Such research is also essential for investigation of the physiological bases of memory, for the development and testing of drugs that influence memory, and for the development of systems of artificial intelligence that mimic living organisms.

Stages of Information Processing

Memory involves the delayed effects of experience. For experience with stimuli and responses to influence behavior some time later, three things have to happen. First, information about the stimuli and responses has to be acquired and encoded in the nervous system in some fashion. This is the *acquisition stage* of information processing. Once encoded, the information has to be stored for later use. This is the *retention stage* of information processing. Finally, when the information is needed at the end of the retention interval, it has to be recovered from storage. This is the *retrieval stage*.

All studies of learning and all studies of memory involve the acquisition, retention, and retrieval stages of information processing. However, which stage is the focus of interest differs, depending on whether learning processes or memory processes are of primary concern (see Table 13.1). Studies of learning focus on the acquisition stage of information processing. In studies of learning, the circumstances of acquisition are manipulated or varied while the conditions of retention and retrieval are kept constant. In contrast, in studies of memory, the conditions of acquisition are kept constant while the retention interval and the conditions of retrieval are varied.

TABLE 13.1 Differences Between Experiments on Learning and Experiments on Memory

Phase	Learning Experiments	Memory Experiments
Acquisition	Varied	Constant
Retention interval	Constant (long)	Varied (short and long)
Retrieval	Constant	Varied

The Matching-to-Sample Procedure

A variety of different techniques have been used to study memory mechanisms in animals. Memory procedures often require special controls to ensure that the subject's behavior is guided by its past experience rather than by some clue that is inadvertently presented in the test situation. In addition, special procedures have to be designed to isolate particular memory processes. To facilitate illustration of these complexities, I will describe one technique for the study of memory mechanisms in detail.

I will focus on the **matching-to-sample** procedure. This is perhaps the most versatile procedure for the study of memory mechanisms and can be used to investigate many different aspects of memory. Although our discussion will focus on the matching-to-sample technique, the issues addressed are relevant to all memory tasks.

In the matching-to-sample procedure, the subject is first exposed to a sample stimulus. The sample is then removed for a retention interval, after which the subject receives a multiple-choice memory test. Several alternatives are presented, one of which is the same as the previously presented sample stimulus. If the subject selects the previously presented sample, it is reinforced.

The matching procedure has been used with a variety of species including dolphins, rats, and people (Baron & Menich, 1985; Forestell & Herman, 1988; Wallace, Steinert, Scobie, & Spear, 1980), and the procedure has been adapted for various types of sample stimuli, including visual, auditory, and spatial cues. Figure 13.1 illustrates a version of the procedure for use with pigeons.

Pigeons are typically tested in a Skinner box that is provided with three response keys arranged in a row. Each trial begins with a start cue, which might be illumination of the center key with a white light. One peck at the start cue results in presentation of the sample stimulus on the center key. In the example, the sample stimulus is a triangle. After a while, the sample stimulus is turned off and a retention interval begins. At the end of the retention interval, the subject receives two test stimuli on the side keys. One of the test stimuli is the same as the previously presented sample (a triangle), whereas the other is different (a square). Pecks at the side key containing the

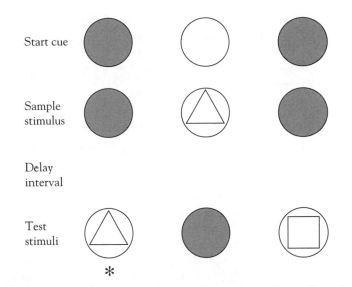

F I G U R E 13.1   **Illustration of a matching-to-sample trial used with pigeons.**
The trial begins with a start cue presented on the center key. The sample stimulus (a triangle) is then presented, also on the center key. The sample is then turned off, and a retention interval begins. At the end of the retention interval, the subject receives two test stimuli on the side keys, one of which matches the sample stimulus. Pecks at the matching test cue are reinforced, as indicated by the asterisk.

sample stimulus are reinforced. Pecks at the alternate test stimuli have no consequence.

SIMULTANEOUS AND DELAYED MATCHING-TO-SAMPLE

As you might suspect, the difficulty of a matching-to-sample procedure depends in part on how long the retention interval is between presentation of the sample stimulus and the subsequent choice test (Grant, 1976). To facilitate learning of a matching-to-sample task, it is useful to begin training without a retention interval. Such a procedure is called **simultaneous matching-to-sample.** In simultaneous matching-to-sample, each trial again starts with a start cue on the center key. This is then followed by presentation of the sample stimulus on the center key. The test stimuli are then presented on the side keys while the sample remains on the center key. Because the sample stimulus is present simultaneously with the test stimuli, the procedure is called simultaneous matching-to-sample.

After subjects have learned to make the accurate choice in a simultaneous matching procedure, a retention interval can be introduced between presentation of the sample and presentation of the test stimuli, as illustrated in Figure 13.1. Because in this case the test stimuli are delayed after presentation of the sample, the procedure is called **delayed matching-to-sample.**

PROCEDURAL CONTROLS FOR MEMORY

Introducing a retention interval is necessary to make sure that the subject has to remember something about the sample stimulus to respond accurately when the test choices are subsequently presented. However, having a retention interval in the procedure is not enough to be sure that the subject is using memory based on the sample stimulus. The sample and test stimuli also have to be varied.

Consider, for example, a procedure in which every trial was exactly the same as the trial illustrated in Figure 13.1. To respond accurately with repetitions of this trial, the subject would just have to learn to peck the left key when the side keys were illuminated. The pigeon would not have to remember anything about the shape of the visual cue that was projected on any of the response keys.

To force pigeons to pay attention to and remember information about the specific stimuli that are presented in a matching procedure, the sample stimulus used and the position of the test stimuli have to be varied across training trials. Figure 13.2 illustrates various types of trials in a matching procedure involving two shape stimuli (triangle and square) and two pattern stimuli (a vertical grid and a horizontal grid). There are eight possible trial types. With each sample stimulus, two types of test trials are used, one in which the correct stimulus appears on the left and one in which the correct stimulus appears on the right. If the eight trial types appear randomly during training, the subject cannot be consistently accurate unless it uses information based on the sample to guide its choice responses.

Types of Memory

Memory is not a homogeneous process. There are different kinds of memory based on what kind of information is remembered, what types of manipulations influence the nature of the memory, and how long the memory lasts. In animal research, distinctions between reference and working memory, active and passive memory, and prospective and retrospective memory have received special attention.

REFERENCE MEMORY AND WORKING MEMORY

What kinds of memory are required to respond successfully in a matching-to-sample procedure? In our discussion of procedural controls for memory, we

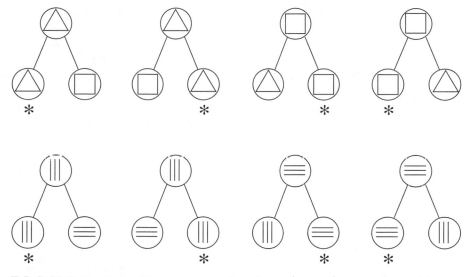

F I G U R E 13.2 **Various types of trials used to make sure that subjects in a matching-to-sample procedure are responding on the basis of information obtained from the sample stimulus.**
For each trial type, the sample stimulus is presented on top, and the two choice stimuli are presented below. The correct choice is identified by an asterisk.

were concerned with making sure that responses to the test stimuli on a particular trial were based on what the subject remembered from having been exposed to the sample stimulus on that trial. Such memory is called **working memory.**

Working memory is memory for information that is needed to respond successfully on one trial or task but is not useful in responding on the next trial or task. Because the sample stimulus is varied from one trial to the next in a matching procedure (see Figure 13.2), information from the sample presented on one trial does not help in picking the correct test stimulus on the next trial. Thus, working memory is of limited duration.

The control procedures that we discussed previously (variations in the sample stimulus and the position of that stimulus during the choice test) ensure that matching-to-sample procedures involve working memory. However, to respond successfully, subjects have to remember more than just information based on the sample on a particular trial. They also have to remember general features of the matching procedure that remain constant from one trial to the next. For example, they have to remember to peck the start cue and to peck one of the test stimuli after the retention interval. In addition, they have to remember that correct responses are reinforced and where to obtain the reinforcer once it is delivered. Such memory is called **reference memory.** Because reference memory involves constant features of a task, it is of considerably longer duration than working memory.

The distinction between working and reference memory is applicable to all sorts of situations. Baking a cake, for example, involves both working and reference memory. As you create the batter, you have to remember which ingredients you have already included and which ones to add next. That kind of information is useful only for the task at hand; it will not help you bake the next cake. Therefore, such information involves working memory.

To bake a cake, you also have to have some general cooking skills. You have to know about cooking pans, ovens, various cake ingredients, and how to measure and mix those ingredients. These general skills are useful not just for the cake you happen to be baking but also for any future cakes you might want to bake. Therefore, such information involves reference memory.

Active and Passive Memory

Working and reference memory are distinguished by the type of information that is retained and, related to that, how long the information is remembered. Memory mechanisms can also be distinguished by the kinds of procedures that influence them. A fundamental issue is whether memory can be modified or influenced by other psychological processes. This is the basis for the distinction between active and passive memory.

Passive memory processes are assumed to be automatic and not subject to modification by other psychological processes. A prominent passive memory process that has been entertained in connection with matching-to-sample procedures is the **trace-decay hypothesis** (Roberts & Grant, 1976). According to this hypothesis, presentation of the sample stimulus activates a neural trace that automatically decays after the end of the stimulus. Information about the sample is available only as long as the trace is sufficiently strong. The gradual fading or decay of the neural trace of the sample stimulus is assumed to produce progressively less accurate recall of information based on the sample.

The initial strength of a neural trace is assumed to depend only on the physical intensity and duration of the sample stimulus. (More intense and longer stimuli presumably activate a stronger neural trace.) However, regardless of its initial strength, the neural trace is assumed to gradually fade with time. Consistent with these assumptions, subjects respond with less accuracy in delayed matching-to-sample procedures as the retention interval between the sample stimulus and the choice test is increased; in addition, responding is more accurate with longer sample stimuli (Grant, 1976).

According to the trace-decay hypothesis, information about the sample stimulus is lost automatically during the retention interval and nothing can be done about that. However, several lines of evidence suggest that memory loss is not an automatic, passive process that is immune to modification by other psychological processes. Contrary to the trace-decay hypothesis, memory for a sample stimulus improves with practice (D'Amato, 1973). Memory can also be improved by making a stimulus surprising (Maki, 1979). Finally, a considerable body of evidence suggests that memory mechanisms can be brought under stimulus control (Rilling, Kendrick, & Stonebraker, 1984). Animals can be conditioned to remember a sample stimulus in one situation but not in another.

The preponderance of evidence suggests that working memory in a matching-to-sample procedure is not the kind of automatic, passive process that is assumed by the trace-decay hypothesis. Rather, it is an active process that can be influenced by various psychological processes such as learning, surprisingness, and stimulus control.

RETROSPECTIVE AND PROSPECTIVE MEMORY

So far, we have established that the matching-to-sample task involves both working and reference memory and that working memory is best characterized as an active rather than a passive process. Another important issue concerns the contents of working memory, or what the subject remembers during the retention interval that enables it to select the correct stimulus during the choice test at the end of a trial.

Retrospective memory. The most obvious possibility is that the subject stores information about the sample stimulus during the retention interval and then uses that information to select the correct test stimulus. According to this scenario, the subject registers or encodes information about the sample stimulus when the sample is presented for a particular trial. After the retention interval, the subject uses its memory of the sample to determine which test cue best resembles the sample. It then selects the test stimulus that best matches the sample.

Remembering attributes of the sample stimulus is a form of **retrospective memory.** Retrospective memory is memory for stimuli (or other types of events) that were encountered previously. It is memory that is retroactive, or involves past events.

Retrospective memory is perhaps the most obvious possibility for the contents of working memory in a matching task. However, just because a hypothesis is obvious does not make it correct. What else might a subject keep in mind during the retention interval that would enable it to respond correctly during the choice test?

Prospective memory. Recall that in the typical matching procedure, a limited number of different trial types are repeated over and over again in a random order. Figure 13.2, for example, illustrates a procedure in which there are four possible sample stimuli: a triangle, a square, a vertical grid, and a horizontal grid. For each sample, there is a unique, correct test stimulus. Because of this, the matching procedure involves pairs of sample and test stimuli.

Let us represent a sample stimulus as "S" and its correct test stimulus as "T." Different sample-test stimulus pairs can then be represented as S1-T1, S2-T2, S3-T3, and so on. Given these S-T pairings, subjects could select the correct choice stimulus in a matching task by thinking of T after presentation of the sample S on a particular trial and storing that information during the retention interval. This would be a form of **prospective memory.**

Prospective memory involves information about a possible future event. Prospective memory involves remembering something that is predicted to occur in the future, or prospectively.

Deciding between retrospection and prospection. Retrospective memory involves remembering the sample stimulus S during the retention interval. Prospective memory involves remembering the correct test stimulus T during the retention interval. How can we distinguish between these possibilities experimentally?

In a matching-to-sample procedure, the sample stimulus S and the correct test stimulus T are physically the same stimulus. If the sample is a triangle, the correct test stimulus is also a triangle. This makes it virtually impossible to decide whether subjects are storing information about stimulus S or stimulus T during the retention interval. To distinguish between retrospective and prospective memory, we have to change the matching procedure somewhat so that the correct test stimulus is not the same physical stimulus as the sample stimulus. Such a procedure is called **symbolic matching-to-sample.**

A symbolic matching-to-sample procedure is illustrated in the left column of Figure 13.3. Each row represents a different trial type in the procedure. The symbolic matching procedure is based on symbolic relations between sample and test stimuli rather than the identity relation. In Figure 13.3, responding to the vertical grid is reinforced after presentation of a triangle as the sample stimulus, and responding to the horizontal grid is reinforced after presentation of a square as the sample. In a sense, the vertical grid is a symbol for the triangle sample, and the horizontal grid is a symbol for the square sample.

As with the standard matching procedure, in a symbolic matching task the correct test stimulus appears equally often on the left and the right, and there is a delay between the sample and the test stimuli. Therefore, the task involves working memory just as the standard matching procedure. However, with symbolic matching, the contents of working memory are distinctly different depending on whether the subject is using retrospective memory or prospective memory. These differences are shown in the center and right columns of Figure 13.3. On trials with the triangle as the sample, retrospective memory involves retention of information about the triangle. In contrast, prospective memory involves retention of information about the vertical grid test stimulus, which is the correct choice after a triangle sample.

Using symbolic matching-to-sample tasks, investigators have found that

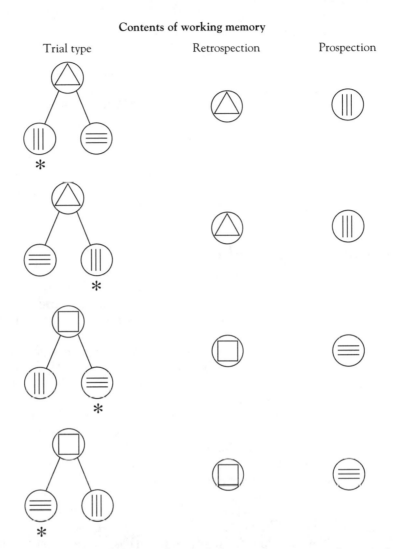

Contents of working memory

FIGURE 13.3 Diagram of a symbolic matching-to-sample procedure and illustration of the difference between retrospective and prospective working memory.

For each trial type, the test stimuli are shown below the sample stimulus, and the correct test stimulus is indicated by an asterisk.

pigeons use prospective rather than retrospective memory (for example, Roitblat, 1980; Santi & Roberts, 1985). Research using other kinds of memory tasks has also provided evidence of prospective memory. However, not all instances of working memory involve prospection or memory for events that are predicted to occur in the future. Whether subjects remember

TABLE 13.2   Difference between Proactive and Retroactive Interference

Proactive interference
Extraneous events → Target task → Memory test
Retroactive interference
Target task → Extraneous events → Memory test

a past event (retrospection) or a future event (prospection) appears to depend on which form of memory is more efficient in solving a particular task (Cook, Brown, & Riley, 1985; Zentall, Steirn, & Jackson-Smith, 1990).

Sources of Memory Failure

Instances of the failure of memory can be as informative about memory mechanisms as instances of successful remembering. Therefore, investigators of memory mechanisms in animals have also studied situations in which memory fails.

Memory may fail for a variety of different reasons. An organism may not remember something because it never encoded (learned) the information in the first place. Memory failure may also result from failure to effectively retrieve information that was effectively encoded (stored). Finally, an organism may perform poorly in a memory task because it remembers several different things and is unable to choose correctly among those alternatives. I will describe examples of each of these different sources of memory failure in the course of discussing two primary issues in the study of forgetting, interference, and retrieval failure.

INTERFERENCE

Memory failure due to interference has been extensively investigated in both human and animal studies. Interference refers to memory failure that results from exposure to stimuli or events that are extraneous to the memory task the subject is tested on. If you were presented with a single visual pattern in an otherwise darkened room, you would show good retention of that stimulus several minutes later. In contrast, if you saw numerous visual stimuli before or after the stimulus that you were tested on, your memory for the test item would be much worse. Exposure to various visual stimuli before and after the test item would interfere with your memory for the test item.

Different kinds of interference effects occur, depending on whether the interfering events occur before or after what the subject is to be tested on (see Table 13.2). If the extraneous stimuli that disrupt memory occur before the target event, the phenomenon is called **proactive interference.** In proactive interference, the interfering stimuli act forward or proactively to disrupt memory for the target stimulus. In contrast, if the extraneous stimuli occur after the event the subject has to remember, the phenomenon is called **retroactive interference.** In retroactive interference, the extraneous stimuli act backward, or retroactively, to disrupt memory for the target event.

Proactive interference in matching-to-sample. Both proactive and retroactive interference have been investigated in animal studies using delayed matching-to-sample procedures. In early studies of proactive interference, an explicit extraneous stimulus was presented before the start of a matching-to-sample trial (and thus before presentation of the sample stimulus for that trial). Subjects performed less accurately on trials preceded by the extraneous stimulus than on control trials conducted in the absence of the extraneous stimulus (Medin, 1980).

Proactive interference is a fairly general phenomenon and can occur even in the absence of the presentation of an explicit interfering stimulus before a matching-to-sample trial. The matching-to-sample task involves repeated training trials. If those trials are presented close enough together, what occurs on one trial can disrupt performance on the next trial. Thus, proactive interference may occur because of the close scheduling of successive training trials (Edhouse & White, 1988; Jitsumori, Wright, & Shyan, 1989).

To see how proactive interference may develop between training trials, let us consider again the matching-to-sample task that was summarized in Figure 13.2. In this task, one of four sample stimuli could occur on any particular trial (triangle, square, vertical grid, or horizontal grid). Let us assume that the subject receives a trial in which the triangle is the sample stimulus and the correct choice, and this is followed by a trial in which the square is the sample and correct choice. To respond accurately on the trial with the square sample stimulus, the subject has to disregard the fact that the triangle was correct on the preceding trial. If the subject failed to disregard what was correct on the preceding trial, it would make an error on the square trial by choosing the triangle (see Figure 13.2).

Proactive interference caused by earlier matching trials is particularly interesting because it is a case in which subjects perform poorly on a memory task not because they remember too little but because they remember too much. The disruption of performance is caused by the fact that subjects remember what happened on an earlier trial and are then confused about the correct response on the current trial. This illustrates the general rule that memory failure can occur for a variety of reasons, not all of which involve the loss of information over time.

Retroactive interference in matching-to-sample. Retroactive interference has been investigated in matching tasks by presenting extraneous stimuli during the retention interval after presentation of the sample for a matching trial. In some studies with pigeons, for example, the sample and choice stimuli were various visual cues projected on pecking keys. As a test for retroactive interference, on some trials the house lights were turned on during the delay interval after presentation of the sample stimulus; on other trials, the pigeons spent the delay interval in darkness. Illumination of the house lights during the retention interval exposed the pigeons to various visual features of the experimental chamber after presentation of the sample and produced retroactive interference. The birds were much less likely to select the correct test stimulus after illumination of the house lights during the delay interval than if they spent the delay interval in darkness (Roberts & Grant, 1978; see also Grant, 1988).

In contrast to proactive interference, which results from remembering too much, retroactive interference seems to result from failure to retain required information during the delay interval. Presentation of extraneous stimuli during the delay interval disrupts the rehearsal processes that are required to effectively store information based on the sample, and that causes subjects to perform poorly during the memory test (Wright, Urcuioli, Sands, & Santiago, 1981). Thus, retroactive interference is caused by failure to adequately learn the information required for the memory test.

RETRIEVAL FAILURE

The studies of proactive and retroactive interference we have considered illustrate two different causes of poor performance in a memory task. Proactive interference caused by scheduling successive matching trials close together results from remembering too much. Information needed to respond correctly on a given trial is confused with information remembered from the preceding trial. In contrast, retroactive interference is caused by not remembering enough. Information needed to respond correctly is unavailable when the subject has to choose between the test stimuli because the information was not learned in the first place. Another common reason for poor performance on a memory task is that the subject is unable to effectively retrieve information that it previously learned.

If poor performance on a memory task is due to retrieval failure, then procedures that facilitate retrieval will facilitate performance. Retrieval of information is facilitated by presentation of stimuli that were previously associated with the target information. Such stimuli are called **retrieval cues.**

Remarkably insignificant features of the environment may become associated with a learning task and facilitate retrieval of information relevant to that task. In one study (Borovsky & Rovee-Collier, 1990), for example, 6-month-old infant babies received an instrumental conditioning procedure in their playpen at home. The experimental setup is illustrated in Figure 13.4.

Each infant was placed in a baby seat in the playpen with a mobile positioned above in plain view. The mobile was gently attached to one of the infant's feet with a satin ribbon. By moving its foot, the infant could

F I G U R E 13.4 Experimental situation used by Borovsky and Rovee-Collier (1990) to study the effects of retrieval cues on the memory of human infants for an instrumental conditioning task.
The instrumental response was moving a leg, and the reinforcer was consequent movement of a mobile located in the infant's view. (Courtesy of Susanna Douglas, Austin, Texas.)

make the mobile move. Thus, the instrumental response was a leg movement, and the reinforcer was movement of the mobile.

Infants readily learn the leg-movement task, but under certain circumstances they show substantial forgetting in as little as 24 hours. Does this rapid forgetting reflect a failure to effectively acquire or encode the instrumental contingency or failure to retrieve what was learned the day before? If the instrumental contingency was not learned effectively in the first place, nothing can counteract the poor performance that is evident 24 hours later. In contrast, if the forgetting is due to retrieval failure, then the presentation of retrieval or reminder cues should restore the performance.

What might be an effective retrieval cue for the infants in this situation? Borovsky and Rovee-Collier (1990) found that the pattern of the cloth liner that covered the sides of the playpen served as an effective retrieval cue for the instrumental response. Sometimes, the liner for the playpen had a striped pattern; on other occasions the liner had a square pattern. Infants for whom the striped patern was in the playpen during training responded better 24 hours later if they were tested with the striped liner than if they were tested with the square liner. The reverse results were obtained with infants for whom the other liner was used during original training.

The results of this experiment are remarkable because nothing was done to direct the attention of the infants to the cloth liners. The square and striped patterns were both familiar to the infants, and the patterns were not predictive of reinforcement. They served merely as background cues rather than discriminative stimuli. Nevertheless, the pattern present during original training became associated with the instrumental task and helped to retrieve information about the task during the memory test 24 hours later.

A variety of different stimuli have been found to be effective as retrieval cues in various learning situations, including exposure to a conditioned stimulus in extinction (Gordon & Mowrer, 1980), internal cues induced by psychoactive drugs (Spear, Smith, Bryan, Gordon, Timmons, & Chiszar, 1980), and exposure to the nonreinforced stimulus in a discrimination procedure (Campbell & Randall, 1976). In addition, retrieval cues have been found to counteract a variety of instances of failed memory including forgotten early life experiences (Richardson, Riccio, & Jonke, 1983) and amnesia caused by electroconvulsive shock (Gordon & Mowrer, 1980).

Suggested Readings

KENDRICK, D.F., RILLING, M.E., & DENNY, M.R. (Eds.). (1986). *Theories of animal memory*. Hillsdale, NJ: Erlbaum.

MILLER, R.R., KASPROW, W.J., & SCHACHTMAN, T.R. (1986). Retrieval variability: Sources and consequences. *American Journal of Psychology, 99,* 145–218.

SPEAR, N.E. & RICCIO, D.C. (1994). *Memory*. Boston: Allyn & Bacon.

Technical Terms

Delayed matching-to-sample	Retroactive interference
Matching-to-sample	Retrospective memory
Proactive interference	Simultaneous matching-to-sample
Prospective memory	Symbolic matching-to-sample
Reference memory	Trace-decay hypothesis
Retrieval cues	Working memory

GLOSSARY

Acquired drive   A source of motivation for instrumental behavior caused by the presentation of a stimulus that was previously conditioned with a primary, or unconditioned, reinforcer.

Afferent neuron   A neuron that transmits messages from sense organs to the central nervous system.

Appetitive behavior   The initial component of an elicited behavior sequence. Appetitive behavior is variable, occurs in response to general spatial cues, and serves to bring the organism in contact with releasing stimuli that elicit consummatory responses.

Appetitive conditioning   A type of conditioning in which the unconditioned stimulus or reinforcer is a pleasant event—a stimulus the subject tends to approach.

Associative learning   Learning in which one event (a stimulus or a response) becomes linked to another, with the result that the first event activates a representation of the second.

Autoshaping   Same as *sign-tracking*.

Aversive conditioning   A type of conditioning in which the unconditioned stimulus, or reinforcer, is an unpleasant event—a stimulus that elicits aversion and withdrawal responses.

Aversive stimulus   Noxious or unpleasant stimulus that elicits aversion and/or withdrawal responses.

Behavior   The observable actions of an organism.

Behavior system   A system of responses and corresponding behavioral and physiological control mechanisms that are coordinated to achieve particular functions such as feeding or defense against predation.

Behavioral bliss point   The optimal distribution of activities in the absence of constraints or limitations imposed by an instrumental conditioning procedure.

Behavioral regulation   A mechanism that focuses on the allocation or distribution of an animal's responses. It is assumed that animals work to maintain an optimal distribution of activities.

Blocking effect   Interference with the conditioning of a novel stimulus because of the presence of a previously conditioned stimulus.

Chained schedule   A schedule of reinforcement in which the primary reinforcer is delivered only after the subject has performed a sequence of responses, with each response performed in the presence of a different stimulus.

Compound stimulus test   A test procedure that identifies a stimulus as a conditioned inhibition if that stimulus reduces responding elicited by a conditioned excitatory stimulus.

Concurrent schedule   A reinforcement procedure in which the subject can choose one of two or more simple reinforcement schedules that are available simultaneously. Concurrent schedules allow for the measurement of choice between simple schedule alternatives.

Conditioned drive state   A drive state induced by the presentation of a stimulus that was previously conditioned with a primary, or unconditioned, reinforcer.

Conditioned inhibition   A type of Pavlovian conditioning in which the conditioned stimulus becomes a signal for the absence of the unconditioned stimulus.

Conditioned reinforcer   A stimulus that becomes an effective reinforcer because of its association with a primary, or unconditioned, reinforcer.

Conditioned response   A response that develops to the conditioned stimulus during the course of Pavlovian conditioning.

Conditioned stimulus   A stimulus that initially does not elicit a conditioned response or activate a representation of an unconditioned stimulus but comes to do so after pairings with an unconditioned stimulus.

Conditioned suppression   An aversive Pavlovian conditioning procedure in which conditioned responding is measured by the suppression of positively reinforced instrumental behavior.

Constraints on learning   A limitation on learning resulting from the evolutionary history of the organism.

Consummatory responses   Behavior that brings an elicited behavior sequence to an end; behavior that consummates a sequence of elicited responses.

Contingency   A measure of the extent to which two events are linked, or the extent to which the occurrence of one event depends on the other, and vice versa.

Control condition   A condition in which subjects do not receive a training procedure but are treated identically in all other respects to subjects that are trained. Performance in the control condition is compared to performance in the experimental condition in the basic learning experiment.

Cumulative record   A graphical representation of responding in which the horizontal axis represents the passage of time, and the vertical axis represents the total or cumulative number of responses that have occurred up to a particular point in time. Rate of responding is represented by the slope of the cumulative record.

CS-US interval   Same as *interstimulus interval*.

Delayed conditioning   A Pavlovian conditioning procedure in which the conditioned stimulus begins before the unconditioned stimulus on each trial.

Delayed matching to sample   A procedure in which subjects are reinforced for responding to a test stimulus that is the same as a previously presented sample stimulus.

Differential inhibition   A procedure in which on some trials a stimulus (the CS^+) is paired with the unconditioned stimulus and on other trials a different stimulus (the CS^-) is presented alone. As a result, the CS^+ comes to elicit a conditioned response and the CS^- comes to inhibit that response.

Differential probability principle   Same as the *Premack principle*.

Differential responding   Responding in different ways or at different rates in the presence of different stimuli.

Directed forgetting   Stimulus control of memory, achieved by presenting a cue indicating when subjects will, or will not, be required to remember something.

Discrete trial method   A method of instrumental conditioning in which the subject can perform the instrumental response only during specified periods, usually determined either by placement of the subject in an experimental chamber or by the presentation of a stimulus.

Discriminated avoidance   An avoidance conditioning procedure in which the occurrence of an aversive unconditioned stimulus is signaled by a conditioned stimulus or warning signal. Responding during the conditioned stimulus terminates that stimulus and prevents the delivery of the aversive unconditioned stimulus.

Discrimination control   A control procedure for Pavlovian conditioning in which one conditioned stimulus (the CS^+) is paired with the unconditioned stimulus whereas another conditioned stimulus (the CS^-) is presented without the unconditioned stimulus. The development of responding during the CS^+ but not during the CS^- is considered evidence of Pavlovian conditioning.

Discrimination hypothesis   An explanation of the partial reinforcement extinction effect, according to which extinction is slower after partial reinforcement than after continuous reinforcement because the onset of extinction is more difficult to detect following partial reinforcement.

Discriminative punishment   A type of punishment procedure in which responses are punished in the presence of a discriminative stimulus but not when the discriminative stimulus is absent.

Dishabituation   Recovery of a habituated response as a result of presentation of a strong extraneous stimulus.

Disinhibition   Recovery of a partly extinguished conditioned response as a result of presentation of a novel stimulus.

Drive reduction theory   A theory of reinforcement according to which reinforcers are effective because they reduce the subject's drive state and return the subject to homeostasis.

Drive state   A motivational state that exists when a system is not at its homeostatic level. Return of the system to its homeostatic level reduces the drive state.

Efferent neuron   A neuron that transmits impulses from the central nervous system to muscles.

Elicited behavior   A specific behavior or action pattern that occurs reliably upon presentation of a particular stimulus (its eliciting stimulus).

Equipotentiality   The idea that the rate of learning is independent of the combination of conditioned and unconditioned stimuli that are used in Pavlovian conditioning.

Ethology   A specialization in biology concerned with the evolution and development of behavior.

Experimental condition   A condition in which subjects receive a training procedure. Performance in the experimental condition is compared to performance in the control condition in the basic learning experiment.

Experimental observation   Observation of behavior under conditions specifically designed by an investigator to test particular factors or variables that might influence the learning or performance of the behavior.

External inhibition   Same as *disinhibition*.

Extinction   See *Extinction effect* and *Extinction procedure*.

Extinction effect   Reduction of a learned response that occurs because the conditioned stimulus is no longer paired with the unconditioned stimulus (in classical conditioning) or because the response is no longer reinforced (in instrumental conditioning).

Extinction procedure   The procedure of repeatedly presenting a conditioned stimulus without the unconditioned stimulus or no longer providing reinforcement for an instrumental response.

Facilitation   A Pavlovian conditioning procedure in which a conditioned stimulus is presented on trials when a second stimulus is paired with a US but not on trials when the second stimulus is presented alone. In such a procedure, one cue designates when another cue will be reinforced.

Fatigue   A temporary decrease in behavior caused by repeated or excessive use of the muscles involved in the behavior.

Feedback cue   A stimulus that results from the performance of a response.

Feedback function   The relation between rates of responding and rates of reinforcement allowed by a particular reinforcement schedule.

Fixed interval schedule   A reinforcement schedule in which reinforcement is delivered for the first response that occurs after a fixed amount of time following the last reinforcer.

Fixed ratio schedule   A reinforcement schedule in which a fixed number of responses must occur in order for the next response to be reinforced.

Flavor neophobia   An aversion based on the unfamiliarity of the flavor of a new food.

Focal search mode   A response mode in the feeding system that is activated once a potential source of food has been identified.

Food handling and consumption mode   A response mode in the feeding system that is activated once the animal has come in contact with a food item.

Free-operant avoidance   Same as *nondiscriminated avoidance*.

Free-operant method   A method of instrumental conditioning that permits repeated performance of the instrumental response, in contrast to the discrete trial method.

Frustration   An aversive emotional reaction that results from the unexpected absence of reinforcement.

Frustration theory   A theory of the partial reinforcement extinction effect, according to which extinction is retarded after partial reinforcement because the instrumental response becomes conditioned to the anticipation of frustrative nonreward.

General search mode   The initial response mode of the feeding system. In this mode, the organism reacts to general features of the environment with responses that enable it to come in contact with a variety of potential sources of food.

Habituation effect   A progressive decrease in the vigor of an elicited response that may occur with repeated presentations of the eliciting stimulus.

Habituation of dishabituation   The decrement in the magnitude of a dishabituation effect that results from repeated presentations of the dishabituating stimulus.

Higher-order stimulus relation   A relation in which a stimulus signals a relationship between two other stimuli rather than signaling just the presence or absence of another stimulus. In a higher-order Pavlovian relation, one CS signals whether or not another CS is paired with a US.

Homeostasis   The processes responsible for maintaining the homeostatic level of a system.

Homeostatic level   The optimal or defended level of a physiological or behavioral system.

Hydraulic model   A model proposed by ethologists, according to which certain factors lead to the buildup of a particular type of motivation or drive that increases the likelihood of corresponding modal action patterns. Performance of the modal action patterns reduces or discharges the motivational state.

Instrumental behavior   An activity that is effective in producing a particular consequence or reinforcer.

Interdimensional discrimination A discrimination between two stimuli that differ in several respects.

Interneuron A neuron in the spinal cord that transmits impulses from afferent (or sensory) to efferent (or motor) neurons.

Interstimulus interval The interval in a Pavlovian conditioning procedure between the start of the conditioned stimulus and the start of the unconditioned stimulus.

Interval schedule A reinforcement schedule in which a response is reinforced only if it occurs more than a set amount of time after the last delivery of the reinforcer.

Intradimensional discrimination A discrimination between stimuli that differ in only one stimulus characteristic, such as color, brightness, or pitch.

Law of Effect A rule for instrumental behavior proposed by Thorndike, according to which reinforcement of an instrumental response strengthens the association between the response and the stimulus in the presence of which the response occurred.

Learning An enduring change in the mechanisms of behavior involving specific stimuli and/or responses that results from prior experience with those stimuli and responses.

Long-delay learning A classical conditioning procedure in which the conditioned stimulus is presented long before the unconditioned stimulus on each conditioning trial.

Long-term habituation A type of habituation that results in a response decrement that lasts for a week or more.

Marking stimulus A brief visual or auditory cue presented after an instrumental response that makes the instrumental response more memorable and helps overcome the deleterious effect of delayed reinforcement.

Matching law A rule for instrumental behavior proposed by Herrnstein, according to which the relative rate of response on a particular response alternative equals the relative rate of reinforcement for that response alternative.

Matching to sample A procedure in which subjects are reinforced for selecting a stimulus that corresponds to the sample presented on that trial.

Maturation A change in behavior caused by physical or physiological development.

Memory A theoretical term used to characterize instances in which behavior at one point in time is determined by some aspect of experience at an earlier point in time.

Memory retrieval The recovery of information from a memory store.

Modal action pattern A response pattern that occurs in much the same fashion most of the time and in most members of a species. Modal action patterns are often used as basic units of behavior in ethological investigations of behavior.

Motivation   A hypothetical state that increases the probability of a coordinated set of activities or activates a system of behavior that functions to satisfy a goal such as feeding, predatory defense, infant care, or copulation.

Motor neuron   Same as *efferent neuron*.

Multiple schedule of reinforcement   A procedure in which different reinforcement schedules are in effect in the presence of different stimuli presented in succession. Generally, each stimulus comes to evoke a pattern of responding that corresponds to whatever reinforcement schedule is in effect in the presence of that stimulus.

Naturalistic observation   Observation of behavior as it occurs under natural conditions, in the absence of interventions or manipulations introduced by the investigator.

Negative reinforcement   An instrumental conditioning procedure in which there is a negative contingency between the instrumental response and an aversive stimulus. If the instrumental response is performed, the aversive stimulus is terminated or prevented from occurring; if the instrumental response is not performed, the aversive stimulus is presented.

Negative reinforcer   Same as *aversive stimulus*.

Nondiscriminated avoidance   An avoidance-conditioning procedure in which the aversive stimulus is not signaled by an external warning signal. In the absence of avoidance behavior, the aversive stimulus occurs periodically, as determined by the S-S interval. Each occurrence of the avoidance response starts over again after a certain amount of time without aversive stimulation, as determined by the R-S interval.

Occasion setting   Same as *facilitation*.

One-way avoidance   An avoidance conditioning procedure in which the required instrumental response is always to cross from one compartment of a shuttle box to the other in the same direction.

Operant behavior   Behavior that is defined by the effect it produces in the environment. Examples include pressing a lever and opening a door. Any sequence of movements that depresses the lever or opens the door constitutes an instance of that particular operant.

Opponent process   A compensatory mechanism that ensures that deviations of a system from a preferred or homeostatic level are counteracted so as to return the system to its preferred level.

Orienting response   Movement that brings a sensory receptor in better alignment with the source of a stimulus.

Outcome   Same as *reinforcer*.

Overshadowing   Interference with the conditioning of a stimulus because of the simultaneous presence of another stimulus that is easier to condition.

Partial reinforcement extinction effect   More persistent performance of an instrumental response in extinction after partial (intermittent) reinforcement training than after continuous reinforcement training.

Performance   An organism's activities at a particular time.

Persistence   The continued performance of an instrumental response after an extinction procedure has been introduced.

Positive occasion setting   Same as *facilitation*.

Postreinforcement pause   A pause in responding that typically occurs after the delivery of the reinforcer on fixed ratio and fixed interval schedules of reinforcement.

Predatory imminence   The perceived likelihood of being attacked by a predator. Different species' typical defense responses are assumed to be performed in the face of different degrees of predatory imminence.

Premack principle   Given two responses with different baseline probabilities of occurrence, the opportunity to perform the higher-probability response will reinforce or increase performance of the lower-probability behavior.

Primary reinforcer   A reinforcer that is effective without prior conditioning.

Proactive interference   Disruption of memory by exposure to stimuli before the event to be remembered.

Proprioceptive cue   An internal response feedback stimulus that arises from the movement of muscles and/or joints.

Prospective memory   Memory of a plan for future action. Also called *prospection*.

Punishment   A type of instrumental conditioning procedure in which occurrence of the instrumental response results in delivery of an aversive stimulus.

Puzzle box   A type of experimental chamber used by Thorndike to study instrumental conditioning. The subject was put in the chamber and had to perform a specified behavior to be released from it.

R-S interval   The interval between the occurrence of an avoidance response and the next scheduled presentation of the aversive stimulus in a nondiscriminated avoidance procedure.

R-S* association   An association between the instrumental response (R) and the reinforcer (S*).

Random control   A control procedure for Pavlovian conditioning in which the conditioned and unconditioned stimuli are presented at random times relative to each other.

Rate of extinction   How fast responding declines when an extinction procedure is in effect.

Rate of responding   A measure of how often a response is repeated in a unit of time—for example, the number of responses that occur per hour.

Ratio run   The high and invariant rate of responding observed after the postreinforcement pause on fixed ratio reinforcement schedules. The ratio run ends when the necessary number of responses has been performed and the subject is reinforced.

Ratio schedule   A reinforcement schedule in which reinforcement depends only on the number of responses the subject performs, irrespective of when these responses occur.

Reference memory   The retention of background information a subject needs to respond successfully in a situation. (Compare with *working memory*.)

Reflex   A unit of elicited behavior involving a specific environmental event and its corresponding specific elicited response.

Reflex arc   Neural structures, consisting of the afferent (sensory) neuron, interneuron, and efferent (motor) neuron, that enable a stimulus to elicit a reflex response.

Rehearsal   A theoretical process whereby some information is maintained in an active state, available to guide behavior and/or the processing of other information.

Reinforcer   A stimulus whose delivery shortly following a response increases the future probability of that response (also called *outcome*).

Releasing stimulus   Same as *sign stimulus*.

Reminder treatment   The presentation of a retrieval cue that activates a memory or facilitates memory retrieval.

Renewal effect   Recovery of responding when subjects are returned to the training context after receiving an extinction procedure in a distinctively different environment.

Response deprivation hypothesis   An explanation of reinforcement, according to which reduced access to a particular response is sufficient to make the opportunity to perform that response an effective positive reinforcer.

Response reserve   The idea that reinforcement of instrumental behavior leads to the buildup of response strength, which is then used up in extinction.

Retardation-of-acquisition test   A test procedure that identifies a stimulus as a conditioned inhibitor if that stimulus is slower to acquire conditioned excitatory properties than a comparison stimulus.

Retention interval   The period of time between acquisition of information and a test of memory for that information.

Retrieval cue   A stimulus related to an experience that facilitates the recall of other information related to that experience.

Retrieval failure   A deficit in recovering information from a memory store.

Retroactive interference   Disruption of memory by exposure to stimuli following the event to be remembered.

Retrospection   Same as *retrospective memory*.

Retrospective memory   Memory for a previously experienced event.

S(R-S*) association   A higher-order relation in instrumental conditioning situations, according to which a discriminative or contextual stimulus (S) activates an association between the instrumental response and the reinforcer (R-S*).

S⁺   A discriminative stimulus that signals the availability of reinforcement for an instrumental response.

S⁻   A discriminative stimulus that signals the absence of reinforcement for an instrumental response.

S-R association   The learning of an association between a stimulus and a response, with the result that the stimulus comes to elicit the response.

S-R learning   The learning of an association between a stimulus and a response, with the result that the stimulus comes to elicit the response.

S-R system   The shortest neural pathway that connects the sense organs stimulated by an eliciting stimulus and the muscles involved in making the elicited response.

S-S interval   The interval between successive presentations of the aversive stimulus in a nondiscriminated avoidance procedure when the avoidance response is not performed.

S-S learning   The learning of an association between two stimuli, with the result that presentation of the first stimulus activates a representation or "mental image" of the second.

S-S* association   An association between a stimulus (S) in the presence of which an instrumental response is reinforced and the reinforcer (S*).

Safety signal   A stimulus that signals the absence of an aversive event.

Schedule line   A line on a graph of different rates of instrumental and reinforcer behavior indicating how much access to the reinforcer activity is provided for various rates of instrumental responding on a particular schedule of reinforcement.

Schedule of reinforcement   A program or rule that specifies which occurrence of the instrumental response results in delivery of the reinforcer.

Secondary reinforcer   Same as *conditioned reinforcer*.

Selective associations   Associations that are formed more readily between one combination of conditioned and unconditioned stimuli than between other combinations.

Sensitization effect   An increase in the vigor of elicited behavior that may result from repeated presentations of the eliciting stimulus.

Sensory neuron   Same as *afferent neuron*.

Sensory reinforcement   Reinforcement provided by presentation of stimuli unrelated to a biological need or drive.

Sequential theory   A theory of the partial reinforcement extinction effect, according to which extinction is retarded after partial reinforcement because the instrumental response becomes conditioned to the memory of nonreward.

Shaping   Reinforcement of successive approximations to a target instrumental response, typically used to condition responses that are not in the subject's existing repertoire of behavior.

Short-term habituation   A habituation effect that lasts a relatively short period of time, sometimes less than a minute.

Short-term sensitization   A sensitization effect that lasts a relatively short period of time, sometimes less than a minute.

Shuttle box   An apparatus for the study of avoidance behavior consisting of two compartments connected end-to-end. The avoidance response involves moving from one compartment to the other (shuttling between the compartments).

Sign stimulus   A specific feature of an object or animal that elicits a modal action pattern.

Sign-tracking   A form of appetitive Pavlovian conditioning in which a localized stimulus serves as the conditioned stimulus. As a result, the subject comes to approach (track) and sometimes manipulate the conditioned stimulus.

Simultaneous conditioning   A Pavlovian conditioning procedure in which the conditioned stimulus and the unconditioned stimulus are presented simultaneously on each conditioning trial.

Simultaneous matching-to-sample   A procedure in which subjects are reinforced for responding to a test stimulus that is the same as a sample stimulus. The sample and the test stimuli are presented at the same time.

Single-subject experiment   A type of experiment in which learning is investigated through extensive observations of the behavior of a single individual. The individual's behavior has to be sufficiently well understood to permit accurate assumptions about how the subject would have behaved without the training procedure.

Skinner box   A small experimental chamber provided with something the subject can manipulate repeatedly, such as a response lever. This allows a subject to perform a particular response repeatedly without being removed from the experimental situation. The chamber usually also has a mechanism that can deliver a reinforcer, such as a pellet of food.

Species-specific defense responses   Species-typical responses animals perform in aversive situations. The responses may involve freezing, fleeing, or fighting.

Species-typical behavior   Behavior that is characteristic of most members of a species.

Spontaneous recovery   Recovery of a response produced by a period of rest after habituation or extinction.

SSDR   Abbreviation for species-specific defense response.

Startle response   A sudden jump or tensing of the muscles that may occur when an unexpected stimulus is presented.

State system   Neural structures that determine the organism's general level of responsiveness or readiness to respond.

Stimulus   An event external or internal to the organism that activates sensory neurons and may elicit or cue behavior.

Stimulus dimension   The feature (color, for example) that distinguishes a series of stimuli in a test of stimulus generalization.

Stimulus discrimination   Differential responding in the presence of two or more stimuli.

Stimulus discrimination training (in classical conditioning)   One conditioned stimulus (the CS^+) is paired with an unconditioned stimulus, whereas another conditioned stimulus (the CS^-) is presented without an unconditioned stimulus.

Stimulus discrimination training (in instrumental conditioning)   A procedure in which reinforcement for responding is available whenever one stimulus (the S^+) is present and is not available whenever another stimulus (the S^-)is present.

Stimulus generalization   The occurrence of behavior in the presence of stimuli that are different from the stimulus used during training.

Stimulus generalization gradient   A gradient of responding that may be observed if subjects are tested with stimuli that increasingly differ from the stimulus that was present during training.

Stimulus generalization of habituation   (See *stimulus generalization*.)

Stimulus learning   The learning of an association between two stimuli such that presentation of one of the stimuli activates a neural representation of the other.

Straight-alley runway   A straight alley with a start box at one end and a goal box at the other. Animals are placed in the start box at the start of a trial and allowed to run to the goal box.

Summation test   Same as *compound stimulus test*.

Symbolic matching-to-sample   A matching-to-sample procedure in which the correct test stimulus is physically different from the sample stimulus.

Taste aversion learning   A type of Pavlovian conditioning in which the taste of a novel food serves as the conditioned stimulus and gastrointestinal illness serves as the unconditioned stimulus. Taste aversions can be learned even if the illness is delayed several hours after exposure to the taste.

Temporal contiguity   The simultaneous occurrence of two or more events.

Temporal cues   Stimuli related to the passage of time.

Trace conditioning   A classical conditioning procedure in which the unconditioned stimulus is presented on each trial after the conditioned stimulus has been terminated for a short period.

Trace interval   The time from the end of the conditioned stimulus to the start of the unconditioned stimulus in a trace conditioning procedure.

Trace-decay hypothesis   The idea that exposure to a stimulus produces changes in the nervous system that gradually decrease after the stimulus has been terminated.

Trials-unique procedure   A matching-to-sample procedure in which a different stimulus serves as the sample on each trial.

Two-factor theory   A theory of avoidance learning involving two forms of conditioning: (1) Pavlovian conditioning of fear to a stimulus that signals aversive stimulation and (2) instrumental conditioning of the avoidance response by fear reduction.

Two-way avoidance   A shuttle avoidance procedure in which trials can start in either compartment of a shuttle box, and the avoidance response consists of going from the occupied compartment to the unoccupied compartment.

Unconditioned response   A response that occurs to a stimulus without the necessity of any conditioning.

Unconditioned stimulus   A stimulus that elicits vigorous responding in the absence of prior training.

US devaluation   A procedure that reduces the effectiveness of an unconditioned stimulus to elicit unconditioned behavior.

US inflation   A procedure that increases the effectiveness of an unconditioned stimulus to elicit unconditioned behavior.

Variable interval schedule   A reinforcement schedule in which reinforcement is provided for the first response that occurs after a variable amount of time from the last reinforcement.

Variable ratio schedule   A reinforcement schedule in which the number of responses necessary to obtain reinforcement varies from trial to trial. The value of the schedule refers to the average number of responses needed for reinforcement.

Warning stimulus or warning signal   The stimulus in a discriminated avoidance procedure that reliably precedes scheduled presentations of the aversive unconditioned stimulus.

Working memory   The retention of information that is needed only to accomplish the task at hand, as contrasted with reference memory, which involves background information that is also needed for future, similar tasks.

REFERENCES

ALCOCK, J. (1993). *Animal behavior* (5th ed.). Sunderland, MA: Sinauer.

ALLISON, J. (1983). *Behavioral economics.* New York: Praeger.

ALLISON, J. (1989). The nature of reinforcement. In S. B. Klein & R. R. Mowrer (Eds.), *Contemporary learning theories: Instrumental conditioning theory and the impact of biological constraints on learning* (pp. 13–39). Hillsdale, NJ: Erlbaum.

ALLISON, J., & TIMBERLAKE, W. (1974). Instrumental and contingent saccharin-licking in rats: Response deprivation and reinforcement. *Learning and Motivation, 5,* 231–247.

AMSEL, A. (1958). The role of frustrative nonreward in noncontinuous reward situations. *Psychological Bulletin, 55,* 102–119.

AMSEL, A. (1967). Partial reinforcement effects on vigor and persistence. In K. W. Spence & J. T. Spence (Eds.), *The psychology of learning and motivation* (Vol. 1, pp. 1–65). Orlando, FL: Academic Press.

AMSEL, A., & RASHOTTE, M. E. (1984). *Mechanisms of adaptive behavior: Clark L. Hull's theoretical papers, with commentary.* New York: Columbia University Press.

AMSEL, A. (1992). *Frustration theory: An analysis of dispositional learning and memory.* Cambridge, UK: Cambridge University Press.

ANGER, D. (1963). The role of temporal discrimination in the reinforcement of Sidman avoidance behavior. *Journal of the Experimental Analysis of Behavior, 6,* 477–506.

AZRIN, N. H. (1959). Punishment and recovery during fixed-ratio performance. *Journal of the Experimental Analysis of Behavior, 2,* 301–305.

AZRIN, N. H. (1960). Effects of punishment intensity during variable-interval reinforcement. *Journal of the Experimental Analysis of Behavior, 3,* 123–142.

AZRIN, N. H., & HOLZ, W. C. (1966). Punishment. In W. K. Honig (Ed.), *Operant behavior: Areas of research and application* (pp. 380–447). New York: Appleton-Century-Crofts.

AZRIN, N. H., HOLZ, W. C., & HAKE, D. F. (1963). Fixed-ratio punishment. *Journal of the Experimental Analysis of Behavior, 6,* 141–148.

BABKIN, B. P. (1949). *Pavlov: A biography.* Chicago: University of Chicago Press.

BAERENDS, G. P. (1988). Ethology. In R. C. Atkinson, R. J. Herrnstein, G. Lindzey, & R. D. Luce (Eds.), *Stevens' handbook of experimental psychology* (Vol. 1, pp. 765–830). New York: Wiley.

BALSAM, P. D. (1988). Selection, representation, and equivalence of controlling stimuli. In R. C. Atkinson, R. J. Herrnstein, G. Lindzey, & R. D. Luce (Eds.), *Stevens' handbook of experimental psychology* (Vol. 2, pp. 111–166). New York: Wiley.

BALSAM, P. D., & TOMIE, A. (1985). *Context and learning.* Hillsdale, NJ: Erlbaum.

BARON, A., & MENICH, S. R. (1985). Reaction times of younger and older men: Effects of compound samples and a prechoice signal on delayed matching-to-sample performance. *Journal of the Experimental Analysis of Behavior, 44,* 1–4.

BECHTEREV, V. M. (1913). *La psychologie objective.* Paris: Alcan.

BENEDICT, J. O., & AYRES, J. J. B. (1972). Factors affecting conditioning in the truly random control procedure in the rat. *Journal of Comparative and Physiological Psychology, 78,* 323–330.

BERLYNE, D. E. (1969). The reward value of indifferent stimulation. In J. Tapp (Ed.), *Reinforcement and behavior* (pp. 179–214). New York: Academic Press.

BEST, M. R., BATSON, J. D., MEACHUM, C. L., BROWN, E. R., & RINGER, M. (1985). Characteristics of taste-mediated environmental potentiation in rats. *Learning and Motivation, 16,* 190–209.

BITTERMAN, M. E. (1964). Classical conditioning in the gold fish as a function of the CS-US interval. *Journal of Comparative and Physiological Psychology, 58,* 359–366.

BITTERMAN, M. E. (1975). The comparative analysis of learning. *Science, 188,* 699–709.

BOAKES, R. (1984). *From Darwin to behaviorism: Psychology and the minds of animals.* Cambridge, England: Cambridge University Press.

BOAKES, R. A. (1979). Interactions between type I and type II processes involving positive reinforcement. In A. Dickinson & R. A. Boakes (Eds.), *Mechanisms of learning and motivation* (pp. 233–268). Hillsdale, NJ: Erlbaum.

BOAKES, R. A., POLI, M., LOCKWOOD, M. J., & GOODALL, G. (1978). A study of misbehavior: Token reinforcement in the rat. *Journal of the Experimental Analysis of Behavior, 29,* 115–134.

BOLLES, R. C. (1970). Species-specific defense reactions and avoidance learning. *Psychological Review, 71,* 32–48.

BOLLES, R. C. (1972a). Reinforcement, expectancy, and learning. *Psychological Review, 79,* 394–409.

BOLLES, R. C. (1972b). The avoidance learning problem. In G. H. Bower (Ed.), *The psychology of learning and motivation* (Vol. 6, pp. 97–145). Orlando, FL: Academic Press.

BOLLES, R. C., & RILEY, A. L. (1973). Freezing as an avoidance response: Another look at the operant-respondent distinction. *Learning and Motivation, 4,* 268–275.

BOROVSKY, D., & ROVEE-COLLIER, C. (1990). Contextual constraints on memory retrieval at six months. *Child Development, 61*, 1569–1583.

BOUTON, M. E. (1986). Slow reacquisition following the extinction of conditioned suppression. *Learning and Motivation, 17*, 1–15.

BOUTON, M. E. (1993). Context, time, and memory retrieval in the interference paradigms of Pavlovian learning. *Psychological Bulletin, 114*, 80–99.

BOUTON, M. E., & BOLLES, R. C. (1980). Conditioned fear assessed by freezing and by the suppression of three different baselines. *Animal Learning & Behavior, 8*, 429–434.

BOUTON, M. E., & SWARTZENTRUBER, D. (1989). Slow reacquisition following extinction: Context, encoding, and retrieval mechanisms. *Journal of Experimental Psychology: Animal Behavior Processes, 15*, 43–53.

BOUTON, M. E., & SWARTZENTRUBER, D. (1991). Sources of relapse after extinction in Pavlovian and instrumental learning. *Clinical Psychology Review, 11*, 123–140.

BOWER, G. H., & HILGARD, E. R. (1981). *Theories of learning* (5th ed.). Englewood Cliffs, NJ: Prentice-Hall.

BRAVEMAN, N. S., & BRONSTEIN, P. (Eds.). (1985). *Annals of the New York Academy of Sciences: Vol. 443: Experimental assessments and clinical applications of conditioned food aversions*. New York: New York Academy of Sciences.

BRELAND, K., & BRELAND, M. (1961). The misbehavior of organisms. *American Psychologist, 16*, 681–684.

BROGDEN, W. J., LIPMAN, E. A., & CULLER, E. (1938). The role of incentive in conditioning and extinction. *American Journal of Psychology, 51*, 109–117.

BROOKS, D. C., & BOUTON, M. E. (1993). A retrieval cue for extinction attenuates spontaneous recovery. *Journal of Experimental Psychology: Animal Behavior Processes, 19*, 77–89.

BURKHARD, B., RACHLIN, H., & SCHRADER, S. (1978). Reinforcement and punishment in a closed system. *Learning and Motivation, 9*, 392–410.

CAMP, D. S., RAYMOND, G. A., & CHURCH, R. M. (1967). Temporal relationship between response and punishment. *Journal of Experimental Psychology, 74*, 114–123.

CAMPBELL, B. A., & RANDALL, P. K. (1976). The effect of reinstatement stimulus conditions on the maintenance of long-term memory. *Developmental Psychobiology, 9*, 325–333.

CAPALDI, E. J. (1967). A sequential hypothesis of instrumental learning. In K. W. Spence & J. T. Spence (Eds.), *The psychology of learning and motivation* (Vol. 1, pp. 67–156). Orlando, FL: Academic Press.

CAPALDI, E. J. (1971). Memory and learning: A sequential viewpoint. In W. K. Honig & P.H.R. James (Eds.), *Animal memory* (pp. 115–154). Orlando, FL: Academic Press.

CHARLOP, M. H., KURTZ, P. F., & CASEY, F. G. (1990). Using aberrant behaviors as reinforcers for autistic children. *Journal of Applied Behavior Analysis, 23*, 163–181.

CHURCH, R. M. (1964). Systematic effect of the random error in the yoked control design. *Psychological Bulletin, 62*, 122–131.

CHURCH, R. M. (1969). Response suppression. In B. A. Campbell & R. M. Church (Eds.), *Punishment and aversive behavior* (pp. 111–156). New York: Appleton-Century-Crofts.

CHURCH, R. M., & RAYMOND, G. A. (1967). Influence of the schedule of positive reinforcement on punished behavior. *Journal of Comparative and Physiological Psychology, 63*, 329–332.

COHEN, L. B. (1988). An information processing view of infant cognitive development. In L. Weiskrantz (Ed.), *Thought without language* (pp. 211–228). Oxford: Oxford University Press.

COLWILL, R. M., & RESCORLA, R. A. (1986). Associative structures in instrumental learning. In G. H. Bower (Ed.), *The psychology of learning and motivation* (Vol. 20, pp. 55–104). Orlando, FL: Academic Press.

COLWILL, R. M., & RESCORLA, R. A. (1990). Evidence for the hierarchical structure of instrumental learning. *Animal Learning & Behavior, 18*, 71–82.

COOK, R.G., BROWN, M.F., & RILEY, D. A. (1985). Flexible memory processing by rats: Use of prospective and retrospective information in the radial maze. *Journal of Experimental Psychology: Animal Behavior Processes, 11*, 453–469.

D'AMATO, M.R. (1973). Delayed matching and short-term memory in monkeys. In G. H. Bower (Ed.), *The psychology of learning and motivation* (Vol. 7, pp. 227–269). Orlando: Academic Press.

D'AMATO, M. R., FAZZARO, J., & ETKIN, M. (1968). Anticipatory responding and avoidance discrimination as factors in avoidance conditioning. *Journal of Comparative and Physiological Psychology, 77*, 41–47.

DARDANO, J. F., & SAUERBRUNN, D. (1964). An aversive stimulus as a correlated block counter in FR performance. *Journal of the Experimental Analysis of Behavior, 7*, 37–43.

DAVIS, M. (1970). Effects of interstimulus interval length and variability on startle-response habituation in the rat. *Journal of Comparative and Physiological Psychology, 72*, 177–192.

DAVIS, M. (1974). Sensitization of the rat startle response by noise. *Journal of Comparative and Physiological Psychology, 87*, 571–581.

DAVIS, M., HITCHCOCK, J. M., & ROSEN, J. B. (1987). Anxiety and the amygdala: Pharmacological and anatomical analysis of the fear-potentiated startle paradigm. In G. H. Bower (Ed.), *The psychology of learning and motivation* (Vol. 21, pp. 263–304). San Diego, CA: Academic Press.

DAVISON, M., & McCARTHY, D. (1988). *The matching law: A research review.* Hillsdale, NJ: Erlbaum.

DEAN, S. J., & PITTMAN, C. M. (1991). Self-punitive behavior: A revised analysis. In M. R. Denny (Ed.), *Fear, avoidance, and phobias* (pp. 259–284). Hillsdale, NJ: Erlbaum.

DEICH, J. D., ALLAN, R. W., & ZEIGLER, H. P. (1988). Conjunctive differentiation of gape during food reinforced keypecking in the pigeon. *Animal Learning & Behavior, 16*, 268–276.

DINSMOOR, J. A. (1952). A discrimination based on punishment. *Quarterly Journal of Experimental Psychology, 4*, 27–45.

DINSMOOR, J. A. (1977). Escape, avoidance, punishment: Where do we stand? *Journal of the Experimental Analysis of Behavior, 28*, 83–95.

DOMJAN, M. (1976). Determinants of the enhancement of flavored-water intake by prior exposure. *Journal of Experimental Psychology: Animal Behavior Processes, 2*, 17–27.

DOMJAN, M. (1977). Attenuation and enhancement of neophobia for edible substances. In L. M. Barker, M. R. Best, & M. Domjan (Eds.), *Learning mechanisms in food selection* (pp. 151–179). Waco, TX: Baylor University Press.

DOMJAN, M. (1985). Cue-consequence specificity and long-delay learning revisited. *Annals of the New York Academy of Sciences, 443*, 54–66.

DOMJAN, M. (1994). Formulation of a behavior system for sexual conditioning. *Psychonomic Bulletin & Review, 1*, 421–428.

DOMJAN, M. (1993). The principles of learning and behavior (3rd ed.). Pacific Grove, CA: Brooks/Cole.

DOMJAN, M., & GILLAN, D. (1976). Role of novelty in the aversion for increasingly concentrated saccharin solutions. *Physiology & Behavior, 16*, 537–542.

DOMJAN, M., & NASH, S. (1988). Stimulus control of social behaviour in male Japanese quail, *Coturnix coturnix japonica. Animal Behaviour, 36*, 1006–1015.

DOMJAN, M., & WILSON, N. E. (1972). Specificity of cue to consequence in aversion learning in the rat. *Psychonomic Science, 26*, 143–145.

EDHOUSE, W. V., & WHITE, K. G. (1988). Cumulative proactive interference in animal memory. *Animal Learning & Behavior, 16*, 461–467.

EISENBERGER, R., KARPMAN, M., & TRATTNER, J. (1967). What is the necessary and sufficient condition for reinforcement in the contingency situation? *Journal of Experimental Psychology, 74*, 342–350.

ESTES, W. K., & SKINNER, B. F. (1941). Some quantitative properties of anxiety. *Journal of Experimental Psychology, 29*, 390–400.

FANSELOW, M. S. (1989). The adaptive function of conditioned defensive behavior: An ecological approach to Pavlovian stimulus-substitution theory. In R. J. Blanchard, P. F. Brain, D. C. Blanchard, & S. Parmigiani (Eds.), *Ethoexperimental approaches to the study of behavior.* (NATO ASI Series D., Vol. 48, pp. 151–166). Boston: Kluver Academic Publishers.

FANSELOW, M. S. (1994). Neural organization of the defensive behavior system responsible for fear. *Psychonomic Bulletin & Review, 1*, 429–438.

FANSELOW, M. S., & LESTER, L. S. (1988). A functional behavioristic approach to aversively motivated behavior: Predatory imminence as a determinant of the topography of defensive behavior. In R. C. Bolles & M. D. Beecher (Eds.), *Evolution and learning* (pp. 185–212). Hillsdale, NJ: Erlbaum.

FANSELOW, M. S., LESTER, L. S., & HELMSTETTER, F. J. (1988). Changes in feeding and foraging patterns as an antipredator defensive strategy: A laboratory simulation using aversive stimulation in a closed economy. *Journal of the Experimental Analysis of Behavior, 50,* 361–374.

FELTON, M., & LYON, D. O. (1966). The post-reinforcement pause. *Journal of the Experimental Analysis of Behavior, 9,* 131–134.

FERSTER, C. B., & PERROTT, M. C. (1968). Behavior principles. New York: Appleton-Century-Crofts.

FERSTER, C. B., & SKINNER, B. F. (1957). *Schedules of reinforcement.* New York: Appleton-Century-Crofts.

FOREE, D. D., & LoLORDO, V. M. (1973). Attention in the pigeon: The differential effects of food-getting vs. shock avoidance procedures. *Journal of Comparative and Physiological Psychology, 85,* 551–558.

FORESTELL, P. H., & HERMAN, L. M. (1988). Delayed matching of visual materials by a bottlenosed dolphin aided by auditory symbols. *Animal Learning & Behavior, 16,* 137–146.

FUDIM, O. K. (1978). Sensory preconditioning of flavors with a formalin-produced sodium need. *Journal of Experimental Psychology: Animal Behavior Processes, 4,* 276–285.

GALBICKA, G. (1988). Differentiating the behavior of organisms. *Journal of the Experimental Analysis of Behavior, 50,* 343–354.

GARCIA, J., & KOELLING, R. A. (1966). Relation of cue to consequence in avoidance learning. *Psychonomic Science, 4,* 123–124.

GARCIA, J., ERVIN, F. R., & KOELLING, R. A. (1966). Learning with prolonged delay of reinforcement. *Psychonomic Science, 5,* 121–122.

GOODALL, G. (1984). Learning due to the response-shock contingency in signalled punishment. *Quarterly Journal of Experimental Psychology, 36B,* 259–279.

GORDON, W. C., & MOWRER, R. R. (1980). An extinction trial as a reminder treatment following electroconvulsive shock. *Animal Learning & Behavior, 8,* 363–367.

GORMEZANO, I., KEHOE, E. J., & MARSHALL, B. S. (1983). Twenty years of classical conditioning research with the rabbit. In J. M. Prague & A. N. Epstein (Eds.), *Progress in psychobiology and physiological psychology* (Vol. 10, pp. 197–275). Orlando, FL: Academic Press.

GRANT, D. S. (1976). Effect of sample presentation time on long-delay matching in the pigeon. *Learning and Motivation, 7,* 580–590.

GRANT, D. S. (1988). Sources of visual interference in delayed matching-to-sample with pigeons. *Journal of Experimental Psychology: Animal Behavior Processes, 14,* 368–375.

GREEN, L., & RACHLIN, H. (1991). Economic substitutability of electrical brain stimulation, food, and water. *Journal of the Experimental Analysis of Behavior, 55,* 133–143.

GROVES, P. M., & THOMPSON, R. F. (1970). Habituation: A dual-process theory. *Psychological Review, 77,* 419–450.

GROVES, P. M., LEE, D., & THOMPSON, R. F. (1969). Effects of stimulus frequency and intensity on habituation and sensitization in acute spinal cat. *Physiology & Behavior, 4,* 383–388.

HEARST, E., & JENKINS, H. M. (1974). *Sign tracking: The stimulus-reinforcer relation and directed action.* Austin, TX: Psychonomic Society.

HEARST, E., BESLEY, S., & FARTHING, G. W. (1970). Inhibition and the stimulus control of operant behavior. *Journal of the Experimental Analysis of Behavior, 14,* 373–409.

HEARST, E., FRANKLIN, S., & MUELLER, C. G. (1974). The "disinhibition" of extinguished operant behavior in pigeons: Trial-tempo shifts and novel-stimulus effects. *Animal Learning & Behavior, 2,* 229–237.

HEILIGENBERG, W. (1974). Processes governing behavioral states of readiness. In D. S. Lehrman, J. S. Rosenblatt, R. Hinde, & E. Shaw (Eds.), *Advances in the study of behavior* (Vol. 5, pp. 173–200). New York: Academic Press.

HERRNSTEIN, R. J. (1969). Method and theory in the study of avoidance. *Psychological Review, 76,* 49–69.

HERRNSTEIN, R. J. (1970). On the law of effect. *Journal of the Experimental Analysis of Behavior, 13,* 243–266.

HOGAN, J. A. (1994). Structure and development of behavior systems. *Psychonomic Bulletin & Review, 1,* 439–450.

HOLLAND, P. C. (1977). Conditioned stimulus as a determinant of the form of the Pavlovian conditioned response. *Journal of Experimental Psychology: Animal Behavior Processes, 3,* 77–104.

HOLLAND, P. C. (1986). Temporal determinants of occasion setting in feature-positive discriminations. *Animal Learning & Behavior, 14,* 111–120.

HOLLAND, P. C. (1989). Feature extinction enhances transfer of occasion setting. *Animal Learning & Behavior, 17,* 269–279.

HOLLAND, P. C. (1992). Occasion setting in Pavlovian conditioning. In G. Bower (Ed.), *The psychology of learning and motivation* (Vol. 28, pp. 69–125). Orlando, FL: Academic Press.

HOLLAND, P. C. (1984). Origins of behavior in Pavlovian conditioning. In G. H. Bower (Ed.), *The psychology of learning and motivation* (Vol. 18, pp. 129–174). Orlando, FL: Academic Press.

HOLLIS, K. L. (1984). The biological function of Pavlovian conditioning: The best defense is a good offense. *Journal of Experimental Psychology: Animal Behavior Processes, 10,* 413–425.

HOLLIS, K. L. (1990). The role of Pavlovian conditioning in territorial aggression and reproduction. In D. A. Dewsbury (Ed.), *Contemporary issues in comparative psychology* (pp. 197–219). Sunderland, MA: Sinauer.

HOLLOWAY, K. S., & DOMJAN, M. (1993). Sexual approach conditioning: Tests of unconditioned stimulus devaluation using hormone manipulations. *Journal of Experimental Psychology: Animal Behavior Processes, 19,* 47–55.

HOLZ, W. C., & AZRIN, N. H. (1961). Discriminative properties of punishment. *Journal of the Experimental Analysis of Behavior, 4,* 225–232.

HOMME, L. E., DeBACA, P. C., DEVINE, J. V., STEINHORST, R., & RICKERT, E. J. (1963). Use of the Premack Principle in controlling the behavior of nursery school children. *Journal of the Experimental Analysis of Behavior, 6*, 544.

HONIG, W. K., & JAMES, P. H. R. (Eds.). (1971). *Animal memory.* Orlando, FL: Academic Press.

HULL, C. L. (1930). Knowledge and purpose as habit mechanisms. *Psychological Review, 30*, 511–525.

HULL, C. L. (1931). Goal attraction and directing ideas conceived as habit phenomena. *Psychological Review, 38*, 487–506.

HUMPHREYS, L. G. (1939). The effect of random alternation of reinforcement on the acquisition and extinction of conditioned eyelid reactions. *Journal of Experimental Psychology, 25*, 141–158.

JENKINS, H. M. (1962). Resistance to extinction when partial reinforcement is followed by regular reinforcement. *Journal of Experimental Psychology, 64*, 441–450.

JENKINS, H. M., & HARRISON, R. H. (1960). Effects of discrimination training on auditory generalization. *Journal of Experimental Psychology, 59*, 246–253.

JENKINS, H. M., & HARRISON, R. H. (1962). Generalization gradients of inhibition following auditory discrimination learning. *Journal of the Experimental Analysis of Behavior, 5*, 435–441.

JITSUMORI, M., WRIGHT, A. A., & SHYAN, M. R. (1989). Buildup and release from proactive interference in a rhesus monkey. *Journal of Experimental Psychology: Animal Behavior Processes, 15*, 329–337.

KAMIL, A. C., & CLEMENTS, K. C. (1990). Learning, memory, and foraging behavior. In D. A. Dewsbury (Ed.), *Contemporary issues in comparative psychology* (pp. 7–30). Sunderland, MA: Sinauer.

KAMIN, L. J. (1965). Temporal and intensity characteristics of the conditioned stimulus. In W. F. Prokasy (Ed.), *Classical conditioning.* New York: Appleton-Century-Crofts.

KAMIN, L. J. (1969). Predictability, surprise, and attention. In B. A. Campbell & R. M. Church (Eds.), *Punishment and aversive behavior* (pp.279–296). New York: Appleton-Century-Crofts.

KAPLAN, P. S., WERNER, J. S., & RUDY, J. W. (1990). Habituation, sensitization, and infant visual attention. In C. Rovee-Collier & L. P. Lipsitt (Eds.), *Advances in infancy research* (Vol. 6, pp. 61–109). Norwood, NJ: Ablex.

KAZDIN, A. E. (1985). The token economy. In R. M. Turner & L. M. Ascher (Eds.), *Evaluating behavior therapy outcome* (pp. 225–253). New York: Springer-Verlag.

KENDRICK, D. F., RILLING, M. E., & DENNY, M. R. (Eds.). (1986). *Theories of animal memory.* Hillsdale, NJ: Erlbaum.

KIMBLE, G. A. (1961). *Hilgard and Marquis' conditioning and learning.* New York: Appleton-Century-Crofts.

KREMER, E. F. (1974). The truly random control procedure: Conditioning to the static cues. *Journal of Comparative and Physiological Psychology, 86*, 700–707.

LASHLEY, K. S., & WADE, M. (1946). The Pavlovian theory of generalization. *Psychological Review, 53,* 72–87.

LEATON, R. N. (1976). Long-term retention of lick suppression and startle response produced by a single auditory stimulus. *Journal of Experimental Psychology: Animal Behavior Processes, 2,* 248–259.

LIEBERMAN, D. A., McINTOSH, D. C., & THOMAS, G. V. (1979). Learning when reward is delayed: A marking hypothesis. *Journal of Experimental Psychology: Animal Behavior Processes, 5,* 224–242.

LOGUE, A. W., OPHIR, I., & STRAUSS, K. E. (1981). The acquisition of taste aversions in humans. *Behaviour Research and Therapy, 19,* 319–333.

LoLORDO, V. M., & DROUNGAS, A. (1989). Selective associations and adaptive specializations: Taste aversions and phobias. In S. B. Klein & R. R. Mowrer (Eds.), *Contemporary learning theories: Instrumental conditioning theory and the impact of biological constraints on learning* (pp. 145–179). Hillsdale, NJ: Erlbaum.

LoLORDO, V. M., & FAIRLESS, J. L. (1985). Pavlovian conditioned inhibition: The literature since 1969. In R. R. Miller and N. E. Spear (Eds.), *Information processing in animals: Conditioned inhibition* (pp. 1–49). Hillsdale, NJ: Erlbaum.

LORENZ, K. Z. (1981). *The foundations of ethology.* New York: Springer-Verlag.

MACKINTOSH, N. J. (1974). *The psychology of animal learning.* Orlando, FL: Academic Press.

MACKINTOSH, N. J. (1977). Stimulus control: Attentional factors. In W. K. Honig & J.E.R. Staddon (Eds.), *Handbook of operant behavior* (pp. 481–513). Englewood Cliffs, NJ: Prentice-Hall.

MAKI, W. S. (1979). Pigeon's short-term memory for surprising vs. expected reinforcement and nonreinforcement. *Animal Learning & Behavior, 7,* 31–37.

McALLISTER, D. E., & McALLISTER, W. R. (1991). Fear theory and aversively motivated behavior: Some controversial issues. In M. R. Denny (Ed.), *Fear, avoidance, and phobias* (pp. 135–163). Hillsdale, NJ: Erlbaum.

McDOWELL, J. J., & WIXTED, J. T. (1988). The linear system theory's account of behavior maintained by variable ratio schedules. *Journal of the Experimental Analysis of Behavior, 49,* 143–169.

MEDIN, D. L. (1980). Proactive interference in monkeys: Delay and intersample interval effects are not comparable. *Animal Learning & Behavior, 8,* 553–560.

MEDIN, D. L., ROBERTS, W. A., & DAVIS, R. T. (1976). *Processes of animal memory.* Hillsdale, NJ: Erlbaum.

MILLER, D. B. (1985). Methodological issues in the ecological study of learning. In T. D. Johnston & A. T. Pietrewicz (Eds.), *Issues in the ecological study of learning* (pp. 73–95). Erlbaum.

MILLER, N. E. (1951). Learnable drives and rewards. In S. S. Stevens (Ed.), *Handbook of experimental psychology* (pp. 435–472). New York: Wiley.

MILLER, N. E. (1960). Learning resistance to pain and fear: Effects of overlearning, exposure, and rewarded exposure in context. *Journal of Experimental Psychology, 60,* 137–145.

MILLER, R. R., KASPROW, W. J., & SCHACHTMAN, T. R. (1986). Retrieval variability: Sources and consequences. *American Journal of Psychology, 99,* 145–218.

MILLER, R. R., & MATZEL, L. D. (1989). Contingency and relative associative strength. In S. B. Klein & R. R. Mowrer (Eds.), *Contemporary learning theories: Pavlovian conditioning and the status of learning theory* (pp. 61–84). Hillsdale, NJ: Erlbaum.

MINEKA, S., & GINO, A. (1980). Dissociation between conditioned emotional response and extended avoidance performance. *Learning and Motivation, 11,* 476–502.

MORRIS, R.G.M. (1974). Pavlovian conditioned inhibition of fear during shuttlebox avoidance behavior. *Learning and Motivation, 5,* 424–447.

MORRIS, R.G.M. (1975). Preconditioning of reinforcing properties to an exteroceptive feedback stimulus. *Learning and Motivation, 6,* 289–298.

MOWRER, O. H. (1947). On the dual nature of learning: A reinterpretation of "conditioning" and "problem-solving." *Harvard Educational Review, 17,* 102–150.

MOWRER, O. H., & LAMOREAUX, R. R. (1942). Avoidance conditioning and signal duration: A study of secondary motivation and reward. *Psychological Monographs, 54* (entire issue No. 247).

PAPINI, M. R., & BITTERMAN, M. E. (1990). The role of contingency in classical conditioning. *Psychological Review, 97,* 396–403.

PAVLOV, I. (1927). *Conditioned reflexes* (G. V. Anrep, trans.). London: Oxford University Press.

PEELE, D. B., CASEY, J., & SILBERBERG, A. (1984). Primacy of interresponse-time reinforcement in accounting for rate differences under variable-ratio and variable-interval schedules. *Journal of Experimental Psychology: Animal Behavior Processes, 10,* 149–167.

PELCHAT, M. L., & ROZIN, P. (1982). The special role of nausea in the acquisition of food dislikes by humans. *Appetite, 3,* 341–351.

PERRY, D. G., & PARKE, R. D. (1975). Punishment and alternative response training as determinants of response inhibition in children. *Genetic Psychology Monographs, 91,* 257–279.

PREMACK, D. (1965). Reinforcement theory. In D. Levine (Ed.), *Nebraska symposium on motivation* (Vol. 13, pp. 123–189). Lincoln: University of Nebraska Press.

RACHLIN, H. (1976). *Behavior and learning* (pp. 102–154). San Francisco: W. H. Freeman.

RACHLIN, H. C. (1978). A molar theory of reinforcement schedules. *Journal of the Experimental Analysis of Behavior, 30,* 345–360.

REBERG, D. (1972). Compound tests for excitation in early acquisition and after prolonged extinction of conditioned suppression. *Learning and Motivation, 3,* 246–258.

REBERG, D., & BLACK, A. H. (1969). Compound testing of individually conditioned stimuli as an index of excitatory and inhibitory properties. *Psychonomic Science, 17,* 30–31.

REPP, A. C., & SINGH, N. N. (Eds.). (1990). *Perspectives on the use of nonaversive and aversive interventions for persons with developmental disabilities*. Sycamore, IL: Sycamore.

RESCORLA, R. A., & FREBERG, L. (1978). The extinction of within-compound flavor associations. *Learning and Motivation, 9*, 411–427.

RESCORLA, R. A. (1967). Pavlovian conditioning and its proper control procedures. *Psychological Review, 74*, 71–80.

RESCORLA, R. A. (1969). Pavlovian conditioned inhibition. *Psychological Bulletin, 72*, 77–94.

RESCORLA, R. A. (1972). Informational variables in Pavlovian conditioning. In G. H. Bower (Ed.), *The psychology of learning and motivation* (Vol. 6, pp. 1–46). Orlando, FL: Academic Press.

RESCORLA, R. A. (1973). Effect of US habituation following conditioning. *Journal of Comparative and Physiological Psychology, 82*, 137–143.

RESCORLA, R. A. (1985). Conditioned inhibition and facilitation. In R. R. Miller and N. E. Spear (Eds.), *Information processing in animals: Conditioned inhibition* (pp. 299–326). Hillsdale, NJ: Erlbaum.

RESCORLA, R. A. (1988). Pavlovian conditioning: It's not what you think it is. *American Psychologist, 43*, 151–160.

RESCORLA, R. A., & DURLACH, P. J., & GRAU, J. (1985). Contextual learning in Pavlovian conditioning. In P. Balsam and A. Tomie (Eds.), *Context and learning* (pp. 23–56). Hillsdale, NJ: Erlbaum.

RESCORLA, R. A., & GILLAN, D. J. (1980). An analysis of the facilitative effect of similarity on second-order conditioning. *Journal of Experimental Psychology: Animal Behavior Processes, 6*, 339–351.

RESCORLA, R. A., & SOLOMON, R. L. (1967). Two-process learning theory: Relationships between Pavlovian conditioning and instrumental learning. *Psychological Review, 74*, 151–182.

REYNOLDS, G. S. (1975). *A primer of operant conditioning*. Glenview, IL: Scott, Foresman.

RICHARDSON, R., RICCIO, D. C., & JONKE, T. (1983). Alleviation of infantile amnesia in rats by means of a pharmacological contextual state. *Developmental Psychobiology, 16*, 511–518.

RILLING, M. (1977). Stimulus control and inhibitory processes. In W. K. Honig and J.E.R. Staddon (Eds.), *Handbook of operant behavior* (pp. 432–480). Englewood Cliffs, NJ: Prentice-Hall.

RILLING, M., KENDRICK, D. F., & STONEBRAKER, T. B. (1984). Directed forgetting in context. In G. H. Bower (Ed.), *The psychology of learning and motivation* (Vol. 18). Orlando: Academic Press.

ROBBINS, S. J. (1990). Mechanisms underlying spontaneous recovery in autoshaping. *Journal of Experimental Psychology: Animal Behavior Processes, 16*, 235–249.

ROBERTS, W. A., & GRANT, D. S. (1978). An analysis of light-induced retroactive inhibition in pigeon short-term memory. *Journal of Experimental Psychology: Animal Behavior Processes, 4*, 219–236.

ROBERTS, W., & GRANT, D. S. (1976). Studies of short-term memory in the pigeon using the delayed matching to sample procedure. In D. L. Medin, W. A. Roberts, & R. T. Davis (Eds.). *Processes of animal memory*. Hillsdale, NJ: Erlbaum.

ROITBLAT, H. L. (1980). Codes and coding processes in pigeon short-term memory. *Animal Learning & Behavior, 8,* 341–351.

ROSS, R. T. (1983). Relationships between the determinants of performance in serial feature-positive discriminations. *Journal of Experimental Psychology: Animal Behavior Processes, 9,* 349–373.

SANTI, A., & ROBERTS, W. A. (1985). Prospective representation: The effects of varied mapping of sample stimuli to comparison stimuli and differential trial outcomes on pigeons' working memory. *Animal Learning & Memory, 13,* 103–108.

SCHEIN, M. W., & HALE, E. B. (1965). Stimuli eliciting sexual behavior. In F. A. Beach (Ed.), *Sex and behavior* (pp. 440–482). New York: John Wiley.

SCHNEIDERMAN, N., & GORMEZANO, I. (1964). Conditioning of the nictitating membrane of the rabbit as a function of the CS-US interval. *Journal of Comparative and Physiological Psychology, 57,* 188–195.

SCHWARTZ, B. (1981). Reinforcement creates behavioral units. *Behavioural Analysis Letters, 1,* 33–41.

SHAPIRO, K. L., JACOBS, W. J., & LoLORDO, V. M. (1980). Stimulus-reinforcer interactions in Pavlovian conditioning of pigeons: Implications for selective associations. *Animal Learning & Behavior, 8,* 586–594.

SHERRY, D. F., & SCHACHTER, D. L. (1987). The evolution of multiple memory systems. *Psychological Review, 94,* 439–454.

SHETTLEWORTH, S. J. (1975). Reinforcement and the organization of behavior in golden hamsters: Hunger, environment, and food reinforcement. *Journal of Experimental Psychology: Animal Behavior Processes, 1,* 56–87.

SHIMP, C. P. (1969). Optimal behavior in free-operant experiments. *Psychological Review, 76,* 97–112.

SIDMAN, M. (1953). Avoidance conditioning with brief shock and no exteroceptive warning signal. *Science, 118,* 157–158.

SIDMAN, M. (1960). *Tactics of scientific research.* New York: Basic Books.

SIEGEL, S. (1974). Flavor preexposure and "learned safety." *Journal of Comparative and Physiological Psychology, 87,* 1073–1082.

SIEGEL, S. (1975). Conditioning insulin effects. *Journal of Comparative and Physiological Psychology, 89,* 189–199.

SKINNER, B. F. (1938). *The behavior of organisms.* New York: Appleton-Century.

SKINNER, B. F. (1953). *Science and human behavior.* New York: Macmillan.

SKINNER, B. F. (1956). A case history in scientific method. *American Psychologist, 11,* 221–233.

SMALL, W. S. (1899). An experimental study of the mental processes of the rat: I. *American Journal of Psychology, 11,* 133–164.

SMALL, W. S. (1900). An experimental study of the mental processes of the rat: II. *American Journal of Psychology, 12,* 206–239.

SMITH, J. C., & ROLL, D. L. (1967). Trace conditioning with X-rays as an aversive stimulus. *Psychonomic Science, 9*, 11–12.

SMITH, M. C., COLEMAN, S. R., & GORMEZANO, I. (1969). Classical conditioning of the rabbit's nictitating membrane response at backward, simultaneous, and forward CS-US intervals. *Journal of Comparative and Physiological Psychology, 69*, 226–231.

SOLOMON, R. L., KAMIN, L. J., & WYNNE, L. C. (1953). Traumatic avoidance learning: The outcomes of several extinction procedures with dogs. *Journal of Abnormal and Social Psychology, 48*, 291–302.

SPEAR, N. E., & MILLER, R. R. (Eds.). (1981). *Information processing in animals: Memory mechanisms*. Hillsdale, NJ: Erlbaum.

SPEAR, N. E., SMITH, G. J., BRYAN, R. G., GORDON, W. C., TIMMONS, R., & CHISZAR, D. A. (1980). Contextual influences on the interaction between conflicting memories in the rat. *Animal Learning & Behavior, 8*, 273–281.

SPENCE, K. W. (1956). *Behavior theory and conditioning*. New Haven, CT: Yale University Press.

STADDON, J.E.R. (1979). Operant behavior as adaptation to constraint. *Journal of Experimental Psychology: General, 108*, 48–67.

STEWART, J., & EIKELBOOM, R. (1987). Conditioned drug effects. In L. L. Iversen, S. D. Iversen, & S. H. Snyder (Eds.), *Handbook of psychopharmacology* (Vol. 19, pp. 1–57). New York: Plenum.

SULZER-AZAROFF, B., & MAYER, G. R. (1991). *Behavior analysis for lasting change*. Forth Worth: Holt, Rinehart, and Winston.

TESTA, T. J. (1974). Causal relationships and the acquisition of avoidance responses. *Psychological Review, 81*, 491–505.

THEIOS, J. (1962). The partial reinforcement effect sustained through blocks of continuous reinforcement. *Journal of Experimental Psychology, 64*, 1–6.

THEIOS, J., LYNCH, A. D., & LOWE, W. F., JR. (1966). Differential effects of shock intensity on one-way and shuttle avoidance conditioning. *Journal of Experimental Psychology, 72*, 294–299.

THOMAS, G. V., & LIEBERMAN, D. A. (1990). Commentary: Determinants of success and failure in experiments on marking. *Learning and Motivation, 21*, 110–124.

THOMPSON, R. F., & SPENCER, W. A. (1966). Habituation: A model phenomenon for the study of neuronal substrates of behavior. *Psychological Review, 73*, 16–43.

THORNDIKE, E. L. (1898). Animal intelligence: An experimental study of the associative processes in animals. *Psychological Review Monograph, 2* (Whole No. 8).

THORNDIKE, E. L. (1911). *Animal intelligence: Experimental studies*. New York: Macmillan.

THORNDIKE, E. L. (1932). *The fundamentals of learning*. New York: Teachers College, Columbia University.

TIMBERLAKE, W. (1980). A molar equilibrium theory of learned performance. In

G. H. Bower (Ed.), *The psychology of learning and motivation* (Vol. 14, pp. 1–58). Orlando, FL: Academic Press.

TIMBERLAKE, W. (1984). Behavior regulation and learned performance: Some misapprehensions and disagreements. *Journal of the Experimental Analysis of Behavior, 41,* 355–375.

TIMBERLAKE, W. (1994). Behavior systems, associationism, and Pavlovian conditioning. *Psychonomic Bulletin & Review, 1,* 405–420.

TIMBERLAKE, W., & ALLISON, J. (1974). Response deprivation: An empirical approach to instrumental reinforcement. *Psychological Review, 81,* 146–164.

TIMBERLAKE, W., & LUCAS, G. A. (1989). Behavior systems and learning: From misbehavior to general principles. In S. B. Klein & R. R. Mowrer (Eds.), *Contemporary learning theories: Instrumental conditioning theory and the impact of biological constraints on learning* (pp. 237–275). Hillsdale, NJ: Erlbaum.

TIMBERLAKE, W., WAHL, G., & KING, D. (1982). Stimulus and response contingencies in the misbehavior of rats. *Journal of Experimental Psychology: Animal Behavior Processes, 8,* 62–85.

TINBERGEN, N. (1951). *The study of instinct.* Oxford: Clarendon Press.

TINBERGEN, N. (1952). The behavior of the stickleback. *Scientific American, 187,* 22–26.

TINBERGEN, N., & PERDECK, A. C. (1950). On the stimulus situation releasing the begging response in the newly hatched herring gull chick (*Larus argentatus argentatus* Pont.). *Behaviour, 3,* 1–39.

TOMIE, A., BROOKS, W., & ZITO, B. (1989). Sign-tracking: The search for reward. In S. B. Klein & R. R. Mowrer (Eds.), *Contemporary learning theories: Pavlovian conditioning and the status of learning theory* (pp. 191–223). Hillsdale, NJ: Erlbaum.

TOMIE, A., MURPHY, A. L., FATH, S., & JACKSON, R. L. (1980). Retardation of autoshaping following pretraining with unpredictable food: Effects of changing the context between pretraining and testing. *Learning and Motivation, 11,* 117–134.

TURKKAN, J. S. (1989). Classical conditioning: The new hegemony. *The Behavioral and Brain Sciences, 12,* 121–179.

WALLACE, J., STEINERT, P. A., SCOBIE, S. R., & SPEAR, N. E. (1980). Stimulus modality and short-term memory in rats. *Animal Learning & Memory, 8,* 10–16.

WASSERMAN, E. A., FRANKLIN, S. R., & HEARST, E. (1974). Pavlovian appetitive contingencies and approach vs. withdrawal to conditioned stimuli in pigeons. *Journal of Comparative and Physiological Psychology, 86,* 616–627.

WEISMAN, R. G., & LITNER, J. S. (1972). The role of Pavlovian events in avoidance training. In R. A. Boakes & M. S. Halliday (Eds.), *Inhibition and learning* (pp. 253–370). London: Academic Press.

WILLIAMS, B. A. (1988). Reinforcement, choice, and response strength. In R. C. Atkinson, R. J. Herrnstein, G. Lindzey, & R. D. Luce (Eds.), *Stevens' handbook of experimental psychology* (Vol. 2, pp. 167–244). New York: Wiley.

WINTER, J., & PERKINS, C. C. (1982). Immediate reinforcement in delayed reward learning in pigeons. *Journal of the Experimental Analysis of Behavior, 38,* 169–179.

WRIGHT, A. A., URCUIOLI, P. J., SANDS, S. F., & SANTIAGO, H. C. (1981). Interference of delayed matching to sample in pigeons: Effects of interpolation at different periods within a trial and stimulus similarity. *Animal Learning & Behavior, 9,* 595–603.

ZENTALL, T. R., STEIRN, J. N., & JACKSON-SMITH, P. (1990). Memory strategies in pigeons' performance of a radial-arm-maze analog task. *Journal of Experimental Psychology: Animal Behavior Processes, 16,* 358–371.

Name Index

Alcock, J., 16
Allan, R. W., 78
Alltson, J., 109, 110, 111, 112, 115
Amsel, A., 84
Amsel, A., 104, 127, 129
Anger, D., 160
Atkinson, R. C., 21, 100, 148
Ayres, J. J. B., 51
Azrin, N. H., 170, 171, 173, 174, 177

Babkin, B. P., 39
Baerends, G. P., 15, 21
Balsam, P. D., 51, 148
Baron, A., 180
Batson, J. D., 49,
Bechterev, V. M., 151, 157
Beecher, M. D., 165
Benedict, J. O., 51
Berlyne, D. E., 107
Besley, S., 122
Best, M. R., 49
Bitterman, M. E., 50, 52, 54, 68, 124
Black, A. H., 64
Boakes, R. A., 39, 41, 44
Bolles, R. C., 41, 84
Bolles, R. C., 162, 163, 165
Borovsky, D., 190, 191
Bouton, M. E., 41, 65, 118, 120, 121, 129
Bower, G. H., 52, 103, 165
Braveman, N. S., 56
Breland, K., 12, 85
Breland, M., 12, 85

Brogden, W. J., 156, 157
Bronstein, P., 56
Brooks, D. C., 118
Brooks, W., 41
Brown, E. R., 49
Brown, M. F., 188
Bryan, R. G., 192
Burkhard, B., 114

Camp, D. S., 170, 171
Campbell, B. A., 177, 192
Capaldi, E. J., 126, 129
Casey, F. G., 108
Casey, J., 100
Charlop, M. H., 108
Chiszar, D. A., 192
Church, R. M., 9, 170, 171, 173, 177
Clements, K. C., 12
Cohen, L., 28
Coleman, S. R., 54, 55
Colwill, R. M., 84, 86
Cook, R. G., 188
Culler, E., 156, 157

D'Amato, M. R., 162, 185
Dardano, J. F., 174
Davis, M., 26, 30, 31, 32
Davis, R. T., 179
Davison, M., 97
Dean, S. J., 175
deBaca, P. C., 108
Deich, J. D., 78
Denny, M. R., 165, 179, 192
Descartes, R., 13, 24
Devine, J. V., 108

Dinsmoor, J. A., 160, 173
Domjan, M., 12, 14, 17, 30, 32, 45, 46, 48, 68, 75
Douglas, S., 191
Droungas, A., 40, 48, 52
Durlach, P. J., 67

Edhouse, W. V., 189
Eikelboom, R., 43
Eisenberger, R., 111
Epstein, A. N., 68
Ervin, F. R., 57
Estes, W. K., 41
Etkin, M., 162

Fairless, J. L., 62
Fanselow, M. S., 44, 164
Farthing, G. W., 122
Fath, S., 51
Fazzaro, J., 162
Felton, M., 91
Ferster, C. B., 90, 92, 95, 100
Foree, D. D., 140
Forestell, P. H., 180
Franklin, S. R., 44, 39
Freberg, L., 47
Fudim, O. K., 47

Galbicka, G., 78
Garcia, J., 48, 57
Gillan, D. J., 30, 49
Gino, A., 159
Goodall, G., 44
Goodall, G., 170
Gordon, W. C., 192
Gormezano, I., 42, 54, 55, 68

Grant, D. S., 181, 184, 190
Grau, J. W., 67
Green, L., 114
Groves, P. M., 30, 31, 32, 35, 36

Hake, D. F., 171
Hale, E. B., 18
Harrison, R. H., 144, 145, 146, 147
Hearst, E., 39, 41, 44, 122
Heiligenberg, W., 31
Helmstetter, F. J., 164
Herman, L. M., 180
Herrnstein, R. J., 21, 97, 100, 148, 165
Hilgard, E. R., 103
Hitchcock, J. M., 26, 32
Holland, P. C., 39, 41, 52, 66, 67, 68
Hollis, K. L., 12
Holloway, K. S., 45, 46
Holz, W. C., 170, 171, 173, 174, 177
Homme, L. E., 108
Honig, W. K., 129, 148, 179
Hull, C. L., 83, 84, 104, 105, 106, 107, 108
Humphreys, L. G., 123

Jackson, R. L., 51
Jackson-Smith, P., 188
Jacobs, W. J., 49, 140
James, P. H. R., 129, 179
Jenkins, H. M., 41, 124, 125, 144, 145, 146, 147
Jitsumori, M., 189
Jonke, T., 192

Kamil, A. C., 12
Kamin, L. J., 55, 56, 57, 68, 139, 140, 159
Kaplan, P. S., 28, 30, 31
Karpman, M., 111
Kasprow, W. J., 179
Kazdin, A. E., 109
Kehoe, E. J., 42, 68
Kendrick, D. F., 179, 185, 192
Kimble, G. A., 41
King, D., 12, 85
Klein, S. B., 86
Koelling, R. A., 48, 57
Kremer, E. F., 51
Kurtz, P. F., 108

Lamoreaux, R. R., 150
Lashley, K. S., 138
Leaton, R. N., 30, 36
Lee, D., 30, 31
Lester, L. S., 44, 164
Lieberman, D. A., 81
Lindzey, G., 21, 100, 148
Lipman, E. A., 156, 157
Litner, J. S., 162
Lockwood, M. J., 44
Logue, A. W., 49
LoLordo, V. M., 40, 48, 49, 52, 62, 140
Lorenz, K., 19
Lowe, W. F., Jr., 154
Lucas, G. A., 44, 86
Luce, R. D., 21, 100, 148
Lynch, A. D., 154
Lyon, D. O., 91

Mackintosh, N. J., 42, 148
Maki, W. S., 185
Marshall, B. S., 42, 68
Matzel, L. D., 60
Mayer, G. R., 96
McAllister, D. E., 165
McAllister, W. R., 165
McCarthy, D., 97
McDowell, J. J., 100
McIntosh, D. C., 81,
Meachum, C. L., 49,
Medin, D. L., 179, 189
Menich, S. R., 180
Miller, D. B., 7
Miller, N. E., 157, 171
Miller, R. R., 60, 179
Mineka, S., 159
Morris, R. G. M., 162
Mowrer, O. H., 150, 157
Mowrer, R. R., 86, 192
Murphy, A. L., 51

Nash, S. M., 17

Ophir, I., 49

Papini, M. R., 50, 52, 68
Parke, R. D., 174
Pavlov, I. P., 38, 39, 48, 60, 72, 118, 138, 139
Peeke, H. V. S., 36
Peele, D. B., 100
Pelchat, M. L., 49

Perdeck, A. C., 18
Perkins, C. C., 80
Perrott, M. C., 95
Perry, D. G., 174
Petrinovich, L., 36
Pittman, C. M., 175
Poli, M., 44
Premack, D., 107, 108, 109, 110, 111, 115

Rachlin, H. C., 12, 22, 100, 114
Randall, P. K., 192
Rashotte, M. E., 104
Raymond, G. A., 170, 171, 173
Reberg, D., 64, 65, 122
Repp, A. C., 177
Rescorla, R. A., 9, 39, 45, 47, 49, 50, 52, 59, 67, 68, 84, 86, 122
Reynolds, G. S., 100
Riccio, D. C., 192
Richardson, R., 192
Rickert, E. J., 108
Riley, A. L., 163
Riley, D. A., 188
Rilling, M. E., 179, 185, 192
Ringer, M., 49
Robbins, S. J., 118
Roberts, W. A., 179, 184, 187, 190
Roitblat, H. L., 187
Roll, D. L., 56
Rosen, J. B., 26, 32
Ross, R. T., 68
Rovee-Collier, C., 190, 191
Rozin, P., 49
Rudy, J., 28, 31

Sands, S. F., 190
Santi, A., 187
Santiago, H. C., 190
Sauerbrunn, D., 174
Schachter, D. L., 179
Schachtman, T. R., 179
Schein, M. W., 18
Schneiderman, N., 55, 56
Schrader, S., 114
Schwartz, B., 77
Scobie, S. R., 180
Shapiro, K. L., 49, 140
Sherry, D. F., 179
Shettleworth, S. J., 85

Shimp, C. P., 100
Shyan, M. R., 189
Sidman, M., 9, 154
Siegel, S., 30, 39
Silberberg, A., 100
Singh, N. N., 177
Skinner, B. F., 12, 39, 41, 42, 72,
    74, 75, 76, 72, 74, 75, 76,
    83, 84, 90, 92, 100, 167,
    170, 175
Small, W. S., 74
Smith, G. J., 192
Smith, J. C., 56
Smith, M. C., 54, 55
Solomon, R. L., 84, 86, 159
Spear, N. E., 179, 180, 192
Spence, W. K., 84
Spencer, W. A., 28, 29, 30, 31
Sprague, J. M., 68
Staddon, J. E. R., 115, 148
Steinert, P. A., 180
Steinhorst, R., 108

Steirn, J. N., 188
Stewart, J., 43
Stonebraker, T. B., 185
Strauss, K. E., 49
Sulzer-Azaroff, B., 96
Swartzentruber, D., 62, 121

Testa, T. J., 49
Theios, J., 124, 125, 154
Thomas, G. V., 81
Thompson, R. F., 28, 29, 30, 31,
    32, 35, 36
Thorndike, E. L., 72, 73, 74, 81,
    82, 84, 85, 103, 104, 167,
    170, 175
Tighe, T. J., 36
Timberlake, W., 12, 20, 22,
    44, 85, 86, 109, 110, 111,
    112, 115
Timmons, R., 192
Tinbergen, N., 15, 16, 18, 22
Tomie, A., 41, 51, 60

Trattner, J., 111
Turkkan, J. S., 39

Urcuioli, P. J., 190

Wade, M., 138
Wahl, G., 12, 85
Wallace, J., 180
Wasserman, E. A., 39, 44,
Weisman, R. G., 162
Werner, J. S., 28, 30, 31
White, K. G., 189
Williams, B. A., 97, 100
Wilson, N. E., 48
Winter, J., 80
Wixted, J. T., 100
Wright, A. A., 189, 190
Wynne, L. C., 159

Zeigler, H. P., 78,
Zentall, T. R., 188
Zito, B., 41

Subject Index

Afferent neuron. *See* Sensory neuron.
Appetitive conditioning, 40–41
Aquired drive, 106, 193
Appetitive behavior, 193
Associative learning, 38, 193
Autoshaping, 41, 193
Aversive conditioning, 193
Aversive stimulus, 193
Avoidance learning, 149–165

Babies, 30–31
Backward chaining, 95
Behavior system, 20–21, 43–44, 193
Behavioral bliss point, 112, 193
Behavioral regulation, 111–115, 193
Blocking effect, 57–58, 194

Chained schedule of reinforcement, 93–96, 194
Compound stimulus test, 194 (*see also* Summation test)
Concurrent schedule of reinforcement, 96–97, 194
Conditioned inhibition, 60–65, 121–122, 161, 194
Conditioned reinforcer, 80, 193
Conditioned response, 38, 42–44, 67–68
Conditioned stimulus, 38, 194
Conditioned suppression, 41, 48, 56, 194
Constraints on learning, 12–13, 47–49, 85–86, 194

Consummatory behavior, 20, 194
Contextural cues, 51, 120, 190–192
Contingency, 59–60, 194
Control conditions, 8, 194
CS-alone control, 50
CS-US interval, 55–57
Cumulative record, 88–89, 194

Defensive behavior, 44, 162–165
Delayed conditioning, 55, 195
Differential inhibition, 61–62
Directed forgetting, 185, 195
Discrete-trial method, 73–74, 195
Discriminated avoidance, 152–154, 195
Discrimination control, 51–52, 195
Discriminative punishment, 172–173, 195
Dishabituation, 30–31, 195
Disinhibition, 118–119, 195
Drive-reduction theory, 104–107, 195

Efferent neuron, 196 (*see also* Motor neuron)
Elicited behavior, 14
Equipotentiality, 48–49, 196
Escape behavior, 174–175
Ethology, 15, 196
Experimental conditions, 8, 196
Experimental observations, 6–7, 196
External inhibition, 118–119, 196

Extinction, 65, 116–130, 196
Eyeblink conditioning, 41–42

Facilitation, 66–67, 196
Fatigue, 3–4, 196
Feedback cues, 160, 196
Feedback functions, 98–100, 196
Feeding system, 20, 44
Fixed interval schedule, 91–93, 196
Fixed ratio schedule, 90–91, 196
Flavor neophobia, 29–30, 196
Focal search mode, 21, 196
Food handling and consumption mode, 21
Free-operant avoidance, 154–156, 196
Free-operant method, 75–76, 196
Freezing behavior, 44, 163
Frustration theory, 127–129, 197

General search mode, 20, 197

Habituation effects, 26–31, 197
Habituation, dual process theory of, 32–35
Habituation, long term, 30, 198
Habituation, short term, 30, 202
Heterogeneous chain, 94
Higher-order stimulus relation, 197
Homeostasis, 25–26
Homeostatic level, 25, 197
Homogeneous chain, 94–95
Hydraulic model, 19, 197

Instrumental behavior, 71, 197
Instrumental conditioning, 70–86
Interdimensional discrimination, 146–147, 197
Interneuron, 33, 197
Interstimulus interval, 197 (*see also* CS-US interval)
Interval schedule, 91–93, 99–100, 197
Intradimensional discrimination, 147, 197

Law of effect, 82, 102–104, 110, 197–198
Learning, controls for, 9–10, 49–52
Learning, definition of, 6, 198
Learning, levels of analysis, 4–5
Long-delayed learning, 57, 198

Marking stimulus, 80–81, 198
Matching law, 97, 198
Matching-to-sample, 180–182, 183, 184, 186–188, 189–190, 198
Maturation, 2, 198
Memory mechanisms, 178–192, 198
Modal action pattern, 15–16, 198
Motivation, 4, 45–47, 104–107, 198, 204
Motor neuron, 33, 198
Multiple schedule, 144, 198

Naturalistic observations, 6, 198
Negative reinforcement, 158, 160, 174–175, 198–199
Negative reinforcer, 199
Nictitating membrane conditioning, 56
Nondiscriminated avoidance, 199 (*see also* Free operant avoidance)

Occasion setting, 199 (*see also* Facilitation)
Operant behavior, 71, 199
Operant conditioning, 70–86 (*see also* Schedules of reinforcement)
Opponent process, 25–26, 199
Orienting response, 24–25
Overshadowing, 139–140, 199

Partial reinforcement extinction effect, 123–129, 199
Pavlovian conditioning, 37–69
Performance, 4, 199
Postreinforcement pause, 90, 91, 92, 199
Predatory imminence, 164–165, 199
Premack principal, 107–109, 199
Proactive interference, 188–189, 199
Proprioceptive cue, 200 (*see also* Feedback cue)
Prospective memory, 185–188, 200
Punishment, 166–177, 200
Puzzle box, 73, 200

Quail, 17–18

R-S interval, 154–156, 200
Random control, 50–51, 200
Ratio schedule, 90–91, 98–99, 200
Reference memory, 182–184, 200
Reflex, 13–15, 24, 200
Reinforcement, theories of, 102–115
Reinforcer, 71, 200
Releasing stimulus, 19, 200
Reminder treatment, 200 (*see also* Retrieval)
Renewal effect, 120–121, 201
Repetitive behavior, 19
Response deprivation hypothesis, 109–111, 201
Retardation-of-aquisition test, 64, 201
Retrieval, 179–180, 190–192, 198, 201
Retroactive interference, 189–190, 201
Retrospective memory, 185–188, 201
Runway, 74–75

S-R learning, 38, 45–47, 82, 201
S-R system, 32–35, 201
S-S interval, 154–155, 201
S-S learning, 38, 45–47, 83, 201
Safety signal learning, 160–162, 201
Salivary conditioning, 39

Schedules of reinforcement, 87–101, 123–126, 144, 174, 202
Secondary reinforcer, 202 (*see also* Conditioned reinforcer)
Selective association, 48–49, 202
Sensitization effects, 26–27, 31–32, 202
Sensitization, short term, 31–32, 202
Sensory neuron, 33, 193, 202
Sensory reinforcement, 106–107, 202
Sequential theory, 126–127, 128–129, 202
Sexual conditioning, 45–47
Shaping, 12–13, 77–80, 202
Shuttle box, 153, 202
Sign stimulus, 17–18, 202
Sign tracking, 41, 44, 202
Signaled punishment, 172–173
Simultaneous conditioning, 54, 202
Single-subject experiment, 9–10, 202
Skinner box, 40, 76, 203
Sodium appetite, 47
Species specific defense responses, 163, 203
Species-typical behavior, 16, 203
Spontaneous recovery, 29–30, 32, 118, 203
Startle response, 26, 203
State system, 32–35, 203
Stickleback fish, 15
Stimulus control, 131–148
Stimulus discrimination training, 142–147, 203
Stimulus generalization, 135–138, 144–146, 203
Stimulus generalization, of habituation, 28–29, 203
Stimulus learning, 4, 203 (*see also* S-S learning)
Summation test, 63–64, 203
Symbolic matching-to-sample, 186–188, 204

Taste aversion learning, 48–49, 56–57, 204
Temporal contiguity, 54, 204
Temporal cues, 159–160, 204
Trace conditioning, 55, 204

Trace decay, 184, 204
Two-factor theory of avoidance,
    157–160, 204
Two-factor theory, 84

Unconditioned behavior, 11–22
Unconditioned response, 38

Unconditioned stimulus, 38, 204
US devaluation, 45–47, 204
US inflation, 47, 204
US-alone control, 50

Variable interval schedule, 93,
    204

Variable ratio schedule, 91, 204

Warning stimulus, 152, 204
Working memory, 182–184, 204